# Memories *of* Loving You

# Memories *of* Loving You

## *Our Forgiven Love*

CH (LTC-R) David Lee Druckenmiller

XULON ELITE

Xulon Press Elite
555 Winderley Pl, Suite 225
Maitland, FL 32751
407.339.4217
www.xulonpress.com

© 2023 by CH (LTC-R) David Lee Druckenmille

Foreword by: U.S. Army CH COL-R Stephen Cook

All rights reserved solely by the author. The author guarantees all contents are original and do not infringe upon the legal rights of any other person or work. No part of this book may be reproduced in any form without the permission of the author.

Due to the changing nature of the Internet, if there are any web addresses, links, or URLs included in this manuscript, these may have been altered and may no longer be accessible. The views and opinions shared in this book belong solely to the author and do not necessarily reflect those of the publisher. The publisher therefore disclaims responsibility for the views or opinions expressed within the work.

Unless otherwise indicated, Scripture quotations taken from the King James Version (KJV) – *public domain*.

Paperback ISBN-13: 978-1-66288-809-0
Ebook ISBN-13: 978-1-66288-810-6

My dear,

Finding you to love was a great joy.

Loving you for a lifetime is still a wonderful adventure.

Knowing your love is still there through the greatest of hardships,

the most challenging situations, failures of our own making, and the battles

we have fought together, gives me the amazing strength to love you even more.

The past is no longer important. The present leads into the future, but the future is

absolutely everything! Come my dear, walk with me in the garden.

written by
**David Lee Druckenmiller**

# Author's comments:

**THIS UNIQUE NARRATIVE** is inspired by my understanding of God's Word, The Holy Bible. The story is based on my study and my life experience. I do use artistic creativity to draw you into deeper thought and a creative imaginary experience. I do believe that the Holy Spirit inspires me through God's Word, and I believe He leads me in my persuasion, as I paint an intellectual image for the reader's mind to consume. I do this with the hope that you will go to God's Word and study for yourself. Scripture is inspired by God and it has stood firm for thousands of years. The Bible has always triumphed over dismissive atheistic scrutiny to enlighten those who seek truth and understanding! I hope this is fun, informative, and self-reflecting for you.

The first section of this story is about *first love*, the beginning of man in the Garden of Eden. It is told through my vision of what the first family, male and female, might have experienced based on what we know happened. Why was this first husband and wife driven from the garden?

I believe I stay true to the context of what caused the fall of man. It is about the War between Good and Evil in our world.

The second portion of this story is about *my life, my memories, my marriage, my struggle, and my failure.* The story is laced with biblical truths for the reader to discover. I hope what I say causes deeper understanding and draws the reader into searching God's Word, where the real truth is revealed. I hope that my story will inspire couples to love each other more. I hope your family becomes and stays strong in this difficult deceitful world we are walking in today. I hope your children are saved from the evil that is pervasively spreading through a progressive deceit of wokeness, which has become the "Borg" agenda of world control to enslave freedom and establish evil dominance through the Marxist Socialist Media Communication. We are already walking upon the stepping stones that will crescendo into the perilous times spoken of in scripture. (2 Timothy 3:1-5) We are told that it is a Tribulation Period of seven years, which is the hardest suffering those who dwell on the earth will ever face. Are you ready? Is your family ready? Facing the Beast of Artificial Intelligence, spawned by the Antichrist

*Author's comments:*

and His global control over humanity, is being ushered in by political potentates.

This dual story is a comparison to what happened in my life. It is a story that reveals how the Lord walked with me to do what is right! It is my struggle to overcome the attack of evil. It is our story of family and how we were able to step back on the path that leads to righteousness, as we continue our journey as a family. We love the Lord and we hope that you find the same forgiveness and blessings on your journey. It is the Lord Jesus Christ, the Savior, who is our Champion. He is the one who walks upon the water and reaches down into the deep sea of darkness to rescue the fallen when they cry out, "Lord Save me." If you need a Champion, look to Jesus Christ and find the Lord! PS: You do need a Champion!

I was born in Sandusky, Ohio and grew up in Swanton, Ohio. I met and fell in love with my grade school sweetheart, Sally Mikola. Our, on and off, relationship for a few years, led to marriage in 1975. The journey of our lives together took us across the country and overseas. It was an amazing experience! This life adventure together took a terrible turn in 2019. This is the story you are about to read. This period of heartache in our lives became a battle to survive. My telling of it is a journey to remember the

*Memories of Loving You*

love we had. Through the gift of forgiveness, we are now Golden Year Newly Weds on our honeymoon. We are living an amazingly beautiful life as one, and we walk in the garden together.

Chaplain LTC-R, David Lee Druckenmiller,
ABS, BS, MDIV, CHOBC, CHOAC, CAS3, CGSC

# Table of Contents

**Foreword** - Endorsement by DR. Stephen L. Cook,    **xxv**
Doctor of Ministry, Chaplain (Colonel),
Retired United States Army

**Author's Introduction**    **xxix**

---

**Chapter One:** *The Original Garden of God's Love*    **1**

---

| | |
|---|---|
| The garden was disturbed. | *The struggle between the light and the darkness.* |
| Life in the Garden before it was disturbed. | *The garden was good.* |
| Two but yet one. | *Male and female created as one.* |
| One command is a warning. | *The knowledge of good and evil.* |
| Disobedience dishonors God. | *Separation from the only source of Life!* |
| Death entered the garden. | *The whole world groans in pain.* |
| She reveals her transgression. | *She admits to Adam that she ate the forbidden fruit.* |

| | |
|---|---|
| Their eyes were open to good and evil. | *They were both naked and hid themselves from God.* |
| The consequence of their action. | *Man is held responsible.* |
| Judgment for sin is inevitable. | *Nothing is ever forgotten.* |
| Driven from the Garden. | *The first family is sent out into a fallen world full of hardship.* |

---

**Chapter Two:** *Falling in Love and Creating a Family*  **45**

---

| | |
|---|---|
| Our world is at war. | *End State Mission.* |
| The struggle of humanity continues. | *It became our fight.* |
| Self-Reflection. | *My need for a foundation of faith.* |
| Still trying to Find Myself. | *Explaining who I am and my struggle between two positions.* |
| Family trouble. | *Happiness became a struggle for life.* |
| Humanity has lost something precious. | *When promises are broken families suffer.* |

*Table of Contents*

| | |
|---|---|
| I'm just a creature created by God. | *Living my life in a fallen world.* |
| God's Miracle of Humanity. | *Man became a living soul - Genetic Pooling* |
| | *The marvelous DNA miracle continues.* |
| My Beginning. | *I became a unique Individual.* |
| God Reveals Himself. | *Wise men and women seek to know.* |
| Finding the Savior. | *The example of God's love for man is revealed.* |
| The following is the story of my ongoing struggle. | *I need forgiveness too…* |

---

**Chapter Three:** *The Storm of Destruction came upon us!*     **90**

---

| | |
|---|---|
| A storm rising against us. | *The hardest trial I have ever faced.* |
| Life before the war. | *The enemy is real and the enemy is out there.* |
| My First World. | *My life is filled with understanding and memories.* |

| | |
|---|---|
| The turmoil of this world today. | *The context upon the sea of life.* |
| The real enemy we all face. | *The serpent predator stalks his prey.* |
| Mission intent. | *The Victory has already been won and freedom offered.* |
| Cold Stone Death. | *Author's Poem about Death and Resurrection.* |
| War upon the Earth. | *The theater of the coming conflict is developed.* |
| Global Borg. | *The collective is growing around us.* |
| I am just one step behind. | *Becoming a Good Warrior.* |
| The Attack begins. | *The Life I remember is under attack.* |

**Chapter Four:** *Alliances and Enemies* — **120**

| | |
|---|---|
| Knowing the Beauty of a Woman. | *A "Virtuous Woman" completes a man.* |
| The enemy: the devil reveals himself. | *The enemy invades and declares war.* |

*Table of Contents*

| | |
|---|---|
| Destroy one and destroy all. | *Sin always spreads around the fallen.* |
| Finding another world. | *A Peaceful Shore, the World of TARA!* |

**Chapter Five:** *Safe Zone to Prepare for Battle* — **137**

| | |
|---|---|
| Stand up and walk. | *Never give up and never give in to the enemy.* |
| I must find shelter. | *Making friends and enemies.* |
| My Time Tunnel. | *A time-traveling tube back to my other world.* |
| Every day was a new start. | *Trying to settle into my new life.* |
| Settling down in a peaceful place | *Trying to make a new home – a new life.* |
| Tara becomes home. | *Making a new life and making friends.* |

**Chapter Six:** *Living in Another World* — **161**

| | |
|---|---|
| Two-world reality. | *Time travel is real and I experienced it.* |
| Preparation for Travel. | *Is there a plan to restore what is good and right?* |
| Freedom or bondage | *Thinking beyond the box!* |

*Memories of Loving You*

| | |
|---|---|
| Forgive one another. | *The most amazing gift that God offers us is the gift we must give to others.* |
| Transported through dreams of remembrance. | *The first dream that took me there.* |
| First Transport into my past | *The conditions that forced me into the past.* |
| The devil in my story | *D-Day, Facing the Enemy.* |
| Memories of young love. | *Many good memories.* |
| Two become one. | *Married and starting our lives as one.* |

---

**Chapter Seven:** *Memories and Reality* — **186**

---

| | |
|---|---|
| Going back to reality. | *Back to the future.* |
| Got to figure it out. | *Trying to understand what is happening.* |
| After the First Jump into the Past. | *Mission to the Past and Wrestling with My Memory.* |
| Talking to the birds. | *An amazing Spiritual Memory I'll never forget.* |
| Could there be another? | *Another life to live.* |
| The Second Jump into my past. | *I was forced to remember my life and my love that was lost.* |

*Table of Contents*

| | |
|---|---|
| Back to my childhood home. | *Home Sweet Home.* |
| Back to School. | *Another Experience of High School.* |
| A Long and Winding Road. | *Back to Her Door Again - Then I saw her face!* |
| Multi-Tasking Brain at Work. | *Distracted during class.* |
| Remembering those special times. | *Remembering my youthful past.* |
| Puppy love two timer. | *Was I a two-timer because I liked two gals and two families?* |
| Another Love | *There were other girlfriends in High School.* |

---

**Chapter Eight:** *Finding the One You Love*     **326**

---

| | |
|---|---|
| There can be only one | *Finding the one you love.* |
| A Promise to Keep | *A Simple Prayer A Simple Promise.* |
| Who brought me back? | *Complications of these memories demand my attention.* |
| Trying to make better choices. | *The search for wisdom to make the best decisions.* |

| | |
|---|---|
| Another New Day and my gift from God. | *What next? Making myself clean again.* |
| The video of my life keeps playing. | *An acute focus on my personal space.* |
| Good Morning Nature. | *The world was alive and evil hunted prey.* |
| First World Storm Brewing. | *My story about "The Scottish Thing to Do!"* |
| Refocus on Second-World Reality. | *No closure keeps me from moving forward.* |
| Living in the reality of this world. | |
| The Real First Family Foundation. | *The force of evil to destroy families.* |
| The Control of Evil. | *The works of evil are known.* |
| Hate is growing around the world | *Self-theism and false Science takeover.* |
| Destroying truth. | *Sin's grip of hate tightens slowly until capture.* |
| Dreams end and reality moves back in! | *Why do I struggle so much?* |

**Chapter Nine:** *Commander's Intent* — 253

| | |
|---|---|
| What the Lord Wants Me to do! | *Battle-ready armor forced to fit.* |

| | |
|---|---|
| I Fought the Battle Everyday. | *The strategy of my enemy, who continuously attacked.* |
| Memories become dreams. | *Lord, help me!* |
| The Notebook by Nichols Sparks. | *The dramatic story of a living love.* |
| My Notebook. | *Why do I remember these things?* |
| Home Sweet Home. | *This is where I should be!* |
| The Argument of loved ones. | *Reliving the same painful arguments again!* |
| Calm Down Take. | *a break to reflect on what happened.* |
| The Admission of the Truth. | *Confession of truth takes ownership of guilt.* |
| The Pain We Bear. | *Our actions affect others.* |

---

**Chapter Ten:** *Deeper Thinking for the Battle*     **277**

---

| | |
|---|---|
| Return to the present reality. | *Life continues and pain follows.* |
| Parliament Investigation. | *Inquiring minds want to know – Staff Work!* |
| Opening remarks. | *I was defending myself.* |
| Adjournment until later. | *Take time to think deeper.* |

*Memories of Loving You*

| | |
|---|---|
| The Enemy is always there. | *The enemy is waiting to attack at vulnerable moments.* |
| The tactic used to capture and enslave. | *Father of Lies uses temptation to attack.* |
| Attack or defend. | *Trust in the Lord with all your heart…* |
| Anger in the heat of battle. | *Shifting strategies and unknown terrain.* |
| Uncertain Information. | *A command decision must be made.* |
| The real world back home. | *I was sheltered from knowing.* |
| D-Day was launched. | *Immediate Overwhelming force* |
| Real spiritual warfare. | *The devil in my story is Pirate Parana Joe.* |
| Defeated but refusing to surrender. | *I defiantly needed a Champion to rescue me.* |
| My Scriptural life verse. | *My prayer many years ago was to live for the Lord.* |
| Living for the Lord. | *Message I preached after a year of retirement.* |
| Looking at my life. | *Proverbs 3: 1-6* |
| Discharged from service. | *Retreat from the battle.* |

*Table of Contents*

| | |
|---|---|
| Back to the Past. | *Visiting the past is hard to do.* |
| Back to the Future. | *Is this where I lived or am I living in the past?* |

---

**Chapter Eleven:** *The Rescue Mission*     **326**

---

| | |
|---|---|
| Road trip to First World. | *The third time travel experience becomes a road trip.* |
| Good Counsel. | *Discussion of mission needs.* |
| | *Exploring mission capabilities.* |
| Slow Return to My First Life. | *We arrived back home in Tennessee.* |
| Remembering the Savior. | *My Champion walks on water!* |
| Reaching out for help. | *My help comes from the Lord.* |
| Another Prayer of HOPE. | *Prayer changes everything!* |
| The experience is reminiscent of all stories. | *Back to the garden.* |
| The Powerful and Perfect Champion. | *The gate into the garden is open again.* |

*Memories of Loving You*

**Chapter Twelve:** *Mission Analysis, Understanding Success* — **326**

| | |
|---|---|
| What I know to be true. | *If God forgives us of our sins through the work of Jesus Christ, I too must forgive others.* |
| What does forgiveness mean? | *Understanding forgiveness is important to reconciliation!* |
| Back in Time. | *One More Memory to Relive* |
| | The assurance of good choices to live with. |
| Covering up sin. | *The memory of the Ookie-Gookie Mess!* |
| Finding the Freedom of Forgiveness. | *The weight of sin once carried, is unloaded when forgiveness is reality.* |
| The Long and Winding Road back to her door. | *Finding my love again.* |
| Forgiveness is God's tool for Reconciliation! | *Forgiving one another is God's perfect will!* |
| Redemption is at the heart of forgiveness! | *The debt of sin is paid by Christ and we are set free!* |
| **The End** | *No longer on the market for sale, FREEDOM!* |

*Author's comments:*

> The front cover designed by the author to illustrate the story was painted by Clare Harvey.
>
> Clare is an instructor at the North Port Florida Art Center.
>
> She visually brings the story to life. Everything in the painting highlights actual events, which emphasis the memories of love and the will of God.
>
> http://clareharveyart.webs.com

*Scriptural Quotes in this book are all from the **King James Version**. Scripture text from the Holy Bible is used to direct the reader to find a deeper discovery of the meaning, which is found in God's Holy Word.*

*David's Group on Facebook:*
*THE WISDOM OF WHAT GRANDPA SAYS*

*Face Book Group:*
*https://www.facebook.com/groups/850918889888446*

# Foreword:

**WHAT A POSITIVE** presentation of restoration of self with those you love. David presents his story in a unique and inviting composition. He has such a way of engaging the attention of his audience that it is difficult to put this book down.

An amazing presentation of the spiritual warfare we all face in this world. David opens up his heart to the destructive storm faced in his life. His deep descriptive presentation will pull you into the narrative and open your understanding of the battle between Good and Evil. It becomes a positive presentation of hope and restoration from the struggles he endured, as he faced an enemy that beguiled his lovely wife of 46 years and brought the heartache that pulled their lives apart. The journey of this story shares the walk with God through hardship and the joy of the Lord, who restores an even greater love.

David Druckenmiller lives out the saying, "Tough times never last but tough people do." He develops the concept of being persistent, even when life seems to be a roller coaster of hardships. He never lost sight of his need for his Champion, whom he learned to rely upon for his restoration and sustainment through his most difficult trials.

He understands and defines the base problem that separates man and woman from God. Mankind continues to replace God with their own thoughts and concepts. David calls this, "self-theism," instead of atheism. What a simple and descriptive term but so profound. Many self-theists think they are smarter than God. Now, there is a losing proposition.

This is worth repeating: As our world moves farther from the time of the birth of Christ, the crucifixion, and the resurrection, many have developed their own ideas of who and what God is. They elevated their personal ideas above what God describes in the scriptures. They made their own gods and worship their own ideas.

Evil is here among us. Make no mistake about this, evil is real and it's objective is to destroy what God has created to be good. Don't let evil thinking lure you into a world that believes it is above God's existence and/or His wisdom.

David shares the influence of the spiritual battle with his enemy. His story adds to the drama of who we are. It

*Foreword:*

is so real that it hurts to feel the empathy because it is a conflict that forces "Collateral Damage" to the family: His family; Your family; Our Human family. He reminds us that we need our Champion! This world does not offer hope from within. This book, a must-read, displays the eternal hope to all who ask forgiveness from the Lord Jesus Christ.

> Dr. Stephen L. Cook, Doctor of Ministry
> Chaplain (Colonel), Retired

# Author's Introduction:

**A ROMANCE BECAME** a tragic storm of destruction. I realized that my writing began as anger. I wanted to share all the details of the real-life drama we suffered. Our life battle became our reality. The theater of this battle was full of surprise, tragedy, manipulation, infidelity, heartache, confusion, and a few years of fighting with the devil who invaded our family. My life journal became a record of every detail, of how this drama played out. The crescendo of narcissistic manipulation increased and the injury multiplied, as I was attacked constantly until I was weary. I was prepared to walk away from what I strongly believed. I was hurt and I was angry. I never thought this could happen to us. We had a great life together. A young romance that became a family for forty-six years crumbled. How does this happen? Why do bad things happen to good people? How does good triumph over evil? I needed the help of the most powerful warrior on my side. He became my Champion.

I trusted in my Savior, Jesus Christ since I was a young boy. I remember my father, Jack, telling me about Jesus Christ and His Resurrection from the dead in 1964, as we returned from church. I was standing in the back seat of our Chevy station wagon. (Back then it was not against the law.) Leaning over the seat to talk to my father, I asked him about Jesus. I was taught in the Lutheran Sunday School that morning that He arose from the dead to be our Savior. I did not know all the details at the time, but this experience on Easter stayed with me my whole life.

At age fourteen I was confirmed in the Lutheran Church in Swanton, Ohio. Most of my theology that I still believe is rooted in the Lutheran experience! However, I made my profession of faith in the Lord Jesus in 1975 at James Lee Road Baptist Church in Fort Walton Beach, Florida. I was in the Air Force and I was stationed at Eglin Air Force Base. Sally and I were Grade School and High School sweethearts. Yes, a young love blossomed and we got married in March, when I returned from technical school, before reporting to my first assignment at Eglin Air Force Base.

We launched our life adventure together. We left our hometown, Swanton, and drove to Florida. We were just two young kids starting our life together. We loaded the

*Author's Introduction:*

gold Plymouth Duster with everything we could pack and drove down I-75. From that point in time we were happy, even though we were dealing with real life as a married couple. We lived in a small trailer. We went to the beach often. It was Florida! We were happy and together. But, an enemy followed us in the background of her mind. I never knew but she had feelings for her 3rd cousin, who was two years older. He joined the Army when she was a sophomore, he promised to return after she finished school. He promised to marry her. I never knew.

Sally never had closure because her mother kept his letters away from her, and her letters to him were removed from the mailbox. She thought he moved on. He was two years older. He thought I stole her from him. He lived a life of womanizing. He could charm a lady and then his narcissistic control took over. Keeping a lady was difficult and impossible every time. His marriage of 35 years was riddled with his narcissistic tendencies, and for the last ten years, she did not live with him. When they were divorcing, he looked Sally up, his excuse of young love, beguiled her with his memories of their short time experience as kids. For five years, they talked on the phone late at night, when I was asleep, and eventually, she enjoyed their conversation. The drama of our family storm, which became a battle of survival, crept into our lives. I did not know about it, but I knew something was going on. We got married 40 years before he started calling. At 45 years, she told me. At 46 years, I divorced her. It was a very difficult emotional decision for me. The next two years were the most difficult.

This story is real. The telling of this story is based on real events. The drama was destructive to us, as a married couple, and to our family. It was a destructive storm that caused division and heartache, which I never thought possible. We had a wonderful life together until the devil in this story attacked.

After graduation from Baptist Bible College in 1980 with an Associate Degree in Theology, I became a pastor. I was a pastor of a Small Southern Baptist Church for a year, and then, I started a Church in Delta, Ohio. In 1984 I went to Liberty University to complete my Bachelor of Science, and then graduated Liberty Baptist Theological Seminary with a Master of Divinity in 1989. I became a chaplain in the United States Army and served until April 1, 2011. We had a great life! I thought we had a great marriage. Sally always supported me in ministry and the military. I never thought this could happen. I was blindsided.

*Author's Introduction:*

As I was writing this story, things changed in my heart. I hope you see this transformation as you read. I realized that the Lord was still walking with me, and His truth became my Light House. I realized that our story is like every love story. The beguiling of evil in the garden, by an enemy who desires to destroy, is the same devil in my story. The beguiling in the Garden of Eden started the battle against us.

My Champion is the Lord Jesus Christ. From the beginning, God had a plan. The plan is forgiveness! The plan redeems the brokenhearted, and the lost, who are not able to overcome without a Champion. This Champion is the Lord Jesus Christ. God has a plan for you to walk by His side again, in the garden! God has a plan for families! He created male and female, and they became one. The history of all humanity is involved in this story. You are in the drama! You are writing your portion of this story. Make it a good chapter for eternity. The following is my story: "Memories of Loving You."

## *Chapter One:*

# The Original Garden of God's Love

***The garden was disturbed:*** *The struggle between the light and the darkness.*

THE DARKNESS OF night lay over the garden, like a thick blanket, hiding all the creatures that were resting. It was the darkest hour and the canopy above was full of celestial wonder. Trillions of tiny stars scattered throughout heaven sang their silent music into the minds of sleeping creatures. The world was about to be awakened to another new day. A new sunrise would drive the darkness back into hiding. The light will reveal the amazing beauty of this small place within a massive universe. The place of life.

Many of the creatures were still in their slumber. However, there were a few already out of their beds. They were preparing themselves for the dawning of this new day. Every morning was the most beautiful experience to behold, as the light peeks over the horizon to begin the task of revealing the adventure of the day. The sun would rise slowly as the invisible power of the master's light traveled from far away. He would paint a new scene around them as they watched, for they were within the picture they observed. They are part of the story. The story is still being written. You are in the story.

The light battles against the darkness to force it to retreat. A thin edge of light pierced through the darkness over the horizon. Silhouetted with the distant trees and landscape that were held captive through the night, the first assault of the light against the perimeter of the darkness is revealed. The violence released amazing colors into the sky, as the light invaded to regain the territory held the day before. Each new sunrise became the unique power for the emerging beauty of the morning sky. A new day was born again before them. Only a special few return every morning to witness the victory of the light, as the garden awakens. Once again, life is rescued from death.

> Those who are awakened know that Joy comes in the morning! *(Psalms 30:5)*

*The Original Garden of God's Love*

These few hunger for the happiness and peace they witness, as the sunshine rises into the sky above. They marvel at the beauty, as the garden fills with wonder and depth. What they see reaches the distant landscape around them, pulling them into the activities of the day. The handiwork of the Master reveals His presence with them, and they enjoy His glory. Life is precious and each moment is a wonder to behold. Living life to the fullest in the beauty of His presence is the real joy they hunger for.

This cycle repeats every day telling the story of Life. The few who understand are enlightened with hope for their new adventures. They are the ones anticipating the outcome of this spiritual struggle. They are the ones hoping for freedom; so they may enjoy what the Master has given them. They are the ones who love life and understand the beauty of creation. They love the walk with God, who is present with them through the day, for Jehovah is pure light. There is no darkness when He is with them. The world becomes beautiful and full of life when the Lord God comes down to walk among them.

However, the darkness will return to fight. It is a power that hungers to control everything in the garden. It is a power that brings slavery and death. For behind this darkness hides a fallen creature who hungers to destroy the souls of the man, male and female, who are created in the image and likeness of God. The bondage of slavery to evil's control is the mission of the darkness. The removal of any joy for God's creatures to experience is at the core of evil's intent to destroy. Hate spawns hopelessness for those who cannot see. Those who cannot see walk in the darkness of death. They crawl back into their crevices and hopeless lairs when light is revealed. Joy always weakens when there is hopelessness within the soul. Despair dominates those who live in fear.

This war is fought on a global scale against all creation. The battle objectives of darkness are waged against every individual created in God's image and God's likeness. The first battle will soon take place in the garden. The enemy of God, who is the enemy of man, is making plans to force his darkness upon everything God has created. The end state of his evil strategy is to take total control and destroy all eternal hope. This evil creature does not want anyone to walk with God in peace and harmony. He wants all creatures to bow before him. He wants to sit upon the throne of God. He wants the rest of the night to become the darkness of his evil. He wants to inflict pain and hopelessness. He is watching you and preparing for his attack. Yes, you! His wicked strategy is

*The Original Garden of God's Love*

crafted each day against the children of man. He plans his attack against you even now!

The enemy weakens the objective until the conditions are just right, so he can capture his prey. Controlling communication is the first step to battle victory. The enemy knows this and his plan to strike at the weakest point is manipulated. He is the father of lies and he whispers deception into the minds of those who listen. He draws his enemy closer and closer until conditions are ready for him to strike with sudden force to destroy.

Every new day, the waking hour causes concern for the creatures of the night. Nocturnal beings begin their retreat into their dens to hide from the light soon revealed. They scurry into the cracks and crevices, in fear of what the light would soon unveil. Beasts of the night, seeking their prey, return to their lairs, hidden from the beauty and joy that was retaking the world from them. However, there was one who would remain hidden in the day, for he had a plan. It did not matter how long it would take, for time was of no concern in the Garden, yet. He waited and he manipulated the conditions to draw his objective into the kill zone. His ambush was enticing and intellectually seductive. His lust was an attack on the mind of the creature most loved by the Creator. He desired to be like the

Most High. He wanted to sit on the throne above the stars of God. He wants to be worshiped. *(Isaiah 14:12-14)* He wants other creatures to bow to his domain. He is the evil one. His costume is a subtle deception of distraction. Be careful, his trap is set for you. *(Ephesians 6:12)*

***Life in the Garden before it was disturbed.*** *The garden was good.*

Slowly rising over the horizon, the sun filled the garden to reveal the beauty of the world. It was a big garden filled with lush vegetation. Trees anchored into the soil reach upward into the canopy above, stretching their limbs over the earth. Grasses spread over the land to pull their life from the nutrients of the soil, and moisture is absorbed from beneath them, as the sunshine awakened every leaf and pedal with life, to begin this new day. The creatures in the garden must be fed with the life that grows upon the face of the garden. *(The power process of photosynthesis to make chlorophyll needs light, nutrients, and water. This becomes the base for all sustenance to feed every creature in God's Garden.)*

The power of life was being manufactured around them through the water, soil, and sunshine, for all creatures to consume in the cycle of life. Consumed and

*The Original Garden of God's Love*

passed on for all to share, the circle of life begets more life in this world. This power continues to be recreated every new day, within the plants that fill the garden with beauty. This power is intelligently designed by God for life to exist upon the earth. The Creator is the greatest master designer. He designed the experience of life to be filled with depth and diversity of color. He paints the scene of each new day differently than any other day because everything grows and moves when life is a reality.

He continues His creation even today. Plants grow. Animals consume. Life thrives in this world, which He placed within a massive universe. This world is the place of creative life. Of course, the enemy dares to take credit and his rhetoric spews into a rejection of God's Glory and power, which he forces into the minds of the innocent. They become foolish. They become self-theists, which was the sin that the serpent beguiled our first mother with. *(Psalm 14:1, Romans 1:22)*

The picture changes every moment, emerging from the retreat of the darkness, from the dull interruption of slumber, into the transforming experience of being alive. Every morning was a reminder of the first awakening moment of life. A moment every creature has experienced. Some creatures realize this and rush into their day to experience the world given to them. They want to live in this wonderful garden. They want to see the beauty, smell the flowers, and feel the sensation of the world upon their flesh. They want to hear the sounds of life around them and they want to listen for the voice of God. Even the one who walks with God longs for the light to remain with him. Stay with me.

***Two, but yet one.***   *Male and female created as one.*

This day she lay next to the one she loved resting in his arms, just as she had already experienced so many days before. Her eyes caught the first glimmer of light that began chasing the darkness away. Her mind was aroused and she pulled him closer to her heart. The warmth of their togetherness snuggled them closer but he was still asleep. She wanted to rush into her day to experience that first awakening moment again. They had experienced this awakening moment together for many sunrises. They shared the joy of being together as they anticipated their daily walk with the Lord. It was a moment relived every time she awakened. Every day was a new adventure. Life was exciting!

*The Original Garden of God's Love*

She always remembered her first experience of opening her eyes. The immediate awakening of consciousness, to see her Creator smiling upon her, was her first thought every morning. She remembered the first touch of her lover when the Lord brought them together. The excitement she felt on the first day of life would be relived every morning and shared throughout the day. This touch reminds her that she is not alone. She is loved!

She did not grow into her adult experience as a child. She was never a baby. Babies do not remember their awakening moment. They grow into their family experience. She awakened to intellectual understanding when life surged into her body. She was an adult when she opened her eyes. She is the only woman to experience what Adam experienced when he first awakened. She saw the Lord looking upon her after He completed His work. She too walked with God in the garden. They were together.

She was not created separately, but rather, she was created from within her lover. She awakened as a unique individual, but she came from within the man she lay next to. The man whom she loved! The DNA was taken from the strands of cells within his rib and she was designed by her Creator to finish the man, so they could become one together. She was created to help man, for the Lord God realized that it was not good for man to be alone. The completed work of God in man was only good after the Lord created this amazing woman and brought her to Adam. Then, God said it was good.

They were one! Almighty God finished His work in man when the wo**man** was taken from the side of man to complete this creature, who would reflect the glory of God. Man was created in the likeness and image of God. He was given a gift that no other creature was given. With this gift comes great responsibility. They were both given this responsibility together as one. *"This is the book of the generations of Adam. In the day that God created man, in the likeness and image of God made he him; male and female created he them; and blessed them, and called their name Adam, in the day they were created."* (Genesis 5:1-2 KJV) [Only pronouns – he & her, became they and them as one together.]

"And God said, Let us make man in our image, after our likeness: and let them have dominion over the fish of the sea, and over the fowl of the air, and the cattle, and over all the earth, and over every creeping thing that creepeth upon the earth. So God created man in his *own* image, in the image of God created he him; male and

*The Original Garden of God's Love*

female created he them. And God blessed them, and God said unto them, Be fruitful, and multiply, and replenish the earth, and subdue it: and have dominion over the fish of the sea, and over the fowl of the air, and over every living thing that moveth upon the earth. And God said, Behold, I have given you every herb bearing seed, which *is* upon the face of all the earth, and every tree, in the which *is* the fruit of a tree yielding seed; to you, it shall be for meat. And to every beast of the earth, and to every fowl of the air, and to everything that creepeth upon the earth, wherein *there is* life, *I have given* every green herb for meat: and it was so. And God saw everything that he had made, and, behold, *it was* very good. And the evening and the morning were the sixth day." *(Genesis 1:26–31)*

***One command is    The knowledge of good and evil.***
***a warning.***

Awakened from her rest, she silently stepped away from her lover. He was still asleep. Each step was soft and silent as she distanced herself. This morning she wanted to sneak away into the garden as an individual. She wanted to be alone. Adam spent many days alone, waiting for God in the morning before she was awakened to life. She was challenged many times by a beautiful serpent to look upon. A serpent that seemed wise, who challenged her intellectual understanding of her world, whose words stayed within her mind and questioned her thoughts each day.

She was drawn away by these thoughts, spoken by a creature she listened to many times. These thoughts pull her away from her home, to wander deeper into the garden. Drawn away by the serpent's words, she prepared for this day. She set conditions that would not be questioned by Adam, for she started playing a game of, "Find me in the Garden," which became a fun challenge for them both. They played hide and seek often.

They took turns wandering off alone and leaving clues for the other to follow. Then the challenge to find the one he loved became playful and rewarding. Each time the game ended, they were together enjoying life within the fruitful garden. The challenges included unique visual beauty, varieties of sustenance, and physical pleasure of land and water, where they both relished in pleasure as one, to experience the unique individual existence that brought them together in oneness. They were one and they were the beginning of a family! They are the First Family! They will be the First Parents!

*The Original Garden of God's Love*

Often, they would wander down the same adventurous paths into the garden because she wanted to be found. He did too. For life in the garden was a wondrous adventure and they enjoyed being together. Love is a spiritual deep connection of the heart, which grows like a seed, in the garden between lovers. The purpose of a garden is to create more life. It is a place of bonding and growth. In the garden, there is a multiplication of oneness into increasing fruitful ancestry. More unique individuals come from the garden. The original garden was just the beginning. Many gardens will fill the earth through time, and the world will increase by the design of the Creator. A wise man understands!

The path she would take on this early morning journey would lead her deeper into the garden, where she had been many times already in secret. It was an area that Adam stayed away from. He did not want to disobey the one commandment of God that he was given. It seems like a simple command, which could be easy to keep. But it was given to Adam and he shared it with Eve after she was taken from his side. God told Adam that he should not eat the fruit that was in the midst of the garden. The warning to obey the command was, that if he did eat of this fruit, he would surely die. *(Genesis 3)*

**Disobedience dishonors God.** *Separation from the only source of Life!*

Curiosity manipulated Eve to wander down this path again. The one creature of darkness, that stayed out in the light, enticed her many times to take the first step down the wrong path. She wandered closer and closer toward the area which Adam told her was a place to stay away from. She knew that something amid the garden was off-limits. She knew that there were consequences for the disobedience of God's command, but her curiosity pulled her farther each time until she stood next to the forbidden. The one thing the Lord God said they should not do, she entertained. Adam told her that if she ate of the fruit on the tree of, "The Knowledge of Good and Evil," that death would occur. She wondered what that meant. She wondered why.

The beautiful serpent began his beguiling the first time he gazed upon this amazing creature, whom he became jealous of. His first contact with her was filled with compliments and suggestive conversation, after which, his words pulled her down this path many times.

*The Original Garden of God's Love*

Closer and closer she approached the grove where this tree stood. Once she was there, he whispered his enticing words into her ear. He cast doubt and he challenged her thinking with pleasure. He spoke things that were close to the truth but always with some deceit and doubt for God's word. He kept up his assault each time she wandered close to the tree, questioning God's authority. This serpent beguiled her to think that God was withholding what was even better than what she had. God is keeping something from you. It can be yours if you want it. "You can be as God, knowing good and evil," the serpent repeated many times into her thoughts. "Just take a bite and you will see and know what you can become." "Go ahead and eat. The fruit tastes amazing. It is the best in the garden. God is keeping you from the best!" The creature from the dark side, who was cast out from heaven with 1/3 of the rebellious angels, beguiled Eve to eat the forbidden fruit. Maybe just once, but always not enough.

This morning, after many previous temptations, Eve walked closer to the tree, closer than ever before. The serpent grimised within. "Come, there is a ripe one here, just for you," he enticed her. "You will be as God, knowing good and evil." "Take a bite and see!" "Don't let God keep this from you. It is your choice." "Adam knows something he will not tell you." "You are an individual and you can decide…"

Finally, Eve picked one of the fruits off the tree. She picked many fruits off other trees before and this seemed normal. She held it in her hand to look closer. She smelled the fragrance of the fruit. It was different than the other fruits in the garden. By smelling it many times, she held it close to her lips. The sensation of the texture added to her curiosity, pulling her deeper toward her demise. Breath after breath she inhaled the smell and she felt the forbidden presence that pulled at her flesh. His beguiling words stirred the challenge in her mind. "Just try it once," the devil whispered.

She thought of Adam, who was out in the garden looking for her, but she knew he would not come this way. Could she get away with this? Should she just taste the juice if she bites into the flesh? Maybe just a little taste would be ok. "Adam would never know," she thought. "How could he find out?" She reasoned. The truth is she was already drawn away by temptation because of the trap set by the serpent, who was excited about the moments leading her to this point. He leaned forward to whisper his deception again. "Didn't God tell Adam not to eat this fruit because you will be as God, knowing good and evil?"

*The Original Garden of God's Love*

"God is keeping this from you," he whispered again. "Do it! Do it now!!!"

Eve responded, "We should not eat or even touch this fruit, lest we die." "Death is not so bad," the fallen creature declared. "I walked with God at one time and I disobeyed Him. Look at me now. I am so beautiful. I am still here," the serpent hissed.

After listening to his persuasion again, she examined the fruit she already had in her hands. She opened her lips and sank her teeth into the flesh of the fruit, as the juices entered her mouth and were ingested into her being. What just happened was much more than just tasting or eating. It was a conscious decision of her soul to disobey Almighty God. At that moment the world changed for Eve. She felt it in her flesh. She experienced it in her soul. Fear poured down her throat and was absorbed into her body. Death began it's slow process of separation instantaneously.

Cut off from the source of life, which is Almighty God, who is Holy. Sin cannot dwell in His presence. This is why the lying serpent was cast out of heaven. It is the reason he was in the garden, which he wants to destroy. He is the father of lies. He is the evil of darkness. He hates man because he hates God. He hates the woman because she is the matrix of ancestry for all mankind.

She is the vessel of heredity for all humanity. Without her, man would still be alone and incomplete. She is God's completion of man, for she is the only being that can multiply the seed of man within her womb, and grow humanity into a lush garden. A garden that grows with life! This garden was meant to fill the earth with sentient beings created to be the Glory of God. The children were meant to walk with God forever. They were meant to explore and experience the adventure of living. Many adventures still wait.

The Family of God would fill the Earth with intellectual beings who can comprehend complexity to know the creativity of life and experience these adventures. These beings would be able to go beyond instinct and hunger for knowledge to understand. They would be creative and loving. Each child born would be a soul, created in God's image and likeness. Man would have fellowship with the Creator! Man would walk with God in the garden and experience things to be revealed, which eyes have not seen or ears have heard. Yet! The eternal experience will always lead to more understanding and wondrous adventures. *(Our current senses only understand this limited world. More power surrounds us that we cannot yet sense.)*

This rebellious demon, the father of lies, chose his target to destroy. He launched his assault with words. He manipulated the target with psychological warfare. His mission goal was within reach. It was D-Day! He was ready to destroy. He hungered for it!

**Death entered the garden.** *The whole world groans in pain.*

Eve immediately shuttered within her body and soul. Death shook every cell inside her and terror filled her mind. The world around her instantly changed. She felt it's fear in her flesh. Her skin felt the darkness pressing into her. She felt danger from everything around her. The other creatures hissed and stepped away from her. There was danger now, and she was the source. Animals feared what they saw and scurried away from her presence. Her eyes were open to sin and she had an understanding of the evil she was guilty of. She wanted to hide from what she had done. She felt naked and exposed to a dangerous world. Her mind raced with scenarios, as she wanted to take it back. She wanted to do it over and never walk down the path that led her to this place. It was too late.

The deed was done and the consequences piled up. Sin affects the sinner but it also affects others around them. The world was not the same now. The world was in pain. The Animal Kingdom was shattered and the Earth groans.

Her fear caused her to remember Adam. He was out there. He was her lover and she feared being alone. What they had together was so wonderful, but she just knew it could never be the same. How could he love her now? "He is going to be angry at me," she openly spoke, as the serpent laughed at her demise. "Now you know, what God was keeping from you," the evil victor announced with glee.

She cried for the first time. She bawled her eyes out in fear and sorrow. It was a lingering death she was experiencing, which would end in physical death someday. This journey would lead to much suffering and heartache for her. The end of this sinful journey will destroy what could have been eternal happiness. She was meant to be a mother! Her joy of motherhood would begin in great pain and end in deep sorrow because of her act of sin. Much heartache and pain was her future.

She ran back up the path to find Adam. She ran and ran as she cried in fear. She checked all of their favorite places until she saw him overlooking the garden valley.

*The Original Garden of God's Love*

Watching him from a distance, she could see he was anxious. He knew something was different and was already searching for any sign that would lead him to her. He knew that she was in trouble. He could feel the violation of their oneness. How could this be? How did this happen? What was going on? Yes, Adam was confused. He felt alone again. Loneliness is a horrible experience once you understand the oneness of family.

| | |
|---|---|
| ***She reveals her transgression.*** | *She admits to Adam that she ate the forbidden fruit.* |

Eve approached Adam from behind, as he searched the valley below from his vantage point. As silently as she left him in the morning, she walked up to him and touched his back, sending her fears into his flesh. Adam jumped as he turned. He was startled at her touch. The effect of her sin could already be felt. He could see her sorrow. This is how he knew she was in trouble. The world around him was affected and their oneness was violated. He could see her fear when he looked into her eyes. Her tears spoke the tale of her disobedience.

"What is wrong," Adam questioned. "Why do your eyes weep and your body shake?" "I have never seen you like this before!" "Where have you been?" he demanded.

"I am worried about you, something is different." "What can I do?" He asked. He already felt the harm of her actions and he felt fear for the first time.

Holding her in his arms, to comfort her, he continued to question her. After calming her down some, she began to reveal her experience. She shared with Adam all the times she went to the forbidden tree and the words that the serpent whispered in her ears. Then she revealed the details of the moment she took the bite; How her teeth pierced the skin of the fruit and the juices sprayed the elixir of knowledge forbidden into her mouth. She told him how she felt and how this event changed her world. It changed her understanding of everything. It was too late to take it back and she did not know how to move forward.

Her understanding of Good and Evil permeated every thought now, and her choices were different. She no longer just thought about right and wrong. She thought about the conflict of right and wrong and how it affected her relationship with God, as well as, her relationship with Adam, her husband. Her understanding makes the choices between what is good and what is evil. Everything has become a conflict in her mind. Her sin has put everything at war and caused division in the world. The understanding of the knowledge of good and evil divides the world and forces creatures, with this understanding, to take sides. It divides. It separates. It causes hate and violence. But, it leaves in place the "Free Will," of the individual, who must choose good or evil. They were no longer innocent

Of course, there are consequences to the choices made. The individual is responsible for actions taken, based on the choices made. There is accountability because man makes his/her choices based on this moral division. There is more to consider than just right and wrong now. There is a contrast between good and evil. Knowing this difference makes the choice between God's Goodness and Holiness, which allows His presence, and, the disobedience of evil, which violates what is morally good and causes harm. This makes each individual, who makes a choice, responsible for the choice. Choices have consequences. Our choices also affect others. Choose to be a good human being!

The gift that God created in man, male and female, was only created in humanity. Mankind was created in God's likeness and image, which means a lot of things, but specifically, it means that man, male and female, have free will. Man is not a Marionette Puppet on a string being controlled by the Master, nor is he a sock puppet with

God's hand making all the movement. Man is a being created to fellowship with God. Man is created to understand wonders and experience goodness. He was made to walk with God and to discover wonderful things throughout the eternal space. He was not created to be in conflict with his creator. However, being able to experience free will means that there must be a choice. There must be a contrast! Without contrast, there is no free will and no image and likeness of God in a created being.

As Eve wrestled with her explanation to understand what happened, she made excuses for her experience. The fruit she brought with her, she held before her husband, "See, I am holding it now and nothing happens." "Join me, I do not want to be alone," she tried to persuade him. "We can still be together. I love you. I want to be with you. We can do this together…" she whispered in his ear as she softly touched his skin. "We can be together. Join me. Be with me. Love me. Just take a bite and we can be together," her fallen heart cried out.

Adam held her in his arms, listening to her words and feeling her love and sorrow over the separation they both felt. They were uniquely separate individuals but they were one. The goodness of their oneness was broken, but they both felt a loss that they wanted to change. They

*The Original Garden of God's Love*

wanted what they had before. They wanted the joy of being together and still being in fellowship with God. They wanted to walk with God, but they knew this could not happen now. Eve lost something precious and Adam was worried.

Adam cared for Eve. He loved her! The first time God brought Eve to Adam, his heart was racing within. She became his great love and joy. They had fun in the garden. They swam in the beautiful pools of water together. They enjoyed the beauty that surrounded them. A world full of life and color that pulls into the imagination of adventure was the world they shared. They held each other and felt the pleasure of their love together. They slept in each other's arms through the night, and they wandered through the garden holding hands and gathering the fruit of life during each day. They cared for the animals, creatures of all kinds. The fowl of the air above, the beast of the earth, and all the creatures, big and small, were their joy. They were happy at one time. The clock was ticking now, and time waits for no man. Time has a beginning and an end. Time takes you somewhere. Hopefully, you want to be there.

Adam was the most perfect man ever created. He was strong and physically the most attractive man that would ever walk the earth. He was intellectually superior to any man. (No caveman here!) Eve was the most beautiful and intelligent woman who would ever walk the earth, for she was created to be the completion of good for man. It was their oneness together that formed into the perfect union of marriage, which became family. The family would be the heredity of humanity. But every cell and every gene in her body was affected now, and the perfection of humanity would not be the same.

Adam felt the happiness they once enjoyed was gone. The garden around them was empty. The animals all fled. They knew that everything was changing. Only God could make things right again. God must not see them like this. "We must hide," Adam thought. "How can I hide Eve and make this right?" There was no answer as he tried to think things through. The reality is that God is teaching man how bad sin is.

Eve looked Adam in the eye with her loneliness of fear and asked him to take a bite. His heart sank within him, as he pulled her so close he could feel her heart beating. Then he pushed her away at arm's distance to gaze upon her. The moment seemed like it would never end. It had to end. She had fallen in sin and he was still innocent. The eternal and time were embraced for a moment.

*The Original Garden of God's Love*

Adam wanted to be with her because he loved her. He also knew that he must obey the Lord God. These thoughts ran through his mind as he looked at her. His empathy pulled him from what was good toward what he considered. She held the forbidden fruit in her hand and raised it to his face. "See, it looks great and smells wonderful. It tastes amazing," she declared. Adam brushed it away at first but Eve kept trying. She did not want to be alone. She thought the only way to survive was to have Adam at her side. She knew nothing else.

Finally, she convinced Adam to hold the fruit in his hands. He raised it to his face and breathed deeply to take in the smell. It touched his lips as he inhaled. Eve watched Adam consider the choice and she smiled. "I want to be with you my love," she spoke passionately, as she pulled him into her arms. After a long moment of embrace, as they still pressed together tightly, Adam raised the fruit to his lips, opened his mouth, and pierced the fruit with his teeth. Taking a chunk of the fruit's flesh, with all the juice flowing into his mouth, he ingested the fruit from the "Tree of The Knowledge of Good and Evil." He willfully made this choice. He joined her in the moment of his disobedience.

Instantly, Adam knew he lost something very precious. At that moment, the world changed even more; like it changed when Eve took her bite. They both lost the connection to God's Spirit, which was breathed into the body of Adam when he first became a living soul. The created spirit of man that was connected to the source of life, who is God Almighty, was separated from the Lord. The spirit of Adam became dead in trespass and sin. Their bodies began to age because the source of life was removed. *(Like a battery or an electrical connection that keeps the power active and full, they were cut off.)* Their power of life would eventually run out, and their bodies would age and physically die. Sin causes death. Death is the greatest enemy of man. An eternal creature in a state of death is a terrible thing. In fact, it might be the greatest horror of all horrors.

The clock of time started to tick. The measurement of time started because what was innocent and perfect began to decay. The created world was affected when sin entered the world and death by sin, so death passed upon all. In the Second Law of Thermodynamics, everything moves from a perfect and good state to a state of corruption, and destruction becomes their reality. It is the law of sin. The end is not good. The end is evil's vengeance of hate.

***Their eyes were open.*** *They were both naked and hid themselves from God.*

They were exposed to the world they once enjoyed and they were afraid. Their happiness became sorrow. The beauty of the Garden withered. There was no place to hide. Their joy became heartache. Their pleasure became a hardship. They lost something precious and they had no power to overcome. Their shame of nakedness shrouded them from innocence. They just hid from God. Fear entered and their confidence waned. Accountability for disobedience was coming. Good is removed from them.

"Adam, where are you?" "Adam, why are you hiding?" The Lord called out to them both because they were called "Adam" as one. They were the first family. The first couple to exist in this world. They were going to be the first parents. The first grandparents of all humanity. The DNA code God created in man, which would continue the creation of all humanity, was within the flesh now affected by sin. The couple was hiding. They were afraid to face God. They were afraid to walk with God.

The Lord knew where they were, and what was done this day, but He still called out to them. "Adam, where are you?" Finally, Adam revealed himself to the Lord. "What have you done?" The Lord questioned. Almighty God knew what happened, but He wanted them to confess their action of disobedience. Like a loving father, He questioned his child, "What have you done?"

God repeated the question many times, trying to get Adam to respond. Truth and honesty were the virtues created in the man and woman standing before Him, but now they were hiding. Hiding from responsibility. Hiding from accountability. Hiding from their God. They were embarrassed and afraid. They felt guilty. They were guilty. They were so afraid that they blamed others for what they chose to do.

Adam began to blame Eve, but he blamed God for creating her. She gave him the forbidden fruit. She brought it to him. She enticed him to eat. The Lord knew what happened and how it happened. He knew the moment it did happen. There was no good excuse or reason for this to happen. Lust and covetousness entrapped them. Temptation became the tool of sin's entrapment. Eve was beguiled by the serpent, and Adam willingly violated the one command of God, not to eat of this fruit. The one

*The Original Garden of God's Love*

thing that allowed "Freewill" to be created in man, was violated. The choice became the battle, which caused the continuous division of humanity. Sin separates man from God. Sin separates man from others. Sin separated man from life. "The soul that sins dies."

The Lord turned to Eve and asked her, "What is this you have done?" She immediately blamed the serpent who beguiled her. It is his fault because he told me I would know good and evil, making me more like you. "The devil made me do it." "I was tricked." "The fruit looked delicious." "I just wanted to taste it..." "It looked and smelled so good." Her excuses piled up. *(The storyline is created from Genesis chapter three. King James Version)*

Eve was tempted by "Self-Theism," which is making oneself God, knowing good and evil. "God knows that in the day you eat thereof, you will be as God knowing good and evil," the serpent's words hissed in her ears. The words constantly whispered, were like never-ending tinnitus ringing in her mind.

> "And the eyes of both of them were opened, and they knew that they *were* naked, and they sewed fig leaves together, and made themselves aprons. And they heard the voice of the Lord God walking in the garden in the cool of the day: and Adam

and his wife hid themselves from the presence of the Lord God amongst the trees of the garden. And the Lord God called to Adam and said to him, Where *art th*ou? And he said, I heard thy voice in the garden, and I was afraid, because I was naked; and I hid myself. And he said, Who told thee that thou *wast* naked? Hast thou eaten from the tree, whereof I commanded thee that thou shouldest not eat? And the man said, The woman whom thou gavest *to be* with me, she gave me of the tree, and I did eat. And the Lord God said to the woman, What *is* this thou have done? And the woman said, The serpent beguiled me, and I did eat. And the Lord God said unto the serpent Because thou hast done this, thou *art* cursed above all cattle, and above every beast of the field; upon thy belly shalt thou go, and dust shalt thou eat all the days of thy life: And I will put enmity between thee and the woman, and between thy seed and her seed; it shall bruise thy head, and thou shalt bruise his heel. Unto the woman, he said: I will greatly multiply thy sorrow and thy conception; in sorrow, thou shalt bring forth children; thy desire *shall be to thy* husband, and he shall rule over thee. And

*The Original Garden of God's Love*

unto Adam, he said, Because thou hast hearkened unto the voice of thy wife, and hast eaten of the tree, of which I commanded thee, saying, Thou shalt not eat of it: cursed *is* the ground for thy sake; in sorrow shalt thou eat *of* it all the days of thy life; Thorns also and thistles shall it bring forth to thee; and thou shalt eat the herb of the field; In the sweat of thy face shalt thou eat bread, till thou return unto the ground; for out of it wast thou taken: for dust thou *art, a*nd unto dust shalt thou return."*(Genesis 3:7-19)*

***The consequence of***   Man is held responsible.
***their action.***

Everything was exposed. They tried to hide what was already done but it was out in the open for the world to see. They were prostrate in their shame and embarrassment before their Heavenly Father. Their feeble attempt to cover their shame of nakedness failed. There was nothing hidden before this judge. Truth is truth and fig leaves cannot cover sin. They were exposed and the consequence of their transgression demands justice.

Naked and afraid, they groveled in the dust of shame that they laid upon before God's presence. Walking in the garden with the Lord was not possible now. Sharing the beauty of God's creation was not a thought. Time was ticking against them, for the eternal experience of life was no longer theirs. The eternal experience of life was already removed because of their sinful presence in the garden, for what had already transpired affected everything created upon this earth. Fear dominated every creature because they were exposed to the consequences of man's sin. They too were separated from God's glorious presence because of sin's power. The earth travails in pain. *(Romans 8:22)*

The animals ran away from them. The birds flew away to hide. Fish swam deep to escape. All creatures in this world feared man and what man had ingested into their being. They feared what man unleashed upon the world.

The trees withered as they struggled to grow. Flowers would bloom trying to multiply their beauty, but their petals shriveled in time. Death fell upon them and fear divided these amazing beings, both great and small. There was now violence between them. There was a hunger to survive. A motivation to dominate and control the world around them floated to the surface of their reality. The struggle to stay alive became a daily mission

*The Original Garden of God's Love*

in this world that eats the weak. Everything was fallen! Sin destroys joy!

The Lord God, Creator of everything, pronounced a judgment upon each individual being. The result of sin becomes known to them all. The difference between good and evil will be experienced. The importance of the gift of free will must be known to every creature born. Pain is passed on to every child. Sorrow will be known, as they experience the tears of failure and loss. Fear will shroud their decisions and their activities. The garden will become darker with spiritual sorrow, as death brings decay and destruction upon the living. Separation from Almighty God is a horrible thing to behold and to become. Death passed upon all for all have sinned. Fallen from the glory of God's intent. Failed in the attempted glory of self-theism to be as God, knowing good and evil.

***Judgment for sin is*** *Nothing is ever forgotten.*
***inevitable.***

Almighty God judged the serpent who beguiled the woman. The Lord cursed the serpent, whose experience of sin's power in this world will be greater than any other creature. Sin already affected everything, but the Lord told this guilty creature, who beguiled the woman to disobey, that the result of sin's curse would be worse on him than any other being. The serpent was then cast down upon the dust of the earth. Everything he would do would be shrouded in the dust of death's end state, for death will be the plight of all creatures. This snake on his belly will forever feel the death of all creatures because of what he has done.

Death will be ingested every time his beguiling split tongue flickers from his mouth to sense the world. He will crawl within and upon the decomposing emulsification of the dead, that once grew with life. The aspiration to be God has taken him down death's path toward hell's eternal confinement. The serpent became a snake, who crawls in the excrement dust of what once was alive.

Then the Lord pronounced hope for man. He declared that the conflict between the snake and the woman would be a continuing war of hostility and hate. The division of good and evil will be a continuing fight of hatefulness. These battles will be passed on to their children. Evil will hate everything good, and those who accept evil will live with evil. They will always live in hate. There will be violence between man and the spiritual evil that will invade their hearts. This evil will bleed into humanity through the persistence of sin's power. But, there will be hope for man.

*The Original Garden of God's Love*

The seed (demonic fallen angels and followers of evil) of the serpent will cause enmity, hateful warfare, and constant conflict. Conflict with immoral violations of God's Holiness, against the children born to the woman (mankind-humanity). This spiritual evil of immorality will continue to be the experience of sin throughout creation. Some will accept and normalize immoral behavior. What is not naturally normal becomes an abomination against the Holiness of God. Death continues to spread through time, as it's destructive force consumes it's prey. Sin beguiles those who approach, listen, and taste this forbidden fruit of rebellion against the Creator, Almighty God.

Specific battles of spiritual warfare will continue between the serpent and humanity. This is a real conflict, which is at the core of every violence and every hateful action humanity will ever experience. The father of lies will continue to deceive. Knowing good and evil is knowing happiness and hate. It is knowing peace and violence. It is warfare in the soul!

Then God reveals the hope for humanity and the defeat of the serpent. A unique and specific prophecy is declared by God. His purpose and plan for humanity are disclosed for all to hear. Something seemingly impossible is foretold for future generations to understand. The first prophetic announcement is spoken: the seed of the woman will destroy the seed of the evil serpent. There will be a Champion, who will defeat the evil intent of sin's destruction of man. *"And I will put enmity between thee and the woman, and between thy seed and her seed; it shall bruise your head, and thou shalt bruise His heel." (Genesis 3:5)*

This prophetic announcement was concise. The Savior will be born from the seed of the woman. We know that the DNA code passed on through time, which continues the creation of humanity that started in Adam, has specific details to form within the woman. God creates the egg in the woman, females, but, only men, males, produce the seed. This prophecy was specifically referring to a Savior who would be miraculously born to a virgin. This Messiah will crush the head of the serpent. The serpent will bruise the heel of the one miraculously born, but the victory will be evil's defeat. Death, the penalty of sin, will be defeated. Life will conquer death for all who believe.

Then the Lord told Eve that her sin would bring her great sorrow and pain. She will bear children through suffering. These children will experience the pain of her sin. They will know the difference between good and evil. They will make decisions based on what is good and evil. Death, with all its consequences, will pass upon all who will be

*The Original Garden of God's Love*

born into this world. To Eve He said: *"I will greatly multiply thy sorrow and thy conception, in sorrow, thou shalt bring forth children, and thy desire shall be to thy husband, and he shall rule over thee."(Genesis 3:16)*

The pleasure of life and the joy of family will become the sorrow she faces. The pleasure of bonding in oneness will cause her pain when she bears her children. She will need her man by her side in this dangerous world. She will need his help and protection. The family will survive because of her desire for her husband. The family will thrive when he takes responsibility as a man, to guide and protect her and their children. The family will grow when she looks to him as the leader. Her desire will be for him, as he completely provides for her, and the children. She must rely upon him and she must continue to help him be the better man he must become. Family is most important and she nurtures her family to be good. She is a mother! Like a Good King who is loved, he will provide a realm of protection for her that is based on love. Good love and a safe dominion, not a kingdom of evil, but a Kingdom of Goodness and Love. This is Family! Ruling equals a good provider, who provides a safe realm for those he loves. It is not forceful domination and cruelty. It is not enslavement or control! It is willing submission, which is the blessing to another in love, willingly offered by the one who loves.

The Lord turns to Adam and clarifies the charges he is guilty of. Adam listened to Eve after she sinned. He chose between who to honor. He chose who to obey. Adam chose to follow her, rather than trusting God. He ate willingly! He ate to be with her, rather than walk with God.

God did not curse Adam. He cursed the ground around Adam. He cursed the ground that would provide sustenance for his family. He did it for the goodness of Adam. The Lord told Adam that he would have to work hard to provide for his wife and family. He will struggle and fight to provide what his family needs to keep living. Evil will fight against his every effort, and death will take love away from him. Death will be their sorrow as they struggle to live as one. The world needs good strong Godly families!

The sin-cursed ground will fight to reclaim what they need. What grows out of death's dusty soil will be what sustains fallen man. Food for his family will require labor to provide. Hard work filled with failures and success will be placed on the table for his family. The plants will have thorns that pierce the flesh and cause pain. What was easy to gather in the garden will now take hardship to provide. The ground will fill with weeds that steal nutrients from fruitful plants. These thistles will steal food from the table. The health of humanity is at stake. We began dying when sin became the reality. This end is not good without the Lord. Only what becomes new will last, a "New birth" is required!

Preparation of food will be required for flavor. Your food will not be ready at the picking, like in the garden. A hard day of work will be required every day until you die. You will sweat from the labor needed to survive in this fallen world. Then, in the end, you will die. Your body will return to the dirt. It will decay into the soil from which it was made. Because of your sin, you will physically return to dust. "The wages of sin is death." Death separates from God. Death is not good.

***Driven from the Garden.*** *The first family is sent out into a fallen world full of hardship.*

Almighty God called forth His greatest warrior angels, the cherubims who were His guardians. He commanded them to guard the garden with flaming swords that turn every which way to keep sinners from eating from the Tree of Life, lest the sinner would live in the eternal state of death, and there would be no hope. The serpent,

Lucifer, was the Covering Cherub before his fall. Two Cherubs will guard the "Tree of Life." *(Ezekiel 28:12-19) They will protect this tree from evil's violation.*

The Lord pointed to the exit of the Garden and told Adam and Eve to leave. The snake slithered away into this fallen world as Adam and Eve were driven away from God's presence. They were lost in a hostile world. They wandered far away and God closed the entrance of the Garden from them. They had to survive a world of difficulty.

> *"And the Lord God said, Behold, the man is become as one of us, to know good and evil: and now, lest he put forth his hand, and take also of the tree of life, and eat, and live for ever: Therefore the Lord God sent him forth from the garden of Eden, to till the ground from whence he was taken. So he drove out the man, and he placed at the east of the garden of Eden Cherubims, and a flaming sword which turned every way, to keep the way of the tree of life. (Genesis 3:22-24)*

This is the story of the first man, male and female, our greatest grandparents. Similarities of the same story

*The Original Garden of God's Love*

we all experience. The desire for good in life struggles against the evil we now face every day. We may have different scenarios with the complexity of situations, but we all face the choices between good and evil now. We walk upon the soil of hardship and doom. Death is our fate because sin has filled the earth. Our only HOPE is in the Lord! Jesus invites you to come and find His rest. *(Matthew 11;28)*

I wonder how many times Adam and Eve wanted to go back to the garden. I wonder if Adam ever tried to rethink what he did when he ate the fruit that terrible day. Did he feel remorse for his act of sin, which caused this harm to his family? Did he look into the faces of his children and regret his act of disobedience? Eve must have cried many days and nights. She lived with great sorrow. Each child born was a reminder of her sorrow. The intense pain she caused her children was re-lived in the moment she became a mother, but each child born became her joy and happiness too. Did she regret following the serpent down the path to the tree so many times? Did she want to go back and re-live that moment she ate the fruit? Her memories were laced with sorrow, as she lived her life with Adam in a world that was hostile to their existence. The human race multiplied upon the

*Memories of Loving You*

earth. Joy was accompanied by sadness, as they walked away from the Garden of God's Glory on their journey to survive in a fallen world.

## Chapter Two:

# Falling in Love and Creating a Family on the Battlefield of Life

[Battlefield Development for
The Ultimate War Against Humanity]

**MANY GENERATIONS FROM** the original garden, we fell in love, and we started our journey of life in a fallen world. Meet me in the Garden so we can fall in love again.

A garden is a beautiful place of new beginnings. A healthy garden becomes a beautiful peaceful environment, where we discover growth and true oneness. It is a great place to fall in love! When we fall in love in the garden, we join together and become family. We become greater than ourselves and have the ability to increase our oneness. It is where we nurture and grow who we become in life. In the garden, there is nutrition for a healthy relationship. The soil beneath us is our foundation. The rain falls upon us to quench our thirst and sustain us with our daily needs. In the garden, the power of the sunshine will pull us up from the earth to become more together, as we grow in our adventure of life. As a family, we become a garden that grows.

Sustenance is shared in this garden, which feeds the body and soul. Life contributes to life, and the garden grows. It produces many things we must have to exist in our world: all the nutrients we need to live and become strong, and a beautiful world around us to share. We become the garden together. We become family! The Spirit breathed into humanity dwells in this Good Garden of Life we become. Our life in oneness has become our children's lives for many generations.

My love, let us go for a walk through the garden. I want to see this beautiful world of color, and I want to share it with you. I want to feel the breeze upon my flesh and inhale the fresh air together. I want to breathe the air you breathe and see the world through your smile. We must walk through the rain and laugh at each other. We must lay upon every bed of flowers to rest. I want to watch every sunrise and start all over again every morning to love you. When each day is done, I would love to share the beautiful sunset with you as our evening runs into the night. Together, darkness only becomes rest. I will build a home for us and we will experience a growing family. There will be a swing for us to share, so when we are old, we will sit and remember every moment, as our children fill our garden with life. We must go back. We must walk together in love with the Lord.

Come, my love, walk with me in our garden...

A good foundation must be built before the actual story is understood. Bear with me as I speak from my understanding and my heart. This is a love story that struggles against a persistent narcissistic enemy, a snake. It is a story of hardship and loss amid an amazing life together. This life weathered the worst of storms, and yet, fought an enemy who tried to steal your love from me. A Giant Narcissistic Enemy of hate is still defying true love. He beguiles us all. He challenges the Creator's design of our Love. He wants to divide us so he can destroy us and enslave our humanity. He is successful with many. The story is still being written and battles are still being fought. However, the end is much greater than the beginning. The victory is already sealed. It is finished!

When I was young, finding a woman to love was a challenge. Loving a woman for a lifetime is an adventure.

But finding a woman, who loves you back for a lifetime, is an exhilarating happiness that makes a man good. She is the journey. She is the adventure of life! My love is who fulfills and motivates me to be more than I would be without her! She makes me better than I could be: Had I remained alone, I could not be who I am today. Liking who you are and what you become is the paradise of the journey. I did not like myself for a while. Maybe others did not like me too. However, I like myself and who I became because I have you walking with me along the way!

Many have lost their way. We no longer understand the gift we have received from our Creator. We no longer understand the gift that we can give to the one we love. Women do not know who they are and they try to redefine their purpose. Men no longer take responsibility for their actions, and the family suffers. Families are broken and our children are wandering around lost in a world that hungers to consume them. Individual value has lost dignity and purpose, as the collective assimilates the soul. The enemy wants to re-purpose you to keep you from the joy you could know. When this is true, the enemy will persistently attack until all hope is gone and happiness is destroyed... The enemy wants to make you

*Falling in Love and Creating a Family on the Battlefield of Life*

into something you are not. Change the truth into a lie. The hidden serpent hides close to each one of us and he beguiles with deceit. He wants you to transgress what the Lord God has given you.

Love is a great gift that heals. A lifetime of love is the protected perimeter of a safe zone, where family and love flourish and happiness feeds the soul. It is in family where boys become real men and girls know who they are, and become Virtuous Women: Women, who make humanity better, who motivate men to be stronger and to achieve more. A woman who nurtures the family and raises children to thrive with purpose. Women do this to make a man good, the best possible leader he can be outside the family, where he is exposed to the threats of this world. (Proverbs 31:10 – 31)

He should be a champion. *A GOOD MAN is the Champion of his family!* But, the woman is the one who helps nurture and strengthens those whom she loves. (Men, be responsible fathers and grandfathers, and ladies be the gift of a great mother and nurture your family for generations to come!)

Evil waits for the weakness in the perimeter to attack those in the safe zone.

Evil pangs of hunger to destroy the family and the future of humanity.

The battle continues each day. There is HOPE!

This is a spiritual war but it is entrenched within the physical reality of our lives. Just because we cannot physically see the influence of the enemy, does not mean that it is not real. We are surrounded by much that is not seen or felt with our physical senses.

***Our world is at war.*** *End State Mission.*

The first portion of this book is my attempt to explain who I am, how I became who I am, and why I am who I am as a man. The story that follows is a roller coaster of physical, spiritual, and emotional battles that I have fought, and in some ways continue to fight. The enemy never goes away in this world. He lurks at the edge of the safe zone, waiting to infiltrate the perimeter. His trolls and hyenas are there ready to pounce on the prey they stalk. Looking for weakness, they test the barriers and strongholds of defense. They push against weaknesses to create the ability to enter my "Green Zone," which is a safe zone of protection. Their mission is to force the evil they inhabit upon the weak and to destroy what they hate. They hate me! They hate us! They hate God! They hate you!

Fallen men and women, who become activist allies of evil, join in the attack. Some willingly join the force of evil, and some are deceived into the fight, by cunning deception. In reality, there is a continuous battle of evil against us all. The fight is both physical and spiritual. Hate thrives within those who keep it stirred up and they use it to harm others. Demons want to make more demons. Evil wants to spread more evil. Death hungers to claim more souls. Liars desire to make more liars. Wickedness evolves into more wickedness. *Beware, the enemy is out there. The enemy wants you.*

Innocence is captured and held in the dark dungeon of evil's intent. The destructive force of sin is manipulated against the innocent from the beginning. Many are overcome and remain in the clutches of this power. They are lost to the force of sin as they are educated by the drill sergeants and teachers of evil darkness. In time, they think it is normal for them to hate others and actively abuse others. They want to control what others think and destroy freedom. They have become the opposite of love.

They are the arbiters of defiance and hate. It is sad that some think they are right but are so wrong.

Parents who are active on the dark side spread the poison to their children early. Parents who surrender to its power neglect their responsibility to defend their children from the tentacles of evil rhetoric. Some parents are not observant because they are already enjoying the pleasure of sin, as it pulls them deeper into its power. Children become the minions, or the fodder, of this dark force. It is subtle and it is aggressive, to captivate and control for it's own consumption or abuse. Evil is the force driven to mobilize against all that is good. It will use any means of deception to empower its capabilities because it hungers to overthrow the righteous. Evil hates good. Evil is a political ideology of rebellion against God.

There are only two forces. Only two polarizing ideologies that self-conscience beings can enlist their loyalty and pledge their sacred honor. The contrasting ideas of good and evil are on opposite ends of the spectrum. There is a clear defining line that separates these two camps of truth. The truth of evil is supplied by hate, violence, deception, and the hunger to hide and destroy what becomes accepted, and what becomes their perceived enemy.

Those who become soldiers in the force of evil do not have the Champion who can defeat sin. Eternal death, sin's power, becomes the end state for the fallen. I am David and I trust the only Champion, who is my Savior, Jesus Christ. I direct your attention to the only hope available in this world. He is able to redeem you into His protection and Glorious Victory. His victory is eternal, and He shares this end state with all who trust Him. *(Ephesians 1:7)*

The hardship of war lingers in the soul of any warrior who has engaged in any type of physical or spiritual warfare. There are daily challenges but there is a peaceful victory for any individual when that individual has a Champion that no enemy can defeat. This Champion protects what is His. This warrior depends on the only Champion who can defeat the enemy. My Champion is the rock of my Salvation. The enemy is real. The Champion is also real, and His victory is eternal. *(Ephesians 6: 10-20)*

After the explanation of my spiritual foundation, which has made me who I am today, the story of my most difficult battle in life will unfold for you to experience. I felt I needed to share this story because I was forced to walk down into the valley to fight this giant.

Yes, I am David. There is a giant that must be killed! *(A Spiritual Metaphor)*

I realize this same giant has attacked us all. He continues to defy those who serve the Lord. The immense narcissism of this giant openly challenges all who choose to serve their God. This aggressive evil enemy continues his assault against every human being who has ever walked upon this earth. He relishes in his ability to bring destruction upon those whom he hates, and those whom he is able to make his trophy. He uses his captive prisoners to attack others. Evil is real and the devil in my story is an evil narcissistic minion, who was relentless in his attempt to kidnap and possess the mother of my children, my youthful and lifetime love. She was my wife of 46 years until he ripped us apart. Evil is cruel and persistent. But, evil is a cowardly weakness.

To understand me, you need to understand the Champion Savior, Jesus Christ, and why He is my Lord and protector. I invite you to "Believe in the Lord Jesus Christ, and you will be saved." I'll bet you need a Champion. He can be your Champion too! He can redeem you and He is able to set you on the eternal journey of life. You can be "Born Again," and live a life that never ends. Walk in the garden with God, as a "Child of God." The adventure never ends! The Family of God awaits your "New Birth." *(John 3)*

***The struggle of humanity continues.***   *It became our fight.*

The serpent reveals himself and Eve listens to his poison. Persuaded that she is missing something, she crosses into a world of deception and drags her husband with her. Adam is tempted by many new concepts introduced by sin and he receives the forbidden fruit. He willingly eats this fruit, knowing he should not because he loves her. They were one.

The Garden of Eden was a wondrous place of beauty and harmony. *(Genesis chapter three)* Everything was "good," according to the scripture, except for the infiltration of evil that lurked to destroy. An intelligent creature was observing every detail and waiting in the shadows to deceive the first married couple. He was a being that hated them so much that he schemed for their destruction because he despised his Creator. Deep hate was the driving factor behind this evil intention to destroy. Hate always tries to drive away the truth and destroy peace. Evil hates what is good. *(Isaiah 14)*

*Memories of Loving You*

Those individuals with hate, to commit evil, never do the work of God. Hate was the motivation of beguiling temptation that caused the fall of man into sin. Evil divides man from God and others. When you see and witness hate, you see the hand of evil. Hate drives this being that desires power and control over others. This hate-filled being waited for his attack until he could strike at their weakest point. Hate in our world drives division and destruction even today. It will be hate that drives the evil period of rebellion for humanity in the end. *(John 3:20, John 15:23 – 25, Matthew 24:9 – 10)* Beware of hate, for it will become the power of sin that will destroy you. Hate never turns its cheek.

What was beautiful and fun became difficult and ugly. What was peaceful and full of joy became stressful and combative. The fallen struggle of life crawled into the soil of this garden and poisoned the abundance of living with sin. The worms burrowed into the fruit of sustenance and the thorns grew around the pathways to invade, what was amazingly wonderful, to make life a battleground of division. A division that still grows in our world today.

Those who divide others are filled with hate. Hate for everything God intends for the creatures He created to reflect His glory in this world: Hate-filled lies, twisted agendas, misleading ideologies, and enslavement through political control of others. Hate and evil are the primary forces of sin. Like gunpowder in ammunition, these two elements are an explosive force of destruction used by those who <u>lie and deceive</u>. Lies are the casing shells to deliver their bullets, which are sent to kill. To kill you!

Beware of hate. Think for yourself. Eve allowed the serpent to explain his version of what God told Adam. This led her to not accept God's truth. This evil led Eve to deceive Adam and make excuses. Adam blamed her and God after he ate the fruit. Sin has taken humanity away from the garden, away from truth, and away from God's friendship and fellowship. Hate and shallow thinking became elements of deception that caused mankind's fallen nature. These elements still permeate humanity.

Sin spawned pain to destroy the love of human harmony between married lovers. It also spread the growing divisional pain between parents and children, families, communities, and all levels of humanity's growth through time. It still spreads in our world. "Fallen!"

The word, "FALLEN," defines the foundational destruction of the created status and rising potential of the being God created. Lost foundational strength, of the position that was enjoyed by the first human couple, continues to empower the falling momentum of distance between the Creator and His great joy. This loss keeps reoccurring to spread the hate of the serpent. The hate of a fallen evil being, who desires to be God, whispers his hate into the thoughts of the first beautiful woman. He still whispers today. He embodies the fuel that empowers the spread of evil in our world.

*(Who funds the busloads of haters who destroy property and use violence for evil political confrontation and control? Who receives the empowerment to force hateful ideology and false science that deceives the innocent? Who is empowered by the destruction of families, innocent children, freedom, faith, and individuals who stand up for what is good and right? Some evil political potentates hunger to control others and force evil's intent. Socialism is evil. Marxism is evil. The force of evil continues to spread its venom into the minds of our children with lies. Be careful who you listen to and who you allow to teach your children, for evil has a mind to destroy truth and enslave the soul. Real truth is found in the Savior, who defeats evil through the cross and by the resurrection from the dead. Jesus Christ is the Champion of faith. He is salvation for all eternity. dld)*

The only hope was a voice calling out, "Where are you?" "Who told you that you sinned?" "Who told you that you were naked?" The original guidance applies even today, for the day that they ate the fruit they were separated from the only source of life/existence. The Creator reaches out to save. He restores happiness and empowers life. This life needs restoration and hungers for true happiness!

***Self-Reflection.*** *My need for a foundation of faith and finding my story within.*

WHO AM I? Am I able to be honest with myself? Must I be honest with others? This is my attempt to investigate my own heart. This is a self-honest adventure into my mind and memories, which I open and leave on display before others. To understand my story I invite you to understand me. I open with my revelation of faith. This is the basis of what I believe. I invite you to know my Savior, like I know Him. He is my Champion.

We all have our stories. Some stories are joyful and some are sad. They are the stories we have written of our own lives as we live in this world. Sometimes you wish you could rewrite a few chapters or even start all over, but you are writing the story of your life every moment you breathe. You are not a puppet on a string. You are in control. You get up every morning with the pen and power of your choices and you write the details of your day in the logbook of memories. Our actions intertwine with those we love and with those we interact with. These activities influence and direct each coming moment ahead, but you are the director of your story. You have a story too!

The story I reveal is dramatic: It is a story of tragedy and defeat. It is a story of hate, failure, confusion, narcissistic evil, and spiritual warfare. It is a story of young love, and it is a story of overcoming and enduring love, which becomes a Victorious Love! It is filled with deep heartache and sorrow. It is a story to find joy and happiness again, after the victory over the horrible hardships of emotional and spiritual pain inflicted by a spiritual storm of evil. This is a story that became an unexpected violent emotional storm with destructive force: a force that ripped our love apart. The enemy tried to destroy my love, my family, and my reputation. He is still trying.

Like a tempestuous cyclone beating upon a struggling ship, thrashing upon the deep sea of darkness, filled with tenacious predators who hunger for sustenance, this story of love was helplessly lost at sea. I was stranded in a distant land away from my love and my family. This story is based on real events and personal experiences. The struggle and sorrow are real. The events are real. The imagination is based on reality but is creative in telling the story. The devil in my story is real. The peaceful shore is a real place with real people. The "Time Travel" really happened in memories, which I share.

I invite you into my experience. I invite you to learn from my struggles. I offer to you what it took to obtain the victory. You might also need to find your victories to overcome your struggles in life. I share this story with you and I hope you discover a greater love and an enduring victory with the love of your life, your own family, and your friends, whom you walk alongside, during your journey of life. Walk down the path that leads to the eternal future of happiness and peace. Walk with God in His garden!

For me, the past is no longer important. The present pilgrimage in this life only leads into the future. The future is everything! Remember your past and learn from the experience. Live in the present, walking the straight and narrow path, seeking the city of God, as you continue on your journey. Then, believe in the future promises of God because the treasure of the eternal is the glory and adventure of knowing the Lord and walking into His presence as a Child of God. A child of God who inherits eternity! There is a beautiful eternal garden that is beyond imagination, filled with amazing adventures just for you. Jesus said, *"Come unto me, all ye that labor and are heavy laden, and I will give you rest..." (Matthew 11:28-30)* I need His rest!

***Still trying to Find Myself.*** *Explaining who I am and my struggle between two positions.*

Sometimes my thoughts travel between two worlds. These worlds are places where I lived different lives with different relationships. It was my memories from each that anchored me to a reality of existence. Dreams kept me traveling in my adventure of life. Tragedy defined the purpose of my living. Challenges kept my life captivating and real. Then an enemy revealed himself. He attacked me through my family. He caused the second world to become my reality for a while. Then he continued his assault in both worlds against me. Worse than an evil thieving pirate, this narcissist enemy attacked. He persistently attempted to kidnap and enslave a wonderful lady, my wife.

From the beginning of my childhood experiences, which became a normal life, to the complexity of my adult struggles, filled with the duality of two different realities, my memories were etched as a record in my mind. It amazes me how detailed my experiences in life stay with me. Even more amazing is how my thinking keyboard can recall and display these memories again. The ability to experience imagination and to be creative, based on my recorded memories, can empower many adventures. These real memories do empower the travels I share.

At my age, these memories recall much happiness, as well as, many trials and difficulties. However, some memories become nightmares that will mislead. An unseen enemy is lurking to spread a new virus of doubt within me each day. This evil enemy seeks to sift my thoughts and destroy any joy I find in life. Malicious invading viruses constantly attack to corrupt these memories recorded in my mind. The functioning details of Intelligent Design, which is running within my physical being, amaze me. I can remember because my Creator's design recalls my experiences and knowledge. The protection provided in this amazing system of gray matter within my skull protects me from the invading self-theism viruses thrown at me by spiritual enemies. Faith is my victory, and with this constant enemy maneuvering against me, I must keep my guard up. I must be strong in the Lord.

My story is based on real experiences but told with my limited artistic creativity. I hope I can reveal my intention to share this story, as insight into your own life experience. Honesty with yourself is the first step in experiencing a life of joy. When you find this joy you can walk with God. The best adventures are beyond imagination when He is at your side!

There are many trails to wander. The two worlds in my mind are separate and yet connected. Yes, it is still me pounding on the keyboard of my experience! How I lived in these two worlds seems to evade me. I try to figure things out. I guess that's just me. Where do I belong?

Each reality is filled with people I love: People I developed great friendships with. Sometimes I imagine that I stepped through a tear in the time continuum and ended up in a parallel dimension with simultaneous events in each dimension playing out the drama of my experience. Each world takes turns looking for my return. My deliberate absence, from those I care deeply for, wanders through my thoughts. Thoughts that keep pulling me to return. "What should I do?" whispers in my ear. These whispers invade my activity of consciousness all the time my PC Grey Matter is running. I think it runs in the background even when it shuts down. *(The amazing brain created by God Almighty is overwhelmingly captivating to study.)*

Honest consideration must include the world I stand in. Consideration of every element, interwoven through my experience and ability to think, must be integrated for deeper thinking. Finding and understanding every aspect is crucial to finding an honest place to stand in my self-confidence. If I want to understand myself and others better, I must always adapt, to absolutely step beyond my senses, to see what is behind the curtain. Find what is hiding. Find what is good. Discover a better path to walk upon. Take off the blinders of self-aggrandizement and realize there is much more to consider, before stubbornly fighting the wolves or elevating myself in grandeur.

**Family trouble.**  *A struggle for life.*

The end never ends. It might fade but it drags on each day and every night. It was not the "Happily Ever After," but rather, "The Struggle of Life and Love on the Battlefield of Sin." With all the memories that color my thoughts, the long first journey together, which started with a joyful celebration, ends in heartbreak. The experiences shared for many years were marked meaningless by the revelation of infidelity. Evil weeds invaded our garden and the garden struggled to survive. What a reminder of how we treat each other compared to how we should treat each other. Our life experiences blend together with a promise dependent upon personal commitment. I assume that some couples are better at this than others, but success depends on individual character. I am not saying that I will reveal everything. Total disclosure is never a smart thing when you live in a world fallen into sin. A wise man chooses his words. *(Proverbs 15:28; Proverbs 17:27)*

When you get married, you do not purchase the one you promise to love. You do not get a "Title Deed" or a "Pink Slip" of ownership. What you do is enter into a covenant promise before God, family, and society. A covenant relationship not hidden but openly lived before all: a declared promise of fidelity that does live within the soul and grows within our children for generations. Marriage is for the health and welfare of all humanity. The evil power of sin will always try to destroy this great gift of God. When marriage, God's design for family, is attacked, you see evil working to spew hate for God. Hate for the Lord's intent to bless men and women, whom He created to be His glory. Evil hides but still crawls through the branches of the trees in the midst of the Garden, waiting to beguile.

The serpent still hates God and he hates humanity more than ever. (We need the gift of forgiveness.)

Both good and bad expectations guide the christening of the life journey, of a man and woman, who promise to share their lives together. Cognitive life experiences, pressed into our psychological understanding, laced with growing-up memories from our unique historical family of origin, as well as, all lessons learned along the way, step across the threshold to unite two separate individuals as one. Marriage is about loving commitment and it includes the joining of families and generations. *(Marriage is the oneness of family, not the oneness of a village or government control. The government does not own anything! Only tyrants and dictators steal, enslave, and possess.)*

The bonding of the two into one is a commitment of the heart. I have told many couples that marital love is defined as a commitment. It includes personal and sexual bonding that allows the other person in the relationship, the freedom to be an individual while respecting and sharing in the promise of marriage. It is in this covenant promise that the health and welfare of the family grows. It is in this covenant that children are raised into adults, and a couple transform from parents into grandparents. Grandparents should be the shining example of a good life shared. I believe the imprint of our living is pressed into the psyche of our ancestry.

***Humanity has lost*** | *When promises are broken*
***something precious.*** | *families suffer.*

I have lost something precious! Families are weakened and destroyed by the influence of a society that has pushed the immoral ideas of the sexual revolution. This loss has led to murder as a form of birth control. Easy divorce has weakened the idea of family, as a personal commitment and personal accountability for our actions. Society has gained control over the education of our children. The collective whispers the fallen lies of the serpent, who now crawls in the dirt as a snake. He tries to rise above the penalty of the sin he experiences, and he pulls many into the dirt with him.

What humanity has lost is the loving example and safe environment of a family, where a husband and a wife provide, protect, and teach their children how to think and share their lives with each other. Instead, they struggle with the idea of what is morally good for strong honest individuals, who contribute to society, because the snake slithers around the feet of God's created children to destroy. We must teach our children how to be leaders and how to achieve success. We must show them how to pursue the original happiness our Creator has for us. We have lost a lot. "Fallen." We struggle to keep going.

I have told my grandchildren many times that Sally and I are grandma and grandpa. As grandparents, we are just one step up from your parents. A healthy family interacts with children, parents, and even grandparents. Grandparents must have authority and influence in children's lives too. The sad part of this is the loss of the crown jewel of parental and grand-parental influence, when trust, based upon good moral living, as an example for them to follow, is destroyed. Oh, how we fail the ones we deeply love.

The following story is an unfolding drama of a family hurt and society weakened by another bad example. My bad example? Her bad example? Our bad example…

**I'm just a creature created by God.** *Living my life in a fallen world.*

I am a man. I am a creature with a beginning. I have amazing senses built within me that allow me to navigate this world. I can see amazing beauty and I see ugliness. I can hear the peaceful music of nature and the powerful sounds of destructive forces. I smell sweetness when it is in the air. I smell the repulsive odoriferous emulsification of waste. I can savor what is placed upon my tongue, and at the same time, all my awareness of being interacts within my consciousness to create the wonder of a great meal. This is an amazing body! A body designed to interact with the created world I live in. I am connected upon, and into, this celestial ball traveling through the universe we know. However, what we know and understand is only what our senses tell us. We are limited because we are creatures. This means we are created by an intelligent mind and a powerful force, which is Almighty God, Our Heavenly Father, who made us in His image and likeness.

There is so much power and activity that surrounds us all the time. Power and activity that surrounds us and passes through us, which we are not able to sense. I am not able to see everything going on. I do not hear everything. There is so much activity around me and passing through me that I am unaware of at any given moment. I can feel the breeze of the invisible wind. I can feel the heat of the sun's nuclear explosions 92.94 million miles away, and my body uses the energy of the light created to ignite my ability to see color, to comprehend depth and distance. Residential frequency, and a variety of other audible frequencies, surround us and pass through us, which man has been able to harness into digital technologies. What I am getting at is that we are connected to our created world. There is so much more than what we can comprehend. The adventure of eternity, if you walk with the Lord, will be beyond amazing and completely fulfilling.

We are not able to see everything with our eyes or hear everything that surrounds us. Our senses allow us to know our world. Just because you cannot see something does not mean it is not there. Many animals see, hear, and smell much better than humans. Our world and our universe are immensely packed with things we cannot see. I know the eternal surrounds us because I can comprehend the simple and complex evidence that leads me to deeper thinking. It leads me to wonder and creativity.

From the micro to the macro, there is order, diversity, and yet dependency with intelligent interaction between systems. There are limits and requirements at every level of existence. How can anyone who thinks deep into the world around them see anything but the power of intelligence? It is ignorance and even foolishness that entertains the ideas forced into the minds of humanity today through the education of our children. They are taught that something is true but it is not true at all. It is a lie because men reject God. Who are we and what are we if there is no

Creator? What a slippery slope of lies, accepted out of ignorance and shallow thinking, that lead to the present world and the problems we all face. *(Those who profess to be wise become fools. A fool says in his heart, "There is no God." Romans 1: 22-25)*

Can anyone honestly say that Intelligent Design does not exist? Only those who stand and look from a very limited view. Self-theists are the ones who believe in impossible self-spontaneous matter. (mindless matter that becomes intelligent complex beings – who believes this stuff?) Not me.

I do believe in God. I also believe the vast majority of people throughout history try to keep their understanding of God in a box. A box created in their own mind that makes them feel better about themselves. Some imagine the old man with a wrinkled face and a very long white beard and long hair, sitting in a rocking chair holding a cane. Some have created stories and invented gods to a lower level of existence, kind of like a superhero. Some dress their god up in a red suit, who flies presents all over the world. Some make themselves gods to control others so they have power and wealth. Some reject God because they trust only their limited senses. I call them self-theists because they make themselves their own authority of understanding and knowledge. In reality, they are shallow thinkers.

Others are told what to believe by those who are self-proclaimed educators, and superior intellects. They accept the shallow thinking of self-theists and refuse to think for themselves. I call them "Mind Midgets."

Evolutionists create fantasy scenarios to explain origins, even though there is no evidence of evolution, as they teach. The facts are very clear and revealing, but they reject God and have to explain complex existence and orderly systems, that clearly reveal evidence of intelligence and design. They reject God. When you remove even one element from the scientific method, your science is false.

Everything about Creation is so much greater and powerful than any man can explain. True science does seek the truth. Honest science observes all elements and facts possible, including operational function, diversity, dependency, systems, and connections to complex structures, micro and macro order, and design, with the interdependence of it all, which becomes the world we live in. "Heaven declares the glory of God and the firmaments show His handiwork (Craftsmanship)..." *(Psalms 19:1)*

The fact is, God is not a man. God cannot be kept in a box. He, the gender He reveals Himself with to humanity through the Scripture, is not limited to space or time. He is beyond comprehension and He is eternal. He reveals Himself to His creation. He walked among us as the Savior, Jesus Christ, the only begotten Son of God. I believe in Jesus Christ, who defeated death by His Resurrection. His word is truth. Man was created an eternal being. Man still is an eternal being. (Man = both genders)

God created them, male and female, in His likeness and image. (Wo**man** and **man**) A deeper explanation is revealed in the story. When I use the term, man, I refer to both men and women unless specific clarity of context.

### God's Miracle of Humanity

*Man became a living soul- Genetic Pooling.*

*The marvelous DNA miracle continues.*

Our greatest enemy is death. Death is not annihilation or cessation of existence, but separation from the life of God, who breathed into man the breath of life, and man became a living soul. Life is passed to every human ever born, through the miracle of DNA, and genetics. The source of life is God alone. This life connects us as ONE Human Race! The **genetic pooling**, after the flood, when the families settled in different places around the world, thus being isolated geographically, families and tribes procreated within their communities, which through time formed ethnicity, cultures, and societies.

This genetic pooling within a specific group, in geographic isolation at the time, created the markers that dominated differences that resulted in ethnicity and specific traits. A DNA strand has more code information than all the libraries combined in the United States. Scientists are still trying to understand and discover the intelligent complexity of genetics, which reveals intelligence and power that far exceeds man's ability. *(The same principle of genetics is used to make changes in the DNA to develop different canine/dog types. All of the coded information is within the DNA of the specific "Kind," and genetic breeding has been used for over 800 years to develop all the variations we know today as different types of dogs.)*

Genetic pooling to create strong coding of DNA information happens naturally in the wild. It happens when manipulated by intelligent (Yet limited) beings. The variety and variations of creatures on this earth are all the result of miraculous genetic merging into specific pooling of characteristics within a **"Kind."** There is no evidence of evolutionary transition between different "Kinds." NONE! (But they still keep lying to the children!)

Breeding horses, cows, and other animals by intelligent beings, man is established and accepted. It happens because there is created information, including a living process of chemical and element absorption by merging information from the DNA, which God created for life to thrive on the earth. It happens through specific living cells that have the miracle of creative life inside. At no time did mindless matter transform into genetic cells with DNA information to become a living organism, and at no time has any specific species of a kind transformed into another kind. It has never happened! Never will!

Evolution is a fairy tale of ignorance based on limited observation because someone did not believe in God Almighty. That someone tries to explain man's existence without a Creator; without Intelligent Design; without observable evidence that is clearly irrefutable. It takes a watchmaker to make a watch. It takes a manufacturing team of intelligent creatures to make a car, a rifle, a washing machine, or any other tool used by man. The evidence is clear, as I see it!

I admit, that part of this problem is the *"god in the box" complex* that many have accepted for their reality. God Almighty is real. The evidence of truth and existence within our world can be seen in the smallest of microorganisms to the extreme Macro structures and organisms we can observe as man. "I am fearfully and wonderfully made." *(Psalms 139:14) [Note the difference between the small g and Capital G. Small g is false god.]*

***My Beginning.*** *I became a unique Individual.*

Life was passed on to me, as I was conceived in 1955. Life comes from God, who breathed into Adam His breath of life, and Adam/Humanity became a living soul. All human life is connected through procreation to this life from God. His life is within us! I became a unique being/soul, when the two haploid cells from my parents merged, and the complexity of the Intelligent Design DNA, began it's process and operation to form me. This was God's design. I was physically born in 1956. At least, this was when I took my first breath. Sandusky, Ohio in Erie County along the Southern Shore of Lake Erie, I entered the world to begin my journey of life. I am not one to follow astrology or even believe in man's attempt to define things through astrology. If something is a truth, it is a truth of God. Truth never changes. It is always true.

I am told that I am a **Gemini**, which means dual personality, sometimes referred to as the twins. I do believe there is a complex world created by God Almighty, and there is truth that always remains truth, but must be discovered. It is not your truth or my truth. It is true. Can the design of God be seen in the seasons, as signs of understanding? I am sure that God's all-knowing power far exceeds the entire collective understanding of creation itself. Things do have a purpose and a design function!

I believe in God and His design of all things reveals His intelligent design, order, multiplicity, diversity, dependency, and so much more! The sun, moon, and stars were given for signs and seasons according to the Book of Genesis, and they declared the "Glory of God." His glory is seen in the minds of those who seek understanding, rather than, self-aggrandizing explanations based on limited, failed, human senses.

If one looks honestly into the heavens, the power of the Lord God is revealed. But when men only look to themselves for answers, they fail! Mud becoming a complex organism is foolishness. What a mess they make in the minds of our children.

*(Sorry about that Astor-Physicist or Scientist, but your superior IQ and comprehension of complex systems is only possible because of INTELLIGENT DESIGN. The merging of haploid cells that became you came from the genetic design of God Almighty. You have been given a gift! PS: You are not a god. Also, I know many do believe and understand that God is real. Use your gift to bless others!!! Use your gift to discover and teach the truth honestly. Stand your model up against Intelligent Design and allow students to reach conclusions. Don't force your opinions. Open your own eyes and be honest with your mind/soul.)*

**God Reveals Himself.**   *Wise men and women seek to know.*

Yes, I use the male gender for God, as we understand in our language, because, in the Inspired Scripture, God uses this clarity to reveal Himself to us. I do think that we created beings, try to place God in the box of our understanding, so we can comprehend our Creator. I do not think He is just a thought within our understanding. He is the Divine of everything. *(Acts 17:26)* He reveals Himself as a person, but He is uniquely One Supreme God. God is infinitely beyond our ability to comprehend fully. God reaches out to His creatures and reveals Himself. *(1 Timothy 3:16)* He stepped down into His Creation and clothed Himself in Humanity. He reveals Himself, as a person who walked among us, and He is our Savior. *(John 10:30, John 17:31)* Jesus is the Messiah, who was promised to redeem the fallen man.

Jesus Christ is Almighty God. *(John 14:9)* This is a bold profound statement of the truth. Prophetic Scripture, pronounced through continuing revelations of the details to come, was written before the time they were revealed. *(Romans 15:4)* Scripture written to ignite HOPE through Faith, as God Almighty worked His Purpose and Plan for the Ages. Jesus is God manifest in the flesh, we are told in the New Testament book of Hebrews. *(Hebrews 10:20)* He was and is just as much human as any man or woman that ever lived. Yet, He was, and continues to always be, Almighty God.

Wise men do still seek Him! He is the seed placed in the woman, who crushes the head of the serpent.*(Genesis 3:15)* He is the one that was born to a virgin, foretold in The Books of Genesis, and Isaiah, and interwoven throughout the Old Testament. He is the one whom the angels heralded from on high, as the Savior of the world. He is the one who defeated death by His resurrection from the dead.

He is the one they guarded to keep in the Tomb, but He walked out alive. He ascended into heaven and promised to return for all who will personally believe and accept His atoning death to forgive sin. Believe in the Lord Jesus Christ and you will be saved! Jesus is the Lord. There is only one true God!

The Tri-unity, Trinity, of The Almighty, is One God. He is **God the Father**, who is ever present all-powerful, and knowing, who reveals Himself in time to His creatures. Creatures who are created in His likeness and image and charged with the responsibility of stewardship over the created world.

The **Holy Spirit** is God's abiding presence within all who believe and accept the **Lord Jesus**, who is God manifest in flesh to reveal Himself, as Savior and Lord. The Holy Spirit convicts men of sin, of righteousness, and of things to come (Promises/Prophecies that are true.) The Holy Spirit leads believers into all truth. *(John 16:13)* The Holy Spirit indwells every person who calls upon the Lord Jesus, in faith repenting of sin. A repentant sinner, who accepts Christ as Savior, is sealed by the Holy Spirit of God until the day of redemption. *(Romans 8:11)* God's Spirit enters and remains in and with the believer until the day of the truth and the reality of Salvation experienced. He will never leave the individual, nor will He forsake this person of faith. Christians do not believe in three gods. There is only one God and His triunity is evident in all creation. There is a Triunity of One! TRINITY!

When man sinned, death entered a creature created to be eternal. "Death by sin, so death passed upon all, for all have sinned and come short of the Glory of God." *(Romans 5:12)* Yes, we need a Savior. Jesus Christ, the Son of the Living God, said, "I am the way the truth, and the life no man comes to the Father without believing in me." "I am the resurrection and the life. No one comes to the Father without me." *(John 11:25)* "There is one name given among men, whereby we MUST be saved." *(Acts 4:12)* Jesus is the Savior. He is the Creator who stepped down from Eternal Heavenly Glory, clothed Himself as a man, and paid the debt/penalty of sin, which is death. Jesus died on the cross crying out, *"It is finished."* The atonement was finished. The work of Christ through Resurrection Saves!

At that moment of anguish and death, Jesus declared that He accomplished His mission. His death of sacrificial atonement was complete and His death alone became the power to atone. He was crucified, which was a public torturous prolonged death of suffocation if allowed to proceed fully. Scripture declares that Jesus laid His life down willingly. After His death, the Centurion ran a spear into Jesus' side, piercing the heart, and causing water and blood to flow out. The penalty of sin was paid for! After three days, which was a verification of dying, as the decomposition of flesh was evident, He secured victory over death as the guards fell and the stone rolled back for all to see this empty tomb. Jesus walked out alive forevermore. Jesus is coming back again and there is going to be a marvelous feast called the "Marriage Supper of the Lamb," for all believers to celebrate with the Lord, as they begin their eternal adventure in God's presence. *(Revelation 19:6-9)* Come, Lord Jesus! I hope he comes today! I look for Him every moment.

Jesus was miraculously conceived within Mary. He had no earthly father. Mary conceived what God placed within her, and the human process of natural birth began within her womb. The Lord Jesus was miraculously conceived but He was naturally born as a human. He is the only Savior. (Read the Gospels of the New Testament.)

***Finding the Savior.*** *The example of God's love for man is revealed.*

I am not sure if making any parallel to my life experience, of this duality, makes any sense without knowing my Savior. I do know that I struggle even as a believer. I desire to know Christ even more, but I find myself living as a fallen creature, who works hard to walk upon the road leading to righteousness. I know that my work will never save me. Only faith in Jesus Christ my Lord will allow me to enter His Eternal Glory. I do believe that once a person is "Born Again," that person will never lose salvation because a believer in Christ has an advocate with the Heavenly Father. The blood of Jesus Christ covers the repentant believing sinner's sin, and the penalty deserved by sin, and is the force of atonement to wash away sin and make FORGIVENESS a reality.

Forgiveness, which allows reconciliation with the Lord, is an eternal experience. Forgiveness is a moral obligation we have as believers. We are required to love one another, and we are expected to forgive others. *(John 13:34, 1 John 4:7, Ephesians 4:32)* The example of God is the Gospel of Christ, who secured forgiveness for us. Forgiveness is paramount in the act of a loving relationship. *Forgiveness is an example of God's love!* His love sent a Savior to redeem the lost by forgiving sin!

Sometimes failures are the result of not dealing with issues in the best way, or, they are reactions to others who are also struggling, which causes difficulties and failures.

*Falling in Love and Creating a Family on the Battlefield of Life*

We as humans have a hard time getting things right sometimes, proving to me how much my Savior and His forgiveness are needed.

***The following is the story***    *I need forgiveness too...*
***of my ongoing struggle.***

These two worlds, I mentioned early in this book, became a duality of oneness within me. I am not comparing the good and evil struggle, as an individual. Believe me, I do struggle with good and evil. These forces are intertwined throughout my life story. These forces also play out in every human story. No fingers to point or stones to throw here. (Trolls, be careful throwing stones because you end up in the pit.)

I am sharing my experiences of these two worlds that I have lived in, and my struggle to find my way home, hoping to share God's love and purpose, even through the failure and defeat of my story. I am asking the question, "Why do bad things happen to good people?" Why has this conflict invaded my life and my family? Sin creates pain and the sin of others around us spreads the pain of sin into your life. Like Eve, our first mother, who was beguiled into her disobedience of one simple command, and like Adam, who ate what was forbidden because Eve brought the forbidden fruit to Him, we have all fallen short of God's glory. *(1 John 1:8)* Stop blaming others and be responsible for yourself!

We all have the same story wrapped in our own experience of life. Each story has a different journey or a different trail of circumstances, but we all face the hardships of sin. We have our own serpent beguiling and our own hiding from God. We have all sinned and come short of God's glory. We have all been driven from the garden of God's presence, and we hunger to walk with Him again. I trusted Jesus as Lord on May 5th, 1975. I realized I was a sinner. I asked the Lord to forgive me of my sin and I accepted Jesus Christ as my Savior. In time God called me into ministry. I went to Bible College for three years and eventually became a pastor. I went to Seminary for 4 more years, was ordained, and after serving as a student pastor for 6 years, I accepted the call to ministry as a chaplain in the United States Army. I had an amazing career serving soldiers and their families.

I served in the Army for 27 years, 11 months, and 25 days. I loved the ministry and I loved preaching the Gospel of Jesus Christ. I also enjoyed being a staff officer for religious support operations in each command I was sent to serve. I retired in April 2011 and went to

Tennessee to be with my family. I was satisfied with my ministry calling, for the Lord Jesus, and the service I was called to provide for soldiers and their families. It was an amazing life experience. I would do it again. I would love to go back!!!

How this storm happened so quickly evades me still. I was not prepared for this sudden attack against my family. I hope the Lord uses my experience to bring others to Salvation and edify believers in faith and service. We are already walking on the stones that will lead to the prophetic reality of living in the Last Days. It is sad that many, especially our youth, who are educated to reject God's Truth and to believe the lies of self-theism, are falling away from the hope of the Eternal Walk with God Almighty. If you read this story, I point you to the Scriptures, the Holy Bible. I hope you find Jesus Christ as your Savior! He is your only HOPE.

Some have privilege, and some have extra hardship. Some use privilege to abuse and some use their privilege to bless others. It is not the color of skin that determines privilege. It is hard work, life circumstances, intellectual capacity, understanding, physical strength, determination, alliances…, and a multitude of life elements. Those who are using privilege as a weapon in our day are manipulating the vulnerable minds of youth and inexperience to force ideological change for self-gain. The struggle of sin has fallen upon all of us.

My white family, from my mother's side, were forcefully taken from Ninove, Belgium as slaves in the first decade of the 1900s. My great-grandparents both came from the same city but met in Canada while they were slaves under the control of the Gangs of Canada. They met when they were young and allowed to marry. My grandmother was the first of 12 children born. When she was nine, her father told her, and the other children at the time, to put on as many clothes as possible and not to carry anything else because they were leaving. She said, that night she was terrified. She told me this story a few years after my grandpa, Oakley Miller, her husband, passed.

She said she was so scared as her father put her mother and children in the row boat and crossed Lake Eire. They escaped to Michigan. Germaine, my mother's mother, was a dreamer. Her parents were illegal aliens. (White escaping slaves) My mother became an anchor baby. Germaine never became a citizen. When she was young she worked the sugar beat fields, where she met her husband, my grandfather. She married Oakley Miller, who worked for the Sugar Mill. They lived in Blissfield, Michigan until they moved to Fremont, Ohio. PS: They were not indentured! My grandmother told me this family truth before she died. She said that they were trapped and poor back then. I believe her.

My father's father died in an accident when my father was eleven years old. Jack was the eldest of four boys. The youngest boy drowned in the Sandusky River at about age six. Jack worked hard to help the family survive. His Irish grandfather came from hardship too. The two uncles struggled through life. One served in both world wars and the other died alone. I could say so much more, but my point is it took hard work and intellectual integrity to succeed. It was not white privilege. This is a hateful lie being told.

I credit my father's hard work, and my grandparents' struggles to overcome, as the privilege that blessed me. NOT my white skin. Don't believe that hate of today's political rhetoric that is being used to divide us all. This lie of white privilege takes away the success of hard work and determination to succeed. Do not allow thieves to steal what they have not earned, or become activists for a false political cause. I am white and I earned what I have in life. My parents earned what little they had because of hard work. This is the American way. Evil wants to divide good people to force village control.

## Chapter Three:

# A Storm of Destruction came upon us!

***A storm rising against us***   The hardest trial
I have ever faced
snuck up on me.

**THE SATISFACTION OF** life, in my First World, came crashing down around me, when the woman I loved for over 50 years, married 45 years at the time, revealed her transgression. I was shocked. (I am sure that Adam was blindsided too.) What happened was the furthest thing from my mind at the time. As I look back on the period before the confession, I begin to understand the tension and stress that grew within our family.

The devil in our story was a serpent. A snake who beguiled her for 5 years on the phone. He got in her ear and whispered his hissing manipulation until he was able to feed her his fruit. She eventually did eat. This was the beginning of the tear in my time continuum that sent me to a different world to struggle with my memories. I was cast into the turmoil of a tempestuous sea. Pounded by relentless angry waves, I lost the ability to keep track of time. I rose and fell with each crashing wave. Violence fell upon my deck and ripped the sails of my life to shreds. I was tossed about upon a deep and dangerous black sea. This sea was filled with hidden hungry creatures. The fear of the unknown overwhelmed me, as I faced her revelation.

Craven with fear, I struggled to breathe. Gasping for life, my heart longed for a peaceful shore. I needed rest or I was going to perish! I was lost at sea. My helplessness was overwhelming. Fear of the next unknown evil attack forced me to muster every ounce of survival from within. Life and love are too precious to give up, so I used all my might to survive. My struggle to fight back weakened me as time passed. It seemed like the longest storm ever. By God's grace, I must overcome.

As the captain of my ship, I tried to rescue the crew from this disaster. The maiden of my heart was thrown overboard and Joe, the narcissistic pirate, made several attempts to pull her into his ship from the deadly waves. He wanted to make her his own. When he scooped her up, she jumped back in. Her strength weakened each time, as the storms strengthened against her until she was lost at sea, struggling against the dangers beneath the crashing waves. We were both in trouble.

The ship was beaten apart by waves determined to destroy it. Eventually, I was scooped off the deck by an unbelievably huge tsunami. I was thrown into the darkness of destruction. I began to sink deeper into the depths of anguish. My breath left me and turmoil filled my lungs. Direction drifted away from my ability to navigate. The light slowly dimmed from my consciousness until I was gone. Darkness took over and I was lost at sea, suffocating from the tempestuous waters that already filled my lungs. Helpless and weakened, I sank deeper away from the world I knew. I lost myself. I lost my crew. I lost my lifetime love.

This is a hard story to tell! This dark ending took me to another place. I am not quite sure how all this happened, but it did happen. Eventually, two realities came crashing together into a competing struggle inside me. This collision within my heart ignited many internal battles that demanded decisions to be made. I never thought anything like this could develop on my radar of responsibility. The storm surprised me with immediate overwhelming

*A Storm of Destruction came upon us!*

force. All I could do was fight to survive, so I could fight another day.

Enemy forces, both spiritual and physical (seen and unseen), hovered around me, just beyond my ability to detect their positions. These predators hungered to devour me. They waited for weakness in their prey. Driven into a trap, my vulnerability created an opportunity for them to pounce. At first, I was oblivious to any emerging conflict. The tension of war grew over time and the enemy built up resources and strongholds to use against me. Evil was strategically observed, as plans were developed. Evil started this war against me, using communications (media) to create divisions and hate between my friendly forces and family. The first stage of a successful battle/war is to control communication. Develop what others think and believe before the violent conflict begins. Yes, war is violent, both emotionally and physically! This became a war in my heart and an attack on my family. The force of evil is attacking humanity even now.

*(It all happened simultaneously in our real world during the hatred of a political party that viciously assaulted the President of the United States, who was elected by a majority to "Make America Great Again." He was fighting to save the country he loved. He ferociously defended the*

*Constitution and created policies that helped the Middle Class. But, the left lied and manipulated, with liberal media and political powers to support the accusations they concocted to destroy him, to regain power. Eventually, almost all were proven as lies. Enemies of freedom tried to sink his ship of hope for America. Even now they continue to manipulate. Evil is real. It is all around us. Potentates want to bring in the global political government, which is the same old evil. We are already engaged in a horrific spiritual war and you are already involved.)*

This storm became my spiritual war!

**My life before the war.**   *The enemy is real and the enemy is out there.*

One day, in my first world experience, a blip *(Like a Chinese Spy balloon, which I was watching the news on FOX as this event in the real world happened, as I was writing in real-time.)* flickered upon the edge of my radar. It took a while for me to see it because I was distracted by many complexities within my family. My attention was focused on my children and their families, as I became a grandfather to wonderful grandchildren.

After a great career in the military, serving as an officer in the Army, I retired. I served as a chaplain for the last twenty two years of my over thirty three years of military service. The first world of my life was amazing. It was complex and challenging. It was filled with opportunities and responsibilities every day, as the complexity of family and career expanded around me. It was an amazing life in many ways. I felt satisfied with what was accomplished. As a man, I was feeling fulfilled in life. I am not saying I did not have failures and disappointments. I did. However, like Job of the Old Testament, I was happy with my life. I was secure in my faith. I tried to serve the Lord and live before others as a man of faith. I can only imagine the spiritual planning of evil forces as they grimaced together to destroy me. Stand up against evil's plan and evil will attack you too.

***My First World.*** *My life is filled with understanding and memories.*

The first world has always been challenging. It is a world I knew well, with deep roots in generations of history and experiences: memories of achievements and struggling challenges from the beginning. I truly know what it is like to feel defeated and inefficient, as well as, successful and appreciated. I have seen the bottom of the barrel several times and clawed up the ladder again, on my way back to what was normal and fulfilling. I was always determined to overcome obstacles and defeats.

However, I always felt one step back: behind someone else. I became good at making others look good and helped others to succeed. I do like it when someone I help succeeds at what he/she does. I say, *"Do it well. Do it right!"* I am comfortable in a position one step back. The reality for me is that I did not want to be upfront. I became used to being number two. Like a first officer to the Commander, I would strive to run the staff successfully, as I watched for opportunities, obstacles, and every detail involved, so I could advise the one in front to be the best at any and everything that was required of him/her. I wanted that person to be proud of the achievement. I was a part of something greater than myself: being a "Team Player" for the Champion!

As a chaplain, I operated in the same way as an executive officer. I always answered to a senior officer. Even when I had my mission assignment, I was operating under a Commander of the Unit, and also, a senior chaplain above me. When I did go back on active duty in the Army, as a chaplain, God blessed me with a good mentor.

Chaplain (COL-R) Stephen Cook, taught me to be teachable. Learn what successful officers know and become a mentor too. I admit I had a learning curve to climb.

Of course, some did not know how the First Officer/Executive Officer/XO, could multiply the success of a mission. The XO carried the weight of planning, logistics, and personnel, and directed all the staff coordination based on the Commander's Intent for Operations. However, there were a few commanders who used me as an errand boy. I was also good at this! But, I look at those periods of assignments, as these individuals limited the potential, of what could be achieved, and I remember hard personalities who could toot their own horn and discredit others to make themselves look good. Toxic and often narcissistic personalities, who kept a stranglehold on those serving under his/her authority. These individuals limited the potential of greater mission success.

I like it when a specific professional, educated and experienced, is allowed to use his/her ability as a multiplier of mission success. I like open-minded DEEP Thinkers who love what they do: individuals who are committed intellectually to succeed in their field. I like "Team Players," who understand that he/she is contributing to something greater than self! I do want to understand fully. I do want to experience the success of accomplishment. I always wanted the recognition to go to the professionals who do their jobs well. I like to see the pride of achievement experienced, written on their faces when the overwhelming interaction of all elements is interwoven together into a triumph/victory of a Mission. Good staff work creates Integrated Application in Overwhelming Sudden Force in the execution of the Commander's Intent, at all levels, which leads to Mission Success. *(A good example of this is found throughout the TV series, "LAST SHIP," as Captain Chandler and his staff protect and defend the required mission to save humanity. An excellent illustration of good overcoming persistent evil.)*

It feels good to be actively part of something bigger than myself: Contributing my knowledge, creativity, vision, strength, and energy to the achievement of a greater end. I believe diversity is strength! God created diversity and interdependence throughout all creation. The Intelligent Design of coded information in a DNA strand is immensely stuffed with variations of diversity, which allows ongoing possibilities. Everything in creation has the networking of multiple variations that depend on other functions to survive and even contribute to overall operations.

There is no mindless chaos spitting out complex functioning intelligent beings. Things do not magically occur or spontaneously burst forth into life or living beings. Everything, even to the most cellular levels and the macro expanse observed, is built with diversity and interdependence. Structure and Order are on display for clear observation for intelligent beings who comprehend observable evidence. God's creative design and continued support can be seen in everything. You have to honestly look. If you honestly look, you will see God's power and His glory is on display!

However, the force of evil has already convinced many into believing what is not true. Scripture reveals that they profess to be wise but become fools. "The fool says in his heart there is no God." *(Psalms 14:1)* Deception is cast into the minds of those who listen.

"The fool can know. The point is to understand."
*Albert Einstein*

The false science of evolution, and rejection of God for shallow thinking of man, became the foundation of many human failures. Failures that still reach into vulnerable shallow thinking minds. Evolution and the "The Strongest Survive = survival of the fittest," became an excuse for slavery. Some were not as evolved and therefore more like animals to be exploited. False science has led many down a path of hopelessness and failure. The contrast is Faith promises hope for tomorrow! We are all brothers and sisters of the same Human Race. Today's racism is ignorance. It is taught by educators who are willingly ignorant of the truth, and who spread their lies to the shallow thinking drones. They divide us from each other so they can force their ideology of socialism, which empowers elitism over the serfs. Their ideology is a confinement camp run by potentates.

***The turmoil of this world today.***  *What path are you walking on?*

We are better as a society when we respect each other and honor individual achievements, as well as, group success. (Just saying!) The real privilege is living in a free country and being able to achieve your dreams and share your creativity.

In our world today, there are Jealous Mind Pirates, Trollish Street Thugs, and Race Gangster Hyenas who try to claim achievements for themselves or destroy what they do not like. There are Science Manipulators (Chicken Little), Intellectual Cattle Rustlers spreading misinformation (wokeness), and Hoodlum History Horse Thieves, who rewrite historical truth into their fabricated storyline so they can push it into the mind midgets, who end up being middle-class or drone labor, enslaved by forced ideas (Group Think).

Malicious minion tyrants (self-appointed elite class potentates and misled minions) manipulate the media through a collaboration of a daily storyline for their political agenda. They claim accomplishments and the creativity of others for themselves, to feed an activism of hate. Minion drone activists hypnotized through misleading information, take action on behalf of their masters, who hunger to take over truth, so the collective grows and remains Borg. Those who do not assimilate must be isolated, consumed, or destroyed. Those in the collective are already under the control of Queen Borg, who feeds her village of drones with misinformation.

Minions and drones believe lies manufactured through collaboration at the highest levels of evil. Our youth are sold a false bill of goods. Twisted lies and manipulated data are fed to them through the abducted atheistic (really self-theistic) education system. The system of "The Beast," revealed in Scripture, written thousands of years ago, is now being manufactured in the minds of our children for several generations. This World System is pressing against the door of time and this door will soon be opened upon our world. The power of restraint will be removed. Evil will strike with fury. *(Revelation 13)* The Lord God will strike with wrath against this evil during the Tribulations period.

***The real enemy we all face.***   *The serpent predator stalks his prey.*

Since the "Fall of Man," Humanity, manipulated by the evil intent of the serpent, who hates God and wants to set his throne above the Creator, as god, beguiles humanity with his strategic evil forces. This rebellious evil serpent, we know as the Devil/Satan, who was a powerful fallen cherubim/angel, has stalked the earth to overthrow and destroy the one being, whom God declared, was created to be in God's image and likeness. The one creature, man, was given dominion over the earth. God gave man a gift that He did not give any other creature: The gift of living in God's image and likeness in creation. *We, humanity, men and women, are responsible for representing God's glory in this world.* I think we have failed. Only in Christ, there is victory.

*A Storm of Destruction came upon us!*

There is one creature, who was the most beautiful being, a powerful cherubim, in the eternal space, we call heaven. He despises man and seeks to destroy humanity because he rebels against his creator. The serpent, who became a slithering snake, in the garden beguiled the woman to stir up doubt and eventual rebellion against the Lord. He still beguiles humanity today and his following grows around us. He is the "Father of Lies." He seeks to devour any believer. He seeks to sift them as wheat, which means absolute destruction. Evil hates God's truth. *(Luke 22:31)*

Evil lies deceive the innocent. The guise of compassion and social justice is the packing used in the box that is delivered into the minds of the innocent and gullible students being brainwashed by progressive wokeness. The package contains the explosive evil that destroys their understanding of their own existence and purpose. Those who fall into the lair of evil become the drones of activism for the lies spread. These lies are crafted to deceive/beguile the good within them and replace it with the evil of an enemy that will destroy them. I have said many times, "Be careful who you listen to!"

His human following of political activists mimics his behavior, as they beguile others and lash out against

Almighty God. They hate the followers of Christ and seek to destroy any concept or belief in the Lord. This spiritual war is fought every day. God has a Purpose and Plan for the Ages and Mission Success is already defined, as the rescue mission of the Savior is executed to seek and to save the lost. *(Luke 19:10)* Jesus came to save all who come to Him through faith. He does not force Himself upon anyone. He reaches down for those who reach out to Him believing. I hope you hear His voice calling out to you, "Come to Me and I will give you rest." *(Matthew 11:28)*

The history of humanity is riddled with continuous battles/assaults of spiritual warfare led by this evil one and his imps/minions, who are fighting against goodness, holiness, and righteousness, to enslave mankind. *(Isaiah 14:12-17)* Lucifer hungers to place his throne of domination and control upon this celestial planet to regain some level of positional authority over what God has created to be good. Evil has already beguiled man, beginning in the "Garden of Eden," and continuing in every way imaginable. From man driven out of the garden, and throughout human history, every attack is strategically planned and executed by his fallen imps from the spiritual world, and

*A Storm of Destruction came upon us!*

his mind midgets and self-theist drones, recruited in our world. Only the redeemed will survive!

The attempt to create a ONE WORLD GOVERNMENT continues, and the end state, believed by those persuaded to be a member of his collective, and who reject individual sovereignty of each soul, continues to assault the objectives of personal freedom and moral responsibility/accountability. These self-theists are committed to destroying any belief in God. Each lost battle contributes to the mission success of humanity being enslaved by this fallen being, who hates God Almighty. The one world government is being constructed around us today. (In the end, the Lord is victorious.)

The prophecies of Scripture, given by the Lord, are being fulfilled. The shame is that humanity has swallowed the lies that will lead to their own defeat and enslavement. This assault on intellectual comprehension began a long time ago, but a major assault began when evolution was intertwined into science, and was accepted as truth, even when there is NO evidence to support these grandiose hypotheses as theories, just because someone does not understand or believe in God. Many are already brainwashed by this false idea. Some of the most precious loved ones are being influenced by this village's collective wokeness. I pray they escape assimilation.

***Mission intent.*** *The Victory has already been won and freedom offered.*

The Lord God does not fit into any creature's mind box of understanding. He revealed Himself in Creation through Intelligent Design, which there is clear evidence to examine and understand, and He revealed Himself when the *Savior, Jesus Christ,* was born. The Lord foretold, and then He fulfilled His objective that defeats ALL attempts of evil assaults against Creation and Humanity when He CLOTHED HIMSELF in human flesh to walk among us. He was the sole power and individual force, who defeated the evil of sin. He brings reconciliation and forgiveness to man. Jesus Christ, "The Son of The Living God," "God Manifest in The Flesh," cried out from the cross where evil is destroyed, "It is Finished." *(1 Timothy 3:16)*

Jesus paid the price for fallen sinners, as the atonement that forgives sin, paying a debt for sinners, they could never pay themselves. He overcame the power of evil by His resurrection. Fallen men, and the evil behind these self-theists, buried and then guarded the tomb.

These haters of God tried to contain the power of God Almighty. Evil wrangled all forces to keep the stone over the tomb. For three days the lifeless body lay on a cold stone slab-motionless. A sarcophagus of flesh lay waiting for the decay of God's glory and truth. Death, guarded by the fallen, is an attempt to steal victory and declare dominance. The intent ended in the defeat of evil when Jesus rose from death and walked out of the grave alive forevermore. Jesus said, "I am the Resurrection and the Life…" *(John 11: 17 – 27)*

## Cold Stone Death *Resurrection Poem*

*Cold stone and motionless flesh, lay still within this darkness, Sealed within it's grasp of death, a grip like a cold steel harness. The strength of sin destroys all flesh that rots within the grave. Light beyond its borders moves but is sealed from the grave.*

*What moved with life, within the light, was now the dross of death's cruel might. No vision there to see the joy, but tears fell as death destroyed. Silence seems to fill the tomb, where the cold stone will never move.*

*Memories of Loving You*

*Removed from us who walk the earth, who face this fate someday: Fear of sin's cruel grasp that lays men in their graves.*

*The sting that brought this flesh down here, was the darkened hearts of men who jeered. They will follow to the grave someday, where pulling flesh to dust when laid. Here, where a cold stone lay.*

*A cold stench of silence, heavy through the darkness stays, No movement stirred for three days. Bound tight and laid in this cold stone grave.*

*A battle ragged beneath this stone, more fierce than men to claim.*

*A great victory will move this stone to reach beyond this cold stone grave.*

*Death's chamber stirred, when life returned, and breath moved death away. This cold stone could never move, for it's grip was weak to contain, The force of life regained the flesh, and life returned to stay.*

*His miracle prevailed this day! The stone rolled, and its seal did break; the veil of light rushed in. Light filled death's chamber's theme, as darkness fled this cold stone scene!*

*The body that was visage marred and brow with thorns was pierced: hands and feet nailed by spikes and flesh ripped open wide.*

*This body with a heart cut deep, flowed atoning blood from side.*

*His innocent blood covers sin, to break death's grip of sin, so men can walk by His side.*

*Love is what flowed from His heart, which was pierced open on His side, so those redeemed can walk above, where the true light shines.*

*Saved from sin's power, with pure hearts satisfied.*

*Roll back the stone, it's cold death grip, a life is coming through.*

*Jesus Christ the Son of God is alive again, for me and you. He alone walked through the cold stone wall of death: The real victory Jesus knew, as sin cowardly withdrew.*

*Alive from death's darkness, this we hold true!*

*In Him, we abide with eternal life, as our future, which is forever true.*

(Poem written by United States Army Chaplain (LTC) David Druckenmiller

26 March 2005 for Easter Service, NATO Support, Belgium)

**War upon the Earth**   *The theater of the coming conflict is developed.*

The time of the greatest wrath poured out on humanity is moments away. It will be a period worse than man has ever known. It is called, "The Time of Jacob's Trouble." *(Jeremiah 30:7, Matthew 24:15-31)* How can we save our children? Teach them about the Savior, Jesus Christ, and help them understand Scripture! *"Whatsoever is written before time is written for our learning, that we through patience and comfort of the Scripture might have HOPE!" (Romans 15:4)*

When the window of heaven opens to rapture believers, a deceptive hellish fury will arise on earth. The fallen angel who hates Christ, Satan the demonic evil one, leader of rebellious creatures, will march upon this world with his venomous hate and cruelty, in an attempt to destroy humanity. The spiritual battle enters our physical reality. This is a real story that will unfold upon humanity. We see it already assembling. The "Day of the Lord," "The Second Coming of Christ," is almost here.

Those who claim to own diversity, as social justice, and still discriminate against groups they do not like, are the ones furthest from understanding the truth. They are the enslavers of the innocent. Policies that are forced upon the population end in human trafficking, higher taxes, homelessness, manipulation of votes to keep power, and economic decline for those who work hard and have earned their wealth. The lazy are rewarded. They take what is good and re-purpose it for evil. They wear the badge of diversity openly while imprisoning the masses who are unaware of the cage around the bait of enticement. Something that looks good draws these entrapped souls into the zone of no escape. The door slams shut and the "Beast" enjoys his sustenance. (Revelation 13)

Until this coming tribulation begins, believers in the Lord Jesus Christ are called upon to live and speak the truth. I think the quote I heard in a movie once, "Never give up and never surrender," is good for Christians to live. We are encouraged to live for Jesus Christ, as we see the day approaching.

Until then, a diversity of imagination, coupled with creative talent and determination of mission success, multiply the accomplishment for future ability and a better world. This is social hope and a brighter future for all. It is sharing ourselves and honoring human dignity. The contrast is the tyranny of self-theist dictatorial enslavement by individuals who make themselves the masters of others. "I know better than you and you will comply" is not progressive. "IT IS TYRANNY." The government does not own any individual. I know that I do not want their village in my life! It does not take a village to raise a child. Socialism is clothed in enticing deception but ends in the trap of human suffering so the elite prosper. Disguised in compassion, they are ravenous wolves of hate.

Too often, working on a job, I dealt with mind midgets and shallow thinkers. People who run into a situation and do not know anything about what is happening. People who are aggressive idealistic novices. I call them "Mind Midgets," aggressive self-absorbed narcissistic dictators who are hypnotized into believing something more of themselves, or the situation before them. Some people believe they know it all and are the only ones that can succeed. Often, the shallow life experiences of these Mind Midgets are limited by the shallow deceptive education they pursued, which has invaded the student's ability to understand real factual details. Inept activists, motivated by external manipulations of the political evil intentions taught at some institution of higher learning, become hypnotized into drones. They are not allowed to think for himself/herself. Evil walks out of the darkness and demands to be followed. BEWARE, this is the nature of sin. *(Midget is something small. I am only referring to small minds.)*

### ***The Global Borg***   *The enemy is known and the collective is growing around us.*

"Group Think" is "Borg:" mind control and forced compliance. Our **"Progressive Political World"** has already been forced into compliance/submission and the collective integrated link is feeding the data required by the elite. This is leading our world into the control of a "One World Government," and a world controlling narcissistic "Beast," a world system controlled economy, military, church, and society, which will be under the power of "Antichrist." The Data Systems of integrated Big Tech, which grows stronger every day, is the system of the "Beast" foretold in the Scripture. It will be the power of world control and one being will be it's master. His staff will be "The False Prophet, the Beast, the Red

Dragon" and Nation Leaders, who bow down giving the Antichrist their authority. Representatives become patsies of evil. Tyranny is rising before our eyes.

Our children have experienced the education of social compliance and a "wokeness," which is a lie being used to build the "World of Borg," here on earth. It is the dumbing down of intellectual understanding for social integration of the "Collective." At the top of this structural mind control are self-theists who hunger for dominance. The "Puppet Master," over this rising collective, hunger to place his throne of dominance over all humanity. His Trolls and Hyenas viciously attack anyone in opposition to their programming of hate. However, champions still walk out into the arena and fight! We need, and must have, these "CHAMPIONS."

*Warning! The danger of evil, interwoven into human life experience for millenniums, is becoming the dominant social ideology of lies. To conquer individuality and enslave humanity, this evil manipulates information. An evil serpent beguiles all who listen. Eventually, if you listen to the hate and deception long enough, you too, will believe the lies. Our media today has become hateful and extremely deceptive. Many of them get by with twisting information so they can press their ideology into the shallow-thinking mind midgets. The evil one pulls humanity into his "One World of Controlling Dominance." The serpent has become his own god and he tells them that they too will be gods.*

*It will not end well for evil. Sinners are being forced into compliance. The Scripture is being fulfilled openly in our day and the vast majority of individuals have no real understanding of what Scripture reveals because they have been told lies since they were toddlers. The lie of evolution keeps spreading; the ignorance of self-theism, those who call themselves "Free Thinkers," (Who cannot think for themselves); the sexual revolution of irresponsibility for personal pleasure keeps destroying individual respect and keeps tearing families apart; and hatred toward God is being pressed into the minds of our children. This hatred spreads through our culture, society, and families of many decades/generations through the education system. Mind control is invasive in our schools. Education is taken over by Socialism and Marxism ideology. Evil works its plan.*

*They even think that they are smart, but they are educated with unfounded hate and misleading data. Curriculum crafted to pull them into the system of the "Beast."*

*What is being witnessed in our time was prophetically revealed thousands of years ago. The "Purpose and Plan of God for the Ages" can be seen throughout the Bible. Humanity is being taught to embrace evil and reject the Lord. There is a coming world collective: "One World Government," which controls the economy and forces its political agenda on all. It attacks everyone who refuses the takeover. In time the enslaving woke leaders (Self-proclaimed Evil Elite Political Potentates) and their minions will attempt to kill anyone who rejects the agenda of Antichrist.*

*The "Tribulation Period" is just around the corner and we are already walking on the stepping stones of Biblical Prophetic History. What is written is unfolding into reality before our eyes. The masses are ignorant of what is happening. They accept the political lies that are spun. Christ is coming and the Tribulation is a breath away. If you miss the "Rapture" you will face the "Beast" with all the fury of hate for humanity pouring out on the world that rejects God the Father, and the Gospel Truth of Jesus Christ the Savior. Come, Lord Jesus! I hope you find the Lord Jesus Christ before it is too late for eternity. dld*

***I am just one step behind.*** *Becoming the Good Warrior.*

Since I was an awakening toddler, growing into the experience of life, I was treated like I was just one step behind my older brother, at least this is how I felt. This was just something that happened and there is no shame for me in this. I even believe the Lord used my life experiences to prepare me for my journey of life. This first world experience of over sixty years was fulfilling and I was happy almost all the time. I did have my ups and downs but to look in the mirror behind me, I see a good life full of family experiences and friends scattered all over the earth. I have lived in other countries and experienced other cultures. It was/is a good life!

Yes, I have also felt the pride of being recognized for my hard work and unique creativity by others: I have been awarded by leaders in positions of success and authority who have risen to the top of the social ladder. I have prayed before a real king in his own country, standing before thousands. I have prayed before famous generals and military leaders. I provided safety and security to a famous pastor and his family for several years. I shook the hand of a giant, Richard Kiel, and escorted him to an appointment with someone famous. I was friends with a great Pastor, Dr. Jerry Falwell. I drove Colonel Oliver North around one day to various events he was scheduled to attend in a bulletproof BMW. I have been on missions I cannot speak of. I have children and grandchildren I love. I have witnessed answers to prayer and I have experienced the Lord speaking, through personal miraculously undeniable events, as He spoke in the "Still Small Voice," to get my attention. I believe in God Almighty and His Son, my Savior, Jesus Christ the Lord.

So, "Why do bad things happen to good people?" "Why has this happened to me?"

***The Attack begins.***    *The Life I remember is under attack.*

The enemy is out there. My first world crumbled around me. I was attacked by a jealous conniving evil narcissist, who tried to pry my wife away from me, and our family, so he could possess her as his own. This evil sinner owned a struggling failed life of relationships. He reached back into his past and plotted the kidnapping of my wife, Sally. He wanted to possess her. What little I know now about this human demonic imp, is that he became a womanizer. He is a control freak who thinks he owns women. He pursued Sally because he could never keep a lady, and his childish memories, of their brief relationship, became a last attempt to take possession of someone he could own/enslave. He is one of these guys who think women are property. It turns out; that he became a narcissistic self-aggrandized <u>male chauvinist failure</u>. He is blinded by his arrogance like many narcissistic self-theists.

## *Chapter Four:*
# Alliances and Enemies

***Knowing the Beauty***    *A "Virtuous Woman"*
***of a Woman.***         *completes a man.*

**MANY MEN GET** this wrong. Some "Ladies of Faith" have accepted what some men believe about the only two-gender relationship that God created. (ONLY TWO)

Time was not a factor in the "Garden of Eden." Before the "Fall," there was no sin and creation was in the eternal condition. Adam walked with God in the Garden. Gender was not a factor. (No sense of time then but for our consideration it might have been eons, or maybe weeks, months... as we could imagine. We have no idea how long. We have no real concept because we have not experienced eternity yet. "Eyes have never seen what God has prepared for us." Yet!)

Eventually, Almighty God, Creator of our world and existence, said that it was NOT GOOD for man to be alone. What was the reason for God to declare this condition of Adam? I am sure God knew and understood everything about the creature He formed out of the red clay and breathed His life into. So, why explain that it was not good? What was wrong or lacking in this being, whom God created in His likeness and image? God said it was not good! Adam was not good at being alone. Was he a sinner yet? "NO!"

The Lord created the woman, Eve. (Recently the question was posed to a progressive representative of our day, "Can you define what a woman is?" The answer given was absurd. Some of this "woke" nonsense has fed into the progressive gender confusion lie of our day.) Ignorance becomes stupidity and grows into foolishness to be fed to mind midgets.

There are only **two genders:** male and female. The distinction between the two was created for procreation, having children to create generations of humanity. Different organs but the same valued soul: a man with a womb and egg, a man with the seed, and the genetic library in DNA with immense variation that are too inexhaustible for the human mind, which will continue the act of creation throughout the history of mankind… Life comes from God and is passed on through the generations.

The life God breathed into Adam, the first man created, is the origin of life within the human species. Even when God created woman, He took the DNA from within Adam's rib to create her. Since then the life of God's breath continues to be passed on through the DNA structure. A haploid cell from a man and a haploid cell from a woman come together through the intimacy of bonding love to create another unique individual child. (To be protected and nurtured.) Creation continues and families are blessed to fill the earth with a vast diversity of unique individuals. Each soul is valued by the Lord God.

So, when God said it was not good, did He mean He failed? NO! It just means He was not finished. When it is perfect, God is finished, and it was not finished until He brought the woman to the man and they were one. There was more to the creation of man, who reflects God's image and likeness, to make it good. Man was the only creature whom God gave the gift of His Image and likeness. He gave a gift to man (I believe the term "Man" is used to explain the creature God created to reflect His glory in the created world, and it includes both male and female. Depending on the context being used.)

After God created Eve, the woman, He said it was "good," which means complete. Now, consider this, "Did

God create her as a slave or some kind of lower creature to be dominated/ruled over?" "NO!" Adam alone was not complete and God said the situation was not good. The Lord took the DNA from the rib of Adam (the genetic code) and He created the woman. When Eve awakened, God brought the two together and said it was complete, meaning "GOOD!" (Eve had a higher IQ than Marilyn vos Savant, born 8-11-1946. IQ test at age 10 was 228.) The idea of cavemen and cavewomen is nonsense.

Eve was the completion of Adam/Man. So, did God Almighty, Creator of Heaven and Earth, create woman to be a slave or someone inferior to man? Absolutely not!!! She became the completion of God's work. God did not make a lesser being. He made an extremely intelligent woman to help Adam become complete in who he is, and/or, who he/they become. Through this loving process, more human beings would be born. A history of created beings that reflect God's Glory will walk upon the earth to experience God's wonders. Eve was the most intelligent and beautiful lady ever. (Inside and outside) Her children call her mother! A man will never experience the wonder of motherhood. He will be a father: a protector, a provider, a lover, and the one completed by her existence. Good mothers are a blessing to humanity. They are a blessing to good men! However, an evil mother is destructive, hateful, and selfish. Bad mothers harm their children, feeding them the forbidden fruit and lies of the serpent. She beguiles them!

The idea of submission is not ownership or a devalued person's status, but rather, the one fulfilling completion that makes whole the design of God to create humanity with generations of unique individuals who can walk with God in fellowship. <u>Submission is a gift</u> that a person gives to the one loved. It is a gift to make him complete and successful.

Women used to know the gift they possessed and they were cautious when giving it to a man. Wise women still do! It is not a tool for hate or division. It is a gift that unites, empowers, creates, and loves. (It is much much more than just pleasure. It is a good gift given by the Heavenly Father for the health and welfare of humanity.)

A man is wise to honor his mother, cherish his wife, and protect and love his children. He is the protector and patriarch of a family that lives and loves all of God's creation. A man is responsible for the welfare of his children, and the support and protection of his wife/family. The scripture does say that the man shall "rule" over the woman, the matriarch of ancestry within her. Like a Good

*Alliances and Enemies*

King who provides security, sustenance, and love, he is a patriarch who is responsible for living before his family in the glory of God's goodness and provision for them. Like Jesus Christ, who offered himself for the health and goodness of the church, assembly of believers through faith, a father/husband that is good blesses his family with a realm of happiness and growth. A good father is respected! Many men have already blown it! It has taken me a lifetime to begin to understand! To "rule" does not mean to be abusively dominant and controlling. It is what you become and provide for those you love.

Women nurture their children and grandchildren because they love their families. The Virtuous Woman *(Proverbs 31)* is described as a hard-working lady, inside and outside of her home. Her diligence honors her husband who becomes a leader in society. Her children rise and call her blessed. A virtuous woman is called the crown of her husband. *(Proverbs 12:4)* When this does not happen, we, men and women, have failed ourselves, our families, and our society/culture/humanity. Failure affects all humanity.

Foolish men are irresponsible and self-serving. They abuse women and forsake families. The goal of evil works toward the destruction of our families. The place of greatest service is at home with family blessing our children with love and truth! Nothing better than a loving good mother, grandmother, great-grandmother… Men must protect and provide for the goodness of their families. Dead beats don't.

My thoughts, as I continue: The Lord God enjoyed walking in the garden with Adam. He wanted Adam to know and love another being. This would be so fulfilling: sharing your soul with someone you fall in love with! To depend upon and to cherish another person, as you experience life together, is such a wonderful journey. This journey of man and woman is enriched with children and grandchildren for generations. This journey connects us all, and it has filled our world with humanity. Each birth is a new personality: Each child is a different soul with great possibilities. Each being has unique DNA = abilities; Each one experiences life with a variety of adventures to share; Each one is a creative being who can learn and master the world they live in; and each new face could walk with God in the world they discover through living. Each person has the opportunity to walk with God in the eternal realm someday. To perish in sin is to lose this opportunity. "LOST!"

*Alliances and Enemies*

Is a woman less than a man? Is a woman property? Is a woman a slave? **"No"** to each question. Men and women are not the same, nor are we equal in all areas. There is a diversity of personalities, various levels of intellectual capacity, education and experience accomplished, size, function, and so much more. The value of every soul starts equal but various things can degrade personal value or increase personal value. God values each soul. But your value depends upon what you do and how you value yourself. The Lord did not create robots or puppets on strings. He created unique intelligent individuals who have freedom of choice and accountability. He gave us a gift!

Talking about individuals and personal responsibility, accountability, participation, commitment, and more: A person who commits crimes and lives immorally degrades self before others. A person who devalues another individual's personal value, or hurts another individual, devalues their own position in the views of others. So, because of sin, we are not all equally valued. We do not trust everyone. We choose our friends. We choose who we love. We choose who we listen to. We choose who we walk with in life! We choose our friends, good or bad, and these individuals/groups define us in some way.

Who do you walk with? Who do you spend time with? Relationships define each one of us. "If you run with dogs you will get fleas." *(Old saying from a grandmother.)*

Family is home and you have a responsibility to protect, nurture, educate, and love each other. It is all about family!!! The spiritual battle is about you and your family!

**The enemy, the devil reveals himself.** *The enemy invades and declares war.*

This narcissistic chauvinist failure, the devil in my story, grimaces like the Grinch in his planning and execution to kidnap my wife and destroy my family for over five years. He continued his assault for over another year. I suspect he is still stalking from a distance and could attack again. He is like a hungry lion, waiting to pounce on his prey. He wants to destroy so he can appease his evil hunger. (His prey has become stronger!)

This devil was conniving a deeper plan each time he called. Almost every evening for five years, after I went to bed, he called her to manipulate her. I never knew. (I wonder if Adam ever knew.) His beguiling assault was a deceitful romancing, which focused on the matriarch of a wonderful family. Emotionally, he persuaded her with promises until he isolated her for capture. He never cared

*Alliances and Enemies*

about his own family that finally rejected him. He never cared about her family. His beguiling sweet talk isolated her from those she truly loved. He smiled while doing it. Eventually, she anticipated his next call. He kept calling. He kept pursuing. His persistence pressed to cut her off and steal her away. He did not care who it would hurt. He just wanted her and pushed until he could take possession. I cannot help but compare the beguiling of Eve in the Garden of Eden. How many attempts did this devil in the garden make before she sinned?

His promises were decorated with romance, wealth, traveling, and his *self-declared* intellectual superiority. From third cousin youthful memories to a fantasy life of promises, he manipulated her with his words. Beguiling another innocent one into his grasp. His assault affected everyone in our family (specifically Sally: but even me) for over six years. This old man, who was two years older than Sally and me, invaded her life after fifty years of no contact. He began sweet talking with brain-washing dribble of past things and built up his persuasion into glorious promises of a wonderful life with him. It took him five years to set the hook and another year of battles to capture.

He was a third cousin. Sally's family spent time together with his family when she was a young girl. I am sure, as kids, they had good times. I am sure she had feelings for him. When he left for the Army, he promised to return and marry her, but her parents obstructed their communication. Her mother did not allow Sally's letters to leave the mailbox and she kept his letters from reaching Sally. In time, they both thought the other one moved on. She never had closure, which he used to manipulate.

His failed life of womanizing brought him back into her life after his marriage failed and he was rejected through the dating scene many times. His wife left him and his own daughter never talks to him. Even his ability to date was a failure because he can charm a lady to find his way into her life but then he becomes a controlling and mentally abusive jerk. Sally was naive and would talk on the phone with him as he turned on his charm. His charm was conniving and his promises to provide a wonderful life full of romantic experiences were enticing, as he beguiled her for hours each night for over five years. The sixth year became a series of battles, which she returned to me, time and again, but his persistence led to another battle strategy and the war started over and over each time. I became battle-weary. Our family was feeling hopeless. I felt lost and hopeless too.

Unknown to me, this storm grew in her hidden life for those five years. Almost all of their contact was over the phone, as he manipulated her feelings. My life was unknowingly being destroyed. A very slow crescendo of marital stress led me to wonder what was going on. Many times I would say, "I do not feel loved." I did get frustrated, but I always walked away. I thought she was just getting to be a cranky old gal. She became mean with her words. She was good at making things look like my fault when I was frustrated by some event. Unknown to me, he was coaching her every night on the next play, as conflict was stirred around us.

> *\*\*\* (As I continue to share this story, I must admit that this is based on my perspective, my memories, my feelings, and my understanding. Right or wrong, this is how I dealt with my heartache. I also use artistic creativity to tell the story but it is all based on real experience.) \*\*\**

**Destroy one and destroy all.** *Sin always spreads around the fallen.*

It was not just my life; it was our family, our friends, and our relatives on both sides. All the people in our lives, who were touched during our careers, were affected in some way. It was reputation and any respect achieved in life that seemed to be discredited, damaged, and even destroyed by this affair. It started in the mind but spread into the heart with the poison of sinful promises. The crescendo of marital tension and family chaos continued over this period, as he spoke into her ear his poisonous lies. I was oblivious to his manipulations and never expected that she could do this. I was blindsided. I was sucker punched by a coward. I was attacked by a punk!

I am reminded of the evil that entered humanity through the beguiling of the serpent (Genesis chapter three). This deceitful creature got in Eve's ear and eventually talked her into violating God's One Commandment, "You shall not eat of the Fruit in the midst of the garden," this was the only thing forbidden. "You will know wonderful things and your life can be better if you just bite into this fruit, which God keeps from you," the fallen lying angel of darkness persuades the innocent. "Just take a bite and you will be as God, knowing good and evil," the devil in disguise whispered. *(Ad-lib based on scriptural truth – Genesis 3.)*

Well, the evil in this story is a self-absorbed narcissist. His name is Joe and he is the devil in this story. Like Eve, the fruit of his lie was ingested by Sally. I am not sure how long the serpent in the garden whispered these things in her ear, because, before the "Fall," there was only the eternal. Time began when death entered their lives. Eve experienced this first because she was beguiled by the serpent/devil and committed the first sin. She violated the Holiness of God, and God Almighty does not allow sin in His presence. Creatures made to be free moral agents are responsible creatures.

The factor of time began, which all humanity now experiences, ends in separation from God, who is the life source of all creation. "Death by sin, and death passed upon all, for all have sinned and come short of the Glory of God." *(Romans 3:23)* "The wages of sin is death." *(Romans 6:23)* Life and happiness ends when sin overcomes. There is pleasure in sin but it ends in destruction. *(Hebrews 11:25)*

I feel like history (even in a small way) is repeating itself when I think deeper into what has happened to us. This horrific violent life storm, crafted by this evil pirate invader, grew each day until the force of its strength became overwhelming. He released his hurricane upon the coast of our lives. This life storm eventually threw me into the dark tempestuous sea. Like Hurricane Ian, it picked me up and threw me down.

Has this life ended? Will the ocean pull me into its depths? Will my life disappear? Will the breath of life be extinguished from my being? Will I be ingested by the deep dark hidden creatures below? Lost and powerless eternally equals hopelessness. I need a Savior that walks on the water! I need a Savior to help me back into the boat. I must watch for the Lighthouse and find the peaceful shore. Oh, I needed help.

Adam did willingly eat the fruit. He was not enticed by the same thing that Eve was tempted with. He was pulled away because he loved Eve. She brought the fruit of sin to Adam and enticed him to be with her. I can only imagine the scene and the persuasion used. The details are not exposed. We do know that Adam ate the fruit and fell into sin just like Eve, and when God came to walk in the garden with Adam, Adam was hiding and ashamed. That's what sin does at every level. It disgraces the sinner. Sinners hide from the truth but the Lord still calls out to them. He invites all to return through **forgiveness**.

The Gospel of Jesus Christ brings forgiveness into personal reality for anyone who accepts the Lord. "Lord Jesus, I'm over here! Help me, Lord. Save me!" The only one who can walk on the water can save me from the waters of this terrible storm. He will navigate my ship. He will place me on a peaceful shore. I trust Him to be the captain. Lord save me!

What I must say at this point is that without Almighty God, Creator of Heaven and Earth, there is NO HOPE. Sin utterly destroys. Hope and happiness are restored by the rescue mission from heaven, the Savior Jesus Christ the Lord. Without Jesus, I would be in the eternal state of death. Without the only source of life, God Himself, eternal death is unimaginably horrifying.

I do not believe Eve understood this when her teeth pierced the fruit's flesh. The beguiling serpent disguised and hid this fact. He spun his lies and deceit in her mind until it sounded good and appealed to her flesh. Same with Adam, he wasn't thinking about the consequences of his act of sin and how it would affect him, and all who would come thereafter. He just loved Eve and wanted to be with her. He willingly ate the forbidden fruit and disobeyed this one command that God gave him. Sin is sin. What level of sin and how much sin does it take to separate you from the Lord, who is the ONLY source of life? All sin qualifies as separation from the Holy God,

*Memories of Loving You*

who does not allow sin to continue in His presence. The brightness of His glory drives it away.

This story I share has changed me. I struggle to find myself again! The storm hit my life hard and the damage still lies in my first world as scattered debris busted into pieces on the rocks of an angry sea. Clean-up continues.

## Chapter Five:
# Finding a Safe Zone

**Finding another world**  *A Peaceful Shore, the World of TARA!*

IS IT A new beginning or a sanctuary? The second world of my life is adventurous and filled with the unknown waiting to be discovered. This other world did not evolve with lengthy experiences and ongoing responsibilities, but rather, sudden changes in locations and characters. This new world is filled with social challenges that transformed me into a different person. I'm still trying to understand who I have become. I still did not know what to do. I was just stunned and trying to survive.

I found myself in this new world suddenly, as if I was cast away from all that I loved. It was a peaceful shore that allowed me to find safety from the tempestuous gales of my life. In a short period, many sudden storms became one hurricane of destruction in my first world: tempests that stretched my endurance until I collapsed upon the old grainy deck of my life exhausted. Without the ability to hold on to my struggling ship of life, because of the waning loss of any more battle strength, I was lost. The crashing waves tore through me until I was ripped from the deck and thrown into the massive squalls of ongoing uncertainty. I was swallowed by the deep black sea of horrific overpowering waves. Inside, I was an emotional wreck.

Once I was flailing within these powerful destructive waves, I became lost in this sea. I felt lost! My breath was challenged, as I tried to find my way back to the surface. Thoughts faded within me, as the sinking panic of my captivity pulled me into its claws, pinching me harder until there was no escape. This overwhelming and deepening struggle pulled me into the deep dark mouth of uncertain destruction until everything became black… It seemed all was lost. Powerlessly ingested into another place, I lay helpless with no capacity to escape. I was lost in a new illusion of life.

I found myself in a new world. Was this a new life? Was this an opportunity to start over?

My eyes fluttered. Smooth waves slowly lapped against my flesh. I was lying upon some unknown distant shore. Life slowly crept back into my consciousness, and I moved my neck to see where I was. I collapsed as I struggled to escape the elements that were still pulling me back into the delusion that held me. I was weakened from past battles but I fought once again, against all odds, because I love life. I must overcome. I will keep fighting: withdraw, recover, refit, plan strategy, and suddenly engage with overwhelming force. [Like Billy Sunday the Evangelist cried out in his sermons, "Where is the devil? I want to fight him. I will punch him, kick him, bite him and when I'm old and toothless, I'm gonna gum him till I die."]

> *"Listen, I'm against sin. I'll kick it as long as I've got a foot, I'll fight it as long as I've got a fist, I'll butt it as long as I've got a head, and I'll bite it as long as I've got a tooth. And when I'm old, fist less, footless, and toothless, I'll gum it till I go home to glory and it goes home to perdition." — Billy Sunday www.goodreads.com*

Time seemed to vanish into an illusion. Reality swirled around me pulling at my soul to awaken. Was all this a dream of distraction? Was my brain hallucinating, as I traveled through a tunnel of uncontrollable destiny? Where am I? Who am I? Why so many questions within my Soul? Why am I here and why am I experiencing all this confusion? Can I find myself? Can I return to my life or must I just survive in this new place? What day is it? Has months evaded me? What year is it? What planet am I on? How did I get here? What brought me to this place? I must find answers! Are there any answers? God help me! Please!!!

***Stand up and walk.*** *Never giving up and never giving in to the enemy.*

With sand and soil between my toes and the elements of this new place under my nails, I pulled myself from the waters that held me. These waters connected to the world that cast me away into the vastness of the open sea. The view across this vast ocean hides my sense of any direction of return. I slowly got to my feet, wary of all the hardships behind me, as the spectacle of a new world was captured through the pixels of my struggling eyes. So many pixels, capturing the refraction of light from this new place, focused on my optic nerve, painted a new landscape for me. Creative impulses sent synaptic waves transforming into my consciousness. Roused by the vision of my new world, waiting to be discovered, I walked with a weak stride of uncertainty. A cloud of confusion dissipated into a vision of hope.

I was standing in a new world and I was still alive. Why did I end up here? Is it fate? Is it destiny? Is it just something that happened? I found myself in a real place with real people. I must integrate. I must blend in because I must survive. All of my resources from the past were gone and the tattered cloth that covered me revealed my vulnerability. I became a weakened game for any predator lurking to devour. I needed to find shelter. I needed a guide to help me. I need information. I need a protector, someone who knows this place and can warn me of dangers and help me find safety. Feeling lost and helpless in a strange world is scary. I was always one who planned every action and crafted every move to succeed. I was the mentor and champion for many, where I came from, but now I was the novice desiring to become an apprentice. This was a humbling experience. I felt lost in my potential.

***I must find shelter.*** *Making friends and enemies.*

At first, I tried to conceal myself in the thickness of the swamp. Hiding from the villagers, I watched from a short distance until I was approached by a wonderful caring soul. The "Flower Lady of TARA" greeted me with a curious smile. Reaching out to me, she welcomed me into the open for all to see. No more hiding in this land. I was relieved.

I felt welcomed to this place, as I walked upon the shore of hope. In time, I was greeted by more of the occupants and I started my new life among them. Friends! It was so wonderful to find friends and to open my life, as a friend, to these wonderful people. As time passed, I became one of them. I fit in! In time I was known as the "Helper, and Good Neighbor Dave." The skills I brought with me were of great use in this place.

The Flower Lady of TARA, her name was Betty, was a soul to the earth. She tended all the plants and flowers of all her friends. She kept the grass growing, even in the hardship of the grueling sun. No brown spots could escape her touch because her goal was beauty. She shared the glory of flowers against the contrast of a green healthy land. The beauty of God's creation surrounds this new world she tended. Her gift to others grew out of the soil through her hands making TARA a wonderful place to live. Everyone who walked in the Garden of TARA felt a peaceful hope. This was a unique place on God's

*Finding a Safe Zone*

green earth, and Tara's Flower Lady was the guardian of its beauty.

TARA was a welcoming place that drew many creatures to settle within. I even saw a large Black Momma Bear the day after I arrived. She passed through the space I settled on, which was next to my first new friend, Flower Lady. I stood still as she passed relatively close to me. We watched each other closely. I questioned myself, "Was I prey and could I evade," as she walked through my space and crossed the street to the other side. Turning to gaze back at me over her shoulder, I wondered what she was thinking.

Disappearing for a moment behind the home of one of my, soon-to-be new friends, the Irish travelers from Northern lands, Momma Bear peeked back at me again to see where I stood and what I was doing. Sizing me up as she considered her action. I was still standing in the same spot watching her. Then she moved to the next home and disappeared for a moment. She peered back again from the other side. She watched and wondered who this new creature was. This time I moved out of curiosity to watch her. This large powerful Momma Bear hesitated to continue before crossing over to the next dwelling. Again and again, this uncertain traveler passed until she stepped back into the dense forest that surrounds TARA. For many days I felt her eyes gazing at me. Was she still in the forest checking me out? I assume she was checking me out, this new creature that washed up on the shore, to see if he was worthy to dwell here, next door.

Just about twenty feet from my place was this wonderful gal. She became known to me as "Flower Girl," who kept beauty alive and so much more. She also loved all the animals that walked in this land, and, if you had a dog or a pet, she would even travel a distance to help those friends. I watched her care for them with her own hands. Truly nature was her love and its beauty her plan. TARA the Flower Girl tended this world that welcomed me from the hardships and memories, that still followed this man.

Feeling safe after this experience, I decided to build, a place where I could live a good life. The foundation was built next to the "Tube" that became my home. *(I lived in an Allegra Motor Home, I called my tunnel or The Tube.)* Anchored deep into the earth, with pillars strong, a building arose that was a spectacle for some. "Was he adding to this 'Tube,' which was his new home," a few curious nosy ones questioned each day, as the platform deck rose from the earth to stay. A canopy covered this place that I built, with screens hanging to protect me from

*Finding a Safe Zone*

the most dangerous creatures he met. *(I built the deck, gazebo, and shed.)*

Yes, right there in TARA, the land that was perceived safe; some thirsty vampires lay in wait. Hiding from the beauty of each day, they crawled into crevices and dark shadows to stay, until darkness spread over the land each night, and then they came out to prey upon all who stayed out at night. Making all the creatures in TARA their feast, they came out of hiding at the end of each day. Swarming upon each creature with blood, these vampire mosquitoes joined together in their fun. Dining on the life of day creatures they planned, to force them in hiding each night if they can. It was not difficult to perceive, that escaping darkness and hiding away was easy to do if these pests came your way.

Like the *Omega Man*, I fled into my Hidden Fortress, THE TUBE. Barricading these vampire pests from the smell and the opportunity they seek, I take my rest. Each one of these vampire parasites desires to impale my flesh with its sharp syringe to drain me of enough blood to satisfy its cycle of life and reproduction, but together they swarm a victim to drain life away. Like the Living Dead, they wander through the darkness to find a victim. It must not be me. I am a survivor! My goal is to kill as many of these pests who desire to multiply their existence by sucking my life away. "Not me!" "Not Ever!" "I will survive." "I will defeat these hungry vampires who follow me with evil intent."

***My Time Tunnel.*** *A time-traveling tube took me back to my other world every night.*

I slept peacefully on my first night in this home, which I eventually called my "Time Tunnel." It was about one hundred feet from Lake Eustis and Lake Harris waterway. My "Time Tunnel" was an Allegra Motor Home parked by the boat docks of Tara Village in Leesburg, North Central Florida. Each evening, as the sun faded over the horizon, I retreated into the tunnel to escape the lurking dangers that came out in the land of TARA. Then my mind transported me away into my past. Thoughts could not be avoided and memories wrestled my mind for answers. Sleep transported me back through my memories to challenge decisions, actions, and experiences from my first life, which called out to me, beckoning for my return.

Alone with my memories of life, and the imagination of the future, my thoughts awakened to another place every new day. Almost every night an old drama returned,

*Finding a Safe Zone*

different than the last, but sometimes stuck as a series of episodes, to haunt me. Not to be fooled, the outside was trying to get in, the future was negotiating to redirect, and the past was pulling me backward. Seems like I was never alone but I was. I do like my solace, but a heartbreaking torture lay waiting for me when the door sealed for the night. I was alone with my memories until daylight reminded me of where I landed. TARA welcomed me each morning and I smiled once again.

I needed this safe place each morning because every night my nightmares took me into another battle against the Evil Pirate Joe, and his imps of darkness. No matter how the dream began it always ended in the nightmare of the demon pirate keeping me away from my love. He manipulated her to maintain control. He promised her riches and a paradise, but he kept her in a dingy cabin on a stinky ship full of trash. In my dreams, I would find the ship and sneak on board to help her escape.

These dreams always ended up in a horrific fight. I was outnumbered every time. I found myself on the edge of triumph with a blade to his neck. At that moment, I always faded away from the scene and blacked out. My mind would shock me into consciousness and I would sit up gasping for air. Each time I lost her again. I did not know how to stop these dreams. I wanted to move on but I was stuck like a scratched record repeating my attempts to rescue her. What can I do?

Each new day began with the awakening experience that brought me out of the horrible never-ending nightmare that had ripped me away from loved ones. Memories of family flashed throughout my head, as my dreams brought me back into this new reality. While the darkness wrestled around me to keep me captive during those few hours of waking up, I was reminded that I was alone in my tunnel. It was a temporary safe place but also the gateway to my new life. I can escape.

**Every day was a new start.**   *Trying to settle into my new life.*

Each day began very early with an elixir of strong hot dark black tea, Scottish Breakfast Tea. Then I waited all alone watching through each portal of my tunnel to see the darkness fade. The hope of a new day slowly painted its new landscape, filling my life with beauty right before my eyes. The world awakened again, as the creatures wandered back from their safe places to reclaim the land from the darkness.

*Finding a Safe Zone*

During the waking hours of dawn, a few villagers passed my tunnel every morning. I watched from behind the curtains to see who it was. Walking with friends they would pass by. I could hear them coming from a distance because they were enjoying loud conversation. Both serious and joyful topics flowed out of their mouths. Words are released into the awakening landscape. It was like some wanted to make sure the others were up and beckoned for everyone to join them outside.

Truly, the mornings were wonderful at TARA. Most mornings were filled with cool breezes that bring calmness after a storm. Songs from the canopy above began the crescendo of beauty and hope that filled the ears of all who listened. Life started, again and again, each new day after the death of darkness was forced to release its grip from the night. It was always a reminder of the hope our Creator designed, "Joy comes in the morning!" *(Psalms 30:5)* Even when the darkness forces you to retreat into your ark of safety each evening, the hope of a new beginning rises with the dawn, as light recaptures the world from the darkness. Each new day reminded me of the hope of God's promises. I need Hope to survive.

The walkers would slow down and even stop in front of my tunnel to discuss the progress I made on my deck and shed the day before. In the beginning, a few grumpy individuals complained. "Why is he building a deck against his RV?" "Is he building a house?" "Is he adding a room on?" "Who gave him permission to do this?" "He is not supposed to build this," some of them whispered. Many others were amazed at the building and complimented "Good Neighbor Dave." In fact, it became a source of conversation which drew many curious travelers to pass by.

The deck was anchored to withstand any storm. Legs deep into the soil with iron rod re-bar under the large slab driveway and concrete on each pillar, guaranteed that this structure could withstand any storm better than any abode in the village. As the three-level deck system became the platform to enter the tube, it became the base of a gazebo and utility shed that provided me with a workshop, storage, laundry room, closet, and a deep sink. The gazebo became the canopy for inviting new friends to join me and others to come together so we could enjoy our time and extend the day into sunset and dawn, fighting away the dark realm, where these pesky vampire skeeters swarmed. With the gazebo screen nets down, these creatures could not penetrate this safe place.

From the beginning, my first complaint was the assault of these nasty vampire mosquitoes. These zombies, who thirst for living blood, lurk outside every dwelling when the sun goes down. I believe they can smell the blood of their prey. They must like the *Belgium-German-Irish* bouquet of my rare red savory sustenance that flows throughout my body. These hungry pests crave my blood to sustain their annoying persistence, but I conquered this problem by creating my safe abode upon the new impenetrable deck. This deck welcomed my new friends to join together in the interaction of a life filled with friendship and hope. I had good friends. Still do!

**Settling down in a peaceful place.**   *Trying to make a new home.*

Every morning I am awakened to the songs of the birds coming from the tall trees. The owls live above me and they began their day discussing "who" it was that lives under the canopy of the standing tall oaks. Drinking my strong black tea, I would listen to their morning chatter. Their discussions were intense, as they investigated WHO I was. "Who is this creature and why is he here?" they called out to the other varmints hidden in the forest. Every creature was talking that surrounded my space; the chatter in the morning filled my ears with sweet grace. I loved listening to what they would say, as I drank my black tea away.

The solace in the morning was nice for me, but escaping that tunnel darkness each morning, helped me survive. I listened to the owls most of all. I think it was the best part of the day. I even shared it sometimes with the best, as we drank our morning "wake-up elixir" and joined the conversation in our own way. We heard the entire world around us, as beauty filled the air, but my friends and I talked about our own stories, as we began to share another day. I was usually up for several hours before my Jedi friend, Perry, came outside, as the first neighbor awake. (He wore a long brown house coat. He looked like OB1.)

The owls hurled their questions each morning, as creatures in TARA heeded their warning: "Who told him he could stay here?" "Who will ask him what he wants?" "Who does he know here and will he stay in our swamp?" "Is it safe to let him live here or "who" will drive him away?" "Who will protect us from this guy if he stays." "Who thinks we are in danger? Are we in danger today?" "Who knows anything about him?" "Who believes he should stay?" Owls are full of questions and can stir up a fuss. But the traveler had to stay here because he was lost.

*Finding a Safe Zone*

The tiny lizards, my little dragons, crept under my things, just to see if this intruder was worthy to stay. They even sent in their amphibious frog scouts, who crawled through the cracks right where he lay. They reported back to the owls what they saw in his home each day, but the "Flower Lady of TARA" trusted this soul. She kept her eye on him because she too wanted to know. Was he someone worthy to stay or must we pressure him to go?

The Sand Cranes, and the fowl of the forest, would sing as they all discussed. What about this creature? What is all the fuse? He was a curious thing and watch him we must. They watched him build a structure as home; to think he might stay was a concern of their own. This being that lived under their home just kept building his place that became his own home.

Some of them dropped the white stinky his way, thinking it might just drive him away. They even dropped the limbs and sharp seed pods each day, thinking it might just keep him away. The messy moss that sheltered their homes, they dropped on his humble abode. The owls called the puma to check his resolve. Maybe just maybe some danger could solve, what concerned them all, since this being they saw. This guy that they watched awakened each day. He sat on the porch and drank his tea away. A calm and peaceful creature was he, but they all quickly decided to drive him away. It is hard to change and accept what is new when many dangers in life arise suddenly too.

Then one day the owls called everyone to gather, and discuss what they all learned and if anything concerning did matter. Each creature watched him to see if he should stay. Is he worthy of this peaceful place today? This was just their way when someone was new. Does he pass our standards to live among us today, or should we provoke him with hardships, until he is forced away? The discussions continued for days into months, until they were satisfied he could become one of Tara's to trust.

Accepted and safe in this wonderful place, I felt welcomed to live in TARA, as I created my space. I felt like I could find peace and make this my home. But the memories and dangers of things in the past haunted my thoughts to clutter my path. Dividing these worlds where I lived will not pass because it was me, and my life to live, as it lasts.

***Tara becomes home.*** *Making a new life and making new friends.*

Finding the rest my mind needed, from the heartache and anger I wrestled with, was a hard private journey that took time. It was the emotional struggle of my life, but I

*Finding a Safe Zone*

knew I must recover from the storm that brought me here. I refused to die on the shore, giving in to my weakness. Finding the strength to stand on the shores of this new world was the beginning of my healing process. It was my new Adventure of Tara. I was an intruder in a new land surrounded by strangers. These strangers became my neighbors. Tara has been a place of new friendships, and a good life too! But memories held me captive and promises stood in my way too!

Making friends with people you never knew before is an adventure in itself. Each individual is uniquely different, with different history and life experience, which has defined each personal character and variations of habits. They too have traveled to this land and found their peace from lives in distant lands. They too were seeking rest from a previous life that was filled with families, friends, and careers. Some of them found themselves alone, after a life with a spouse they loved. Some accepted closure and moved on to find another they could love. Some accepted their situation and were satisfied with new friends. Some lived alone and some lived with others in need. They helped each other and shared their lives in this close community as friends. These friends slowly moved into my heart to reside. Welcomed by the time we shared, I was happy in the present, and there I did abide.

In the background of my mind was the nightmare that brought me here. Hidden in my heart was a life that I did love and a woman who walked alongside me for the majority of my life. I missed my family. I missed each individual and each memory I shared in my past life, as I made new friends and started a new life. But, as I was living in this new place among new friends, I worried about the harm and the trouble left behind. I did not find closure and I longed for the life I missed. I was learning a difficult lesson.

Could I have done more? Should I have done more? Is it my fault? Did I contribute to the situation? Did I make it worse? Did I fight hard enough or did I give up? The questions swirled in my head. Everything was amplified into much deeper thinking when I closed the door to my time tunnel. Memories became nightmares, and peace became conflict. Anger became sweat and heartache became tears, as an emptiness inside forced me to escape each morning back into Tara, where I found my peace again.

The life I missed seemed so far away. It seemed impossible to return to the things that I loved for a lifetime.

*Finding a Safe Zone*

Yet, my heart grew fonder each day in Tara. Loving new friends seemed right. It was right. These friends gave me purpose, which defined every day. They opened their lives to me and shared their memories, careers, and experiences from distant worlds they lived in. But, here in Tara, they created new friendships through sharing their lives. Their kindness drew me into the tribe as I opened my heart and contributed what I knew to help make their lives better. I gave what I was able to give, as I helped meet certain needs. I think I became a "Good Neighbor." They called me "Good New Neighbor Dave." I am surprised they did not call me, "State Farm," because I was there and I always wanted to help.

As I already stated, the Florida Flower Girl, Betty, was my first friend. She was the first Tara resident that I met and she lived next to the lot I settled in. Every day I would look out my window and see her working in the yard. Her flowers were always beautiful and she was always adding more to her garden. Betty even talked me into getting some pots and planting flowers. In time, she mowed my grass and watered the life that grew from the soil of my lot. When she was away, I took care of her yard. We became very good friends. We would sit and talk over coffee and tea often, and we would go out to eat. She was always checking on me, especially when I stayed in the tube longer than normal. When I stayed inside, I was usually writing. Most mornings I would write about the dreams experienced through the night. For some reason, inside the tube, my dreams were detailed and so vivid that I did not want to lose the experience. This became a habit that drew me deeper into the other world, as well as, push me further into a new adventure.

It was an adventure meeting new friends and spending time with them. John and Sue, who lived across the street were my Canadian Michigan friends. John's background was a Scottish ethnicity, motivated within by generations of clan life, transposed into personality. Sue was a sweetheart Canadian. She was a retired nurse who cared about others. Both John and Sue were retired nurses, and always checked on me. For some reason, my health always bothered me, especially after the storm. They seemed to try and hook me up so I could be happy again. I guess they could see my hidden sadness. I built them a deck entry to their home. The previous steps were tall and steep, which caused me to worry about their safety. Even Betty would tell me I should build them a deck because she worried too. So, I built the deck, which they enjoy every day.

*Finding a Safe Zone*

Then there was Perry, my Irish friend. He too walked out into the freshness of each morning from his dwelling, wearing his long brown "Jedi" robe. In my mind, "I called him OB1." With a cup of coffee in one hand and a Swisher cigar in the other, he would greet me into the day. Often we would sit on the deck and enjoy conversation, while others slept through the most beautiful part of the day. Mornings were the best time! His wife Patti makes the best Sauerkraut Salad! I never had it before but I would like to eat it often! Perry was a Construction Contractor up North and Patti was still an Education Administrator. They were "Snow Birds," who traveled back and forth every year between their two worlds.

Judie lived four dwellings down and across the street. She was a widow for just over a year when we first met. Tom, her husband, was a veteran. I could tell that she loved him and missed him. I think I would have been a good friend if I had the chance to meet him. My impression is that he always made things work, even under simple means. They lived in Tara for over 13 years and Judie was the Office Administrator for Tara when I got there. In time, we became close friends and did a lot of things together. I took down the temporary canvas carport Tom built on the driveway, and I built her a framed shed and carport. I even replaced the flag pole out front and raised the American Flag in Tom's honor again. She was a wonderful lady but she knew I struggled inside with my past.

There were many other friends like Gary the talker, Vladimir (My Russian friend who always thought others were watching him), Mark the traveling trucker, Bob the Marine Chef, Joe the Good Boat Captain, Chanel and Gene the French ladies, David the Michigander, Sandy the Lonely Widow, Mike the Gold Cart Traveler and, of course, Betty the Flower Lady of TARA, as well as many others. A great mixture of ethnicity sharing in the community became my home. They all made Tara a wonderful place to live. Each person was a unique character and each became my friend. I was closer to some but still friends with all, as we shared space in this small community. Tara the Peaceful Village of Friends!

## *Chapter Six:*
# Living in Another World

***A two-world reality.***   *Time travel is real and I experienced it!*

THINGS SETTLED DOWN in my life and a routine developed. As much as I could expect, during the day, my life returned to a new normal. After a long journey of attempted rest every night, I arose from the back chamber of the tube very early, before the waking hours. It was dark outside. Like I always did in my previous life, the internal alarm cracked my eyes open in the darkness to the image on my clock of 4:04 a.m. every day.

I lay there in my thoughts, as the rewind of the recording spun in my head, followed by a fast-forward recall of the nightmare just experienced. All night long my memories from the previous life played inside me. It is hard to start the day without writing. I would wake up with ideas that I just had to record. Staying in the TUBE

*Memories of Loving You*

at night became my transport into the past. Going to sleep was difficult because I knew that when my eyes shut I would time travel back into my other world and re-experience events. Remembering some things brought joy, but some other things caused sadness.

It seemed like I had no control over this reverse transport. Sometimes I wanted to remember, and other times I tried to avoid my memories. There was something about the "Tube," this motor home I was living in, that pulled me away. When I fell asleep in the dark backroom chamber of this tube and began to dream, a gate opened. This gate forcefully pulled me back in the past to an event I already experienced, forcing me to look at myself. I was always trying to figure out what I could have done better.

***Preparation for Travel.*** *Is there a plan to restore what is good and right?*

None of this was planned by me. It just happened. It seemed like I was being forced to reconsider my life. Who am I, and how did I get here? Where am I going? Where should I be? Do I believe in fate or is there randomness in life's adventure? Am I a puppet controlled by a superior force? Like a marionette puppet with strings attached to my hands and feet, am I dancing to music under the master's hand? I never liked the idea that control in my life was directed by God and I have no responsibility. The idea, "Why did God let this happen?" was not something I believed in. God is not the author of confusion and He does not sin. I do believe that the Lord does interact with His creation. "All things do work together for good, for those who love the Lord." *(Romans 8: 28)* "He has not appointed His children to wrath but to salvation." *(1 Thessalonians 5:9)*

Faith is the power that leads to salvation. Forgiveness is the power experienced through repentance, which leads to reconciliation with The Lord God. <u>Forgiveness is the gift God gives</u> to repentant sinners, who trust in Jesus Christ the Savior. Forgiveness can only be given when the person who has caused the harm, understands and takes responsibility for the harm of their sin against the one (1 John 1: 9) offended/damaged.

Taking responsibility for personal sin against another, acknowledging personal responsibility, and confessing to the person harmed is the first stage that leads to forgiveness. This gift of forgiveness is given willingly by the one who was harmed. Jesus demonstrated the harm sin causes when He died on the cross. "Death by sin, so death passed upon all, for all have sinned." *(Romans 3: 23, Romans*

*6:23)* He also demonstrated forgiveness when He rose from the grave alive forevermore! The Gospel of Jesus Christ as Savior must be accepted and personally experienced through faith by calling on Jesus Christ to redeem and save from sin. Whoever calls upon the name of the Lord, Jesus, shall be saved. It is the power of God unto salvation! *(Romans 10: 9-10)*

### *Freedom or bondage.*     *Thinking beyond the box!*

Yes, God's Intelligent Design is in all things created. Everything functions under his power. He sustains life. He is life! In Him, I live and breathe and have my being. The Lord God gave man a gift He did not give any other creature. He created man in His likeness and image. Man, humanity, is created to reflect God's glory in the world we find ourselves living in. We are not gods but we are called upon to be His glory in creation. To be anything less than a free moral agent would make us puppets under the control of another intelligent being. To love and serve God freely is the greatest relationship!

Evil wants to do exactly that: make us puppets under the control of sin. The serpent beguiled Eve into thinking she could know good and evil and become her own god.

*Living in Another World*

The original sin that caused the fall of man is "self-theism." The nature of this sin is similar to the rebellion of Lucifer, the covering of Cherubim when he tried to overthrow God. Lucifer, who is the devil, declared that he would set his throne above the stars of God and that he would be the Most High, God Almighty. God said that he would be brought down and cast into the pit. *(Isaiah 14: 12-17)*

There was war in heaven. *(I remind the reader that in the ETERNAL SPACE, there is no time.)* Michael the Archangel, with the host of heaven, fought Lucifer and the fallen angels that followed in rebellion. Lucifer was cast out of God's presence with one-third of the angels, who became evil spirits/demons. Lucifer the devil, and the fallen angels hate humanity and desire utter destruction of the beings created in God's likeness and image. Our Heavenly Father has established His strategic plan to defeat the devil and to save man. The Lord has a "Purpose and Plan for the Ages." He has already won the victory in the <u>eternal space</u>, which reaches into the fallen created space, where we exist as human beings. The Lord God Almighty sent the Savior into the world to forgive repentant sinners, who trust and follow Jesus Christ. The Savior redeems all who come to Him, asking for forgiveness, believing in His atoning death and victorious resurrection.

Sin separates creatures from a Holy God, who will not allow sin to remain in His presence. Adam and Eve were driven out of the Garden of Eden because of their sin. I am sure they had regrets as they walked away from a beautiful place and into the world that groans with pain *(Romans 8:22)* because of their sin. The eternal experience of Adam and Eve became death, which is not cessation of existence but separation from God, who is the source of life within their being. God formed Adam from the dust, and red clay of the earth, and breathed life into the flesh. It was God's breath, Nephesh, that awakened man as a soul, a living self-conscious being/sentient, made in God's image.

The first couple walked out of the garden, as they were driven away by God, who placed powerful angels with fiery swords to guard the "Tree of Life." The scripture reveals that if they ate of the "Tree of Life," they would live forever in their fallen condition of sin. There would be no hope. This condition would be "Eternal Death." Imagine the continuing decay and destruction of death eternally, for a creature who was created to be eternal. *(Matt 10:28, 25:41-46, Rev 20:6-10, 21:8, 2 Thessalonians 1:9, Luke 16:19-31, 2 Peter 3:9)*

*Living in Another World*

The man fell into sin, the state of constantly dying forever. In the scripture, the condition of sin leads to a place called hell. This is a place of fire where the worm (soul) dieth not. It is a place of torment experienced forever. It never gets better and it always becomes worse. This place was made to contain Lucifer and the rebellious fallen angels. It was not created for man! It is a place created to separate the sin of Lucifer and the rebellious angels from the Holy Eternal Realm of God's presence. Sinners, fallen man, will also be cast away from God's life and glory if they do not come to the Savior. Jesus said, "I am the resurrection and the life, he that believes in me shall never die." *(John 11:26)*

Time became a factor when sin was committed. Time is a measurement of existence, after the fall into sin. This measurement is the result of decay/destruction; from what was pronounced as "Good" by God, when He created it perfect. Sin destroys! There was no time before the "Fall." The Bible tells us that God loves the creature He made in His likeness and image. He does not want anyone to perish in this eternal death situation. I do not comprehend the full impact of sin's eternally destructive force. I do realize that it is beyond our current ability to understand fully. It is not a good thing. I am sure that no one that ends up there wants to be there for even a moment, let alone, forever. It is not a place where any person or friends will spend time together or enjoy life. You will not have any buddies in this eternal penitentiary and there is no escape. Eternally experiencing death is unimaginable and horrific to comprehend. *(Mark 9:44)*

Our Creator, Almighty God, Heavenly Father to believers, does not want anyone to eternally perish in sin. *(2 Peter 3:9)* He wants all to come back to Him in faith and be saved. He provided the way to salvation through Jesus Christ, who conquers death. He will not force anyone to be saved. As a being created with free will/choice, we have the ability to make a decision. The Lord has provided the way of salvation, which is eternal peace with God, who is the source and power of life. To lose this life is to die.

***Forgive one another.*** *The most amazing gift that God offers us is the gift we must give.*

Nature will not make a way, and you cannot make a way. Man's science cannot make a way. God has made the only way. His way brings reconciliation in your relationship with Him, which is grounded in FORGIVENESS. You can personally experience peace with God and be "born again" unto salvation. Jesus said, "You must be born again, or you cannot enter into heaven." *(Read The Gospel of John, chapter three, to understand how much God loves you and how you can find faith through believing in Jesus. This faith becomes eternal life. John 3:16)*

The work of God in salvation is an amazing experience. It leads to the walk with the Lord through the rest of this life. The greatest example God has given us, which He models before us, is forgiveness, which leads to the reconciliation of your being with Almighty God, Our Heavenly Father. It is the example of God, taking upon Himself the flesh of man as Jesus Christ to be the Savior. Jesus humbled Himself by stepping down into His creation to provide salvation to sinners. Jesus walked among us, humanity. Forgiveness is the wondrous gift God has provided that leads to a relationship in God's presence forever. Walking with God! "Eyes have never seen and ears have never heard the things that God has prepared for them that love the Lord." The most amazing adventures are in eternity for all who are "BORN AGAIN." *(Micah 6:8, Colossians 1:10-11) (1 Corinthians 2:9)*

If forgiveness is God's plan to reconcile a person back into a relationship with Him, is it also the example we must follow? *(Matthew 6: 14–15)* How can we love one another, as believers, if we cannot forgive others for their trespass against us? Our Heavenly Father wants us to forgive others. Forgiveness contains mercy but mercy is not forgiveness. Treating someone with mercy is treating them better than they deserve. When you are harmed by someone there is pain and suffering. The relationship is hurt or even broken. The person harmed has the right to react to the suffering and pain caused. The damaged relationship is not the same. It is either over, or damaged so much it is a dis-functioning mess that causes further harm and more sin. How can there be reconciliation?

*FORGIVENESS AND LOVE* are heavenly qualities lived by those who trust in Jesus Christ! A living sacrifice of forgiveness is a path that leads to righteousness in this life. It is the example we live before others through our faith. *(Ephesians 4:32)*

I CANNOT IMAGINE, HAVING LOVED SOMEONE SO DEEPLY, AS A HUSBAND OR A WIFE, AND NOT BEING ABLE TO FORGIVE. The gift of forgiveness cannot be given to the one who caused the harm until this person takes responsibility and ownership for the sin; stops committing the sin; acknowledges the sin; and asks the one harmed for forgiveness. You can be merciful to someone who does not deserve your time or kindness, but true forgiveness, which contains mercy, is a gift given by the person harmed to the person who caused the harm. It is when the relationship is reconciled that the experience of forgiveness is realized. Those who do not forgive become trapped in pain and anger. They even cast the first stones. *(Matthew 6:15)*

**Transported through**  *The first dream that*
**dreams of remembrance.**  *took me there.*

I did not know, nor did I plan, what was happening to me: from the horrific storm that spit me out on the shores of Tara, settling down in this peaceful world, to the overpowering of "The Tube," my time travel chamber that took me into the past during the night. This was all unexpected. In reality, I did not want to experience this storm.

I began the adventures of my memories. I am not sure if it was a real transport but it was real for me. I was there and it happened. Maybe it was like a spiritual virtual reality. When it happened, I felt the pulling of my flesh through the gate of my memories.

I found myself watching my life as it played like a video before me. It was like watching a movie that was rewound and then replayed. As I watched the memory episode, I was pulled into the drama of myself, at the

*Memories of Loving You*

point of the experience being observed. Reflecting on what was happening, as it happened, my thoughts convinced me that I had to watch these previous experiences to understand the context of what was currently happening in my life. The one thing I had to my advantage is all of my experiences of my past were remembered, as well as, all the events playing out in my life in Tara. My first world could not escape me. I could not ignore or forget anything. Why was I there, and how did this happen, were the questions I faced. My heart and my soul searched for healing.

| ***First Transport into my past.*** | *The conditions that forced me into the past.* |
|---|---|

After a long hot day working in the sun, I retreated into the motor home at dusk, just before the bloodthirsty vampire mosquitoes, little demons, began their hunt. I started very early in the morning building a deck next to my motorized home. I planned on leaving the motor home in place. I was settling in! I had no plans to travel. That morning I walked out into the fresh air to organize my tools and gather supplies. Then I spent the day building the deck I designed. Many friends stopped by to watch throughout the day and some even helped me when they could. Of course, I was trying not to think of the pain within me that brought me to this place. I was trying to stay busy so I would not think of the past so much. Keeping busy did work sometimes. Painful memories stalked me at every opportunity. How do I shut down? How can I stop the constant recall? Behind my smiles there was heartache. I think I was able to hide my pain from others most of the time. It was a skill that became natural for me because it was part of my life experience since birth. A deformity inside me caused pain several times a day when nature called for me to take action. My earliest memories as a boy always included this hidden pain, because of the medical procedures I endured, which never fixed the problem. I learned to hide my physical pain. I became very good at this. *(This problem was not fixed until I was almost 50 years old.)*

Retreating for the night, I turned my TV on to keep me company. I cleaned up from the sweat and soil from the day's activity. I was exhausted. I knew that I pushed it way too long, but I enjoyed the creativity of construction. I wanted to get done with the project, but it kept growing in front of me, as I added more. I just kept going and going for 10 hours but I spent over two hours getting materials and tools set up. Every day was the same as I built my place: a three-level deck system with a Gazebo, a tool shed, and a laundry room. Electricity and water, with a washer, dryer, and a deep sink, made the comforts of life better. I thought I was there to stay.

That night, after I made something to eat, I went to bed as early as possible. I turned on my ROKU free streaming to watch some clips on YouTube. I looked up educational videos about narcissism. I started watching Dr. Ramani, a clinical psychologist in California. She was very interesting and I started to understand more about narcissism. After the first video clip, I struggled with deeper thought about what she said. Everything she covered fit into the first-world life experience I endured.

***The Devil in my story.*** *D-Day and Facing the Enemy.*

The Devil in my story, Pirate Piranha Joe, was an evil womanizing narcissistic predator, who could never keep a relationship. He was getting older and he was alone in life. He was Sally's third cousin and when they were younger they had feelings for each other. He used memories of their relationship to invade our family and steal my wife. I even called him a "Wife Thief" once, to one of his neighbors. *(I found where he lived and waited outside all day for him to leave or return, which never happened. I wrestled with God in prayer because I wanted to hurt him. I was ready and willing to violate what I believed to hurt him that day. I would have hurt him if he had shown his face. It was a slow long day of wrestling with God and He protected me from myself. Eventually, I left. I must admit, I am glad I drove away.)*

Like an evil narcissistic Pirate, he attacked my family. He did not care who he harmed or what damage he would leave behind. He harmed Sally more than anyone else, but he would never acknowledge his evil. Evil Joe the Pirate searched for her and eventually found her in 2014. He got into her ear, like a beguiling snake that he is, for over five years without me knowing. She kept her secret well. *(I have wondered if Adam knew that Eve was listening to the creature that beguiled her in the garden.)*

During this time, our marriage began to suffer. Our family became stressed. I did not understand what was going on. I knew something was going on with Sally, but I never suspected that she was being persuaded by this pirate to leave me. Everything Dr. Ramani presented about narcissistic evil intentions and persuasion to seduce and control was exactly what happened to Sally. Her naivety and hidden childhood feelings for her cousin were massaged into her mind for years. He manipulated how she felt and continued to dig deeper into her feelings. I never knew this was going on.

I went to bed early and woke up around 4 a.m. every day. She would stay up late and often told me she was sleeping on the couch, or the other room because she was having stomach pain. It was this late night, hidden conversations, for five years, she was hiding from the whole family, that was pulling her away. This evil selfish predator promised wondrous and romantic things, each night, trying to persuade her to leave me. They would talk for hours each night. No good man would do this. He beguiled her until she gave in. What Dr. Ramani was teaching was exactly what was happening. She got my attention. I think I began to understand. So, I started to listen.

I was angry. I was hurt. I was confused. I was embarrassed. I withdrew from what was normal for me. I guess the normal for me had to change. I should have listened to the Spirit of the Lord within me, but I was hiding in pain and stopped listening. When I understood that all of this was an attack by an evil narcissist, and the loved ones I should have protected were also suffering, I started to listen to the Lord. As a pastor, I ran away from the fight in the beginning. Not only "Why" did this happen, but

*Living in Another World*

"How" did this happen? Was this experience a path for me to understand, and remember, God's love?

That night, I started to nod off, as I tried to watch another video clip. I turned my free streaming AP to "Sacred Sounds," and listened to some ambient noise with visual display until I fell asleep. With my eyes shut and my mind, full of memories, resting, a sudden jolt of power grabbed me and pulled me through a gateway. It was a long dark tunnel with a very distant flicker of light, which grew into a past reality. My whole body was gripped with a tightness, like a sudden excruciating cramp, until it released me into another place.

I could barely stand after the pain. Weak and shaking, I instantly remembered this place. I was in my backyard when I was a boy. At first, I felt like I was watching a scene from outside of the setting. It was like a dream, but it was proceeded by this physical jolt of energy. I felt like I was ripped away from reality and squeezed through a knot-hole. I was forced into another place. I was pulled into the past to face my enemy.

I watched young teenagers swimming in a pool. As I watched, I realized one of them was me. I remember when my parents installed an above-ground pool in April 1971. I was swimming with friends. They were close together on the other side of the swimming pool ignoring me. The memory opened into my mind and I realized it was Sally. I recalled inviting her to swim. She asked me if she could bring her cousin too, which I said was all right. He was a cousin – right? Why wouldn't I let him come? Especially if I wanted her to come over that day so I could see her, and he was visiting.

The event confused me at the time because I thought we were getting back together as boyfriend and girlfriend. This was her cousin but they were acting like their relationship was much closer. Watching them together during this revisit of time, I became angry. This anger was tempered with everything I experienced throughout my life, first-world reality. I knew who he was and who he became, as I watched them together. This first real experience confused me as the memory was a present reality again. But, this time I became aggravated because I knew what was going on. I knew she was going to be my wife for over forty six years and we would have a good life and children together.

I also knew the harm he forced into our lives and how things developed, which caused us to divorce in May of 2021. The date of this combined reality experience followed after the long day of work in Tara, which was also filled with me remembering my young life. The date I was experiencing this time duality was May 10, 2022. The date of my first real-life experience in the pool was May 10, 1971. It was exactly fifty one years to the day. I remember because it was the day after my mother's birthday and I was going to be fifteen years old the next month.

My anger became internal frustration, as I watched this event through my own eyes. I also realized that at this time we were not married yet. But, he had his hand on her shoulder and she was in a bathing suit. Their faces were too close a few times. They did not kiss but I could see they both wanted to. I helplessly watched, as we all splashed around in the pool. I felt like I was the unwelcome guest in my pool, and my love was pinning for another before my very eyes.

As this re-occurrence was relived, other memories reloaded in my mind. I could see the little girl that I went to kindergarten with. She was crying as her mother took her back home on the first day. This is my first memory of Sally. Then I remembered that she was the American Legion, "Poppy Queen," of Swanton, Ohio in 1967, sitting in the backseat of a convertible, during that year's small-town parade for Veterans Day. Gold Platinum hair and big brown eyes smiled at me when she went by waving. I smiled at the memory, but I clenched my fists and ground my teeth watching this jerk play with her in the pool. It was the only time I ever met him in the past. We were kids, but I would never forget that day in the pool. I remembered his name.

***Memories of young love.*** *I have many good memories.*

Details from the past were called forward into the moment. Other memories unfolded in my dream that night. The memories about her family and how Sally and I liked each other when we were thirteen. Old memories flashed through my thoughts. I walked for three miles to her house many times to visit her. When I knocked on the side door, her mother would answer and invite me in with a smile. Helen would add another plate to the dinner table and invite me to stay. Sally and I would play board games or cards in the small sitting room. We would watch TV together and sit close to each other. I remember my heart racing at times and I was happy. We were kids!

Her father, Marcus, Muggs, Mikola would work in his garden every day. I would go out and help him. He taught me about gardening. Many times we would pick vegetables fresh for dinner. He always had the best "Beef Steak Tomatoes," corn, cabbage, beans, radishes, melons, zucchini, and much more. I would help with weeding, rotatilling, hoeing, harvesting, cleaning, pruning, mulching, and more. As the memories of her father flashed in my head, I thought about Muggs and how much I liked him.

Muggs was a hard-working truck driver. When I was seeing Sally from age thirteen to fourteen, he was working for Arlington Glass. Muggs and two other drivers would load glass in Toledo, Ohio, and transport the glass to New York City for about ten years. The glass was loaded off the ships in Toledo, Ohio onto the semi-trailer. He would transport the glass that filled the Twin Towers, as it was under construction. When he returned home after each trip, he would clean the truck, and when I was there, I would help. He was a good man and I respected him. I think he knew this because he would let me help him as he taught me some things. Best of all, back then, he allowed me to see his daughter.

Muggs was a WWII Veteran. He was with the third wave on Omaha Beach and he fought as a medic soldier during the Liberation of France and Battle of the Bulge. I fell in love with Sally's family. They became my family too. In this family, I met many wonderful individuals.

*Memories of Loving You*

Larry and Sharon and their two daughters, Sandy and Roger, and their three boys. In time I met Susie and her daughter and Mark her brother, who was in the military during the time I was seeing Sally.

This unique family allowed me to join them daily. So much so that they called me "Furniture," because I was always there. Helen, Sally's mother, was always talking. She kept a sparkling clean house and she set the rules. She was a beautiful lady. Muggs and Helen would bicker about things, but I could see that they loved each other. It seemed like Helen was always moving and talking, and boy, she was a good cook. Muggs too! He would grill steak, lumberjack hamburgers, hot dogs, corn, and anything else needed for the meal. I would stand there and talk, as I watched him grill the meat and pour some PBR, Pabst Blue Ribbon, his favorite beer, on the meat. I carried a plate stacked tall with porterhouse, grilled to perfection, into the kitchen, where Helen set a table full of food to compliment the main staple, STEAK! Muggs always had the steak special cut at Don's Butcher Shop on Airport Highway in Swanton. Don acquired most of the corn-fed beef from local ranches and it was the best.

On weekends, all the family would gather around the large dining table in the kitchen for a cookout. The yard became a playground before and after the meal. There would be thirteen to sixteen family members engaged in conversation as they consumed or played outside all day long. I became part of the weekly family celebration of life. I loved this family and I fell in love with this petite, big-eyed blonde girl.

As I experienced the pool scene again, it occurred to me that it was this event that initiated my breaking up with Sally for a while. This was hard for me because it was about her, and, it was about her family, who I loved. My entire adult life included this complex family that I became a member of. They were my family too!

***Two become one.*** *Married and starting our lives as one.*

I joined the Air Force in 1974. When I returned from Air Force Basic and Technical School, to stand at the altar and watch her walk down the aisle with her father, as he, and the family, gave me her hand in marriage on March 8, 1975, I eagerly said, "I do." We just turned nineteen years old. We started our own family. She left home with me to go to Eglin Air Force Base in Florida, my first assignment. I signed into the unit and immediately took my first thirty day leave. We went down to

Winter Springs, Florida, where her uncle Bob lived. We went to Disney World, Sea World, and many other attractions, as we enjoyed our Honeymoon. We also enjoyed long nights together sharing our love. We were young and full of energy back then. We loved each other and we were happy.

All these flashing thoughts ran through my mind as they became present reality before me. As I watched and recalled so many things about our past, the initial space I found myself in came to a pause. I observed them through my eyes but the body stood firmly in place. Within my mind, all the important memories were relived, as if I was being forced to think deeper in remembrance. It was like reliving, in a few seconds, my whole life, as I was dying. I was not dying but I felt like I could die. There were times I wanted to die, to stop the pain, but I never considered suicide. Life is a precious gift from God and I know that He has good things for me. However, finding the good path, He wants me to travel upon, takes me some time. I know I need the Lord's help every day.

Suddenly, as my anger crawled into my face and the still frame was abandoned, movement on the set came alive. They were still swimming and I was neck-deep in the water, ready to pounce at him. I could end this

*Living in Another World*

now and what happens in the future will never take place. Lunging forward in my anger, I was ready and willing to do what I knew the Lord did not want me to do. For the moment, I just gave in and was prepared to violently rip his head off. I knew what I was capable of and I was ready to dance with this devil to destroy him. As I heard one actor say, "I have skills..."

*(I do not have any memories of Joe before or after the swimming pool. I never knew much about him until many years later.)*

# Chapter Seven:

# Memories and Reality

***Back to the future.*** *Forced back to reality.*

A POWERFUL GRIPPING jolt of energy grabbed me. Ripping me out of my young self, this hand pulled me away, as the scene became distant: Like a Google search on a geographic position of a map, I was pulled further and further away watching my backyard become my childhood house, then the neighborhood were I grew up, then small town Swanton became the Maumee Valley, then Ohio, America from sea to shining sea, and the Earth shrank into a distant vanishing blue sphere. Finally, the darkness with all the distant stars flickering around my reality raced past me, until the surge pulled me back through the small opening into my Tube. I lay on the wet sheets of my bed as my heart raced within me. What happened? Was I dreaming? It felt real! It was real for me!

*Memories and Reality*

As I lay there stunned looking at the ceiling in this dark chamber bedroom, the hole in the roof cavity of the motor home structure, where I had removed the light fixture weeks earlier, because the light fixture did not work, focused my attention back into my present life in Tara. I recalled the few days of trying to repair this light. I replaced bulbs, ballast, and checked wiring. I discovered that there was no electricity to the light, and the switch next to the door on the wall was dead. I gave up on my repair attempt when I could not trace the electric problem, but I left the light fixture off, which left a hole in the ceiling above my bed.

The hole was there for weeks before the first jump. Laying in my sweaty sheets after being yanked through this hole, my mind started to search for reasons how and why this was happening. I even remember two occasions before the jump, in the middle of the night, while sleeping, I felt something slimy and cold hit me on the arm, followed by slight force and another cold impact on my leg (Jump), which instantly forced me to react. Grabbing in the darkness, at whatever this thing was that startled me, my hand gripped a cold struggling mass, as my other hand reached for the light next to my pillow. It was a large green tree frog. This frog was the one who bugged me every night for hours as he croaked. Was he warning me or just trying to irritate me? This experience in the middle of the night happened two times about a week apart. After grabbing the frog, I considered killing it to stop the irritating annoyance every night, but I could not. I took it outside across the street and let it go both times.

Realizing something was going on with this hole in the ceiling, I started to investigate. I assumed the cavity was sealed from the outside. How was this frog getting into my motor home and how was it able to crawl through the tight structure above me? The AC unit was above this area, so the next morning I got on the roof and started to search for answers. Answers I could not clearly find. Speculation and theories reason with my intellect. Like a scientist trying to explain with only physical understanding, I had to just accept that something was real but beyond my ability to explain. Was my experience spiritual? Of course, it had to be!

I began to evaluate what happened in the context of this hole in the ceiling. This hole was a gateway of some kind. (My Artistic Imagination – the frog really happened.) It must be the gateway into my past. With my head swirling with thoughts to understand, I became anxious to figure out how this was happening to me.

***Got to figure it out.*** *Trying to understand what is happening.*

Laying there after the jump, I could not move for some time. I was upset by the experience. The ambient noise of the Sacred Sounds App continued to play on the TV above me. The sound of trickling water from three bamboo stalks splashed into a pool, as the visual scene continued. The sound of splashing water in the present forced me to think about what happened. Was this real? I clearly remembered the incident many years ago, but now it was a present experience to wrestle. Did I want to remember? It seemed like I could not find closure in my heart, so the emotional pain continued within, to be carried around during the day. It was extra weight in the new world of Tara. I tried to keep it secret but I believe some of my new friends could see the struggle of my heart. Sometimes I was evasive, staying in my tube hiding from my troubles.

Finally, my body relaxed from the squeezing power of this newest reminder. My first world was still out there beyond the sea of trouble. I had no closure! The enemy, Joe the Pirate, was sailing into the lives of other women to bring his destructive evil. That is what evil pirates do. He became a womanizer in Europe while in the Army. He never could keep a lady. He sought for one to possess, and his narcissistic nature allowed him to accept his evil intentions, as he justified in his brain, what was immoral.

Sally was out there on the wreckage of her life without me. She escaped from his control but he was searching the ocean to find her. He still wanted to possess her. Every moment she was getting weaker and weaker and I was sheltered from knowing what was really happening. The sadness in her mind was pulling at her, to give in to her helpless situation. The elements of destructive forces preyed upon her to let go. She lost everything. Was anyone looking for her? Would anyone rescue her from her drifting peril and declining existence? Every day she cried and became frail. She gave up hope and just drifted into oblivion.

My children tried to keep me away from what was happening. They were protecting me. It became difficult because I was living in a different world now. I had new friends and new experiences to consider. I tried to forget the past but all I could do was push it into a separate compartment and act like it was not there. It was there! It constantly haunted me as each new experience was recorded next to my old experiences on my old hard drive, brain.

***After the First Jump***     *Wrestling with my memories.*
***into the past.***

The next morning began slowly. I made a pot of tea and sat at the table stunned. Many thoughts poured through me. It took a few still silent hours before I moved again. I tried to let my brain go blank but each time I was close, another thought poured in. I was trying to get this behind me. I kept turning the sail away in a different direction but the winds pulled me back to sea. I wanted to step back unto Tara shores, where I presently resided and have friends.

When I looked out of the window, toward my "Florida Girl's" place and saw her tending the flowers, I was able to step back into the present reality of Tara Village. I grabbed a fresh cup of strong black tea and stepped out of the tube into a new day. I walked over to her and we sat down and enjoyed our tea/coffee, as we shared our morning. I recall the owls in the canopy above making an unusual fuss as I shared my frog experience with Betty, the Flower Girl. She told me that she was annoyed many nights and mornings by the croaking frog. I told her that I launched the frog back into the forest hoping it would go away. She was glad that I did not kill it. Me too!

***Talking to the birds.*** *An amazing spiritual memory I'll never forget.*

Later the same day, as I was walking back from Judie's project, I saw two owls in my driveway. They were just sitting there watching me. I stopped so I would not scare them off. They never moved. They just looked at me with those big eyes. It was as if they were staring me down, but I realized they wanted to tell me something. I walked closer. They kept staring. So, I decided to get as close as I could. I spoke back to them, holding my arm out hoping one would land on it, "Hey guys, what you up to?" I did get close before they spread their wings to catch the uplifting breeze.

The amazing moment was in slow motion. One of the owls disappeared into the canopy above, but the other one landed upon my flag pole that leaned off the Gazebo by the steps. On top of my American Flag, like an Eagle symbol, this owl perched. Looking at me, as I walked up the steps, I came as close as three feet from this beautiful creature. I went inside my Tube to get my camera, hoping he would stay in place. I just had to get a picture! He stayed in place, as I came back out and walked past him down the steps. He just watched me. The only thing that moved on him was his head. He followed my movement waiting. I stepped back and took several pictures. It was as if he was posing for me on purpose. When I was done taking pictures, I told him thank you! He blinked at me a few times as if to say, "Everything will be alright." I felt accepted but I also knew he was referring to my experience at night. At that moment the creatures all began their musical forest melody, led by the frog. I felt like life was an amazing adventure and my travels were meaningful. I just had to find the path I was meant to walk upon.

Suddenly, this majestic animal stretched his wings fully and grabbed the invisible power of the wind, as he forcefully launched upward into the canopy to watch over me. I felt amazing but bewildered. I wanted to know what all this means. After some time, the thoughts that ran in the background faded away. I was able to enjoy my second world full of new friends again. Of course, I told them about my pet owls.

Daily activities kept me engaged. We worked in the yard and helped each other. We would go out to eat, and go to festivals in Eustis, Tavares, Mount Dora, and even the Villages. John and I would go fishing on his boat or the dock. We would swim at the pool in the park or play cards at the clubhouse. I would hang out for a short time with my brother, who did live close by. Keeping busy kept me away from the dreams that became nightmares and sadness. I was trying to be happy. These new friends did bring me happiness and we spent much time together.

I love to cook. So I always made a large pot and shared it with my neighbors. They shared what they made with me too. Food was never an issue of concern, except for making too much. John shared his moose steak. Patty shared her special beans and sauerkraut salad (my favorite!). Betty, the Florida Flower Girl, shared her soups. Besides my soups, I would host fish fries at my place and everyone chipped in. My brother Rex located a company that sold Walleye, which became a favorite for us all. Yes, the days were busy with friends and I was running away from the past. I was desperately trying to find closure. I was trying to move forward. I was trying to forget the jump experience into the past, dismissing it as only a dream. Behind my smile was a world of memories and a love I lost. A smiling sadness was the story behind my face.

After building my new deck, gazebo, and shed, I built John and Sue a double deck, which made it safe for them to enter their RV and to sit outside. I often joined them in conversation. We would watch other neighbors walk by and sometimes engage them in conversation too.

*Memories and Reality*

***Could there be another?***     *No closure but another life to live.*

Judie, the Tara Village office manager, was preparing to retire from her job. She began joining us at the fish fries and contributing her talents in preparation for the event. Her husband, Tom, a military veteran, passed away two years earlier. She always liked the military and we had much in common. We spent time together as friends. We shared meals and watched some movies. In time she wanted a deeper relationship, which I was not ready for. I liked her and enjoyed her personality and company, but I did not have closure. She was hanging on to her first love too, even though he was gone. Their names were on the welcome sign and all the pictures and memories were inside her home. Like me, she did not want to be alone. Judie was an amazing friend but I was not looking to get married. Of course, everyone else was cheering the situation on.

Judie asked me to help her build a new shed and carport. I was anxiously willing to assist because I wanted to keep busy. She paid for the materials and I removed the old metal pipe and tarp carport, as well as other things in the yard. Over several months, I built her a 10×12 shed and a framed carport with a metal roof. I finished her

"She Shed" inside with electricity and insulation, and I mounted her AC. But during these long days of construction creativity, another world and other times continued to play in my thoughts. I was good at hiding my pain. At least I thought I was. I guess some things cannot be hidden and Judie could tell I was wrestling with my past.

One day when Judie made me a nice meal for the work I was doing, she asked me various questions. She was wondering where our relationship would be in six months. My response was slow to answer but I said we were friends. She dropped it for a while. Eventually, she told me that the one thing she worried about was my relationship with Sally. She told me that she knew I still had feelings for Sally and cared for her. I guess I mentioned things from my past and shared current information from back home often. We were friends. I told her we were friends and I did not want to get married at least three times over several months.

In my mind, I worried every day about Sally and wondered what was happening. I knew she was suffering emotionally. So was I. When I received a scrap of news about her situation, I tried to understand more. Her situation was elusive to me. Those whom I love were protecting me from knowing the details. As I look back on

*Memories and Reality*

all this, I admit that I did not have closure. My heart was stuck. I could not move on, even though I tried.

After returning to my motor home, "The Tube." I was stressed. It was a very-very long day of building with a lengthy dinner and conversation afterward. Stress followed me back to my place. I was very tired in my mind, as I cleaned up. I crawled into bed with the TV on, but I fell asleep quickly. When I woke up to go to the bathroom after a few hours, everything was on my mind. Once I lay back down under my silky bamboo sheets and blanket, I turned on the "Sacred Sounds" app to help me go back to sleep. Every muscle was aching from the many days of construction on Judie's place. The water trickled out of the visual bamboo stalks into the pool of water and I drifted away. I was powerless. I was pulled away into my past again.

***The second jump into my past.***   *I was forced to remember my life.*

The sudden jolt of power grabbed me just like it did before. My body clenched with pain. My mind instantly opened. The ambient visual that continued in the room faded in strength and distance, as I was pulled through a tunnel back to the past. There was no planning, nor anticipation, for this event.

I had no control over anything and I felt helpless. My body was tight and stretched out like a board. The velocity increased and my thoughts compared what was happening to what a missile would be like when launched toward a target. The room became dark as the television disappeared in the distance. The darkness became heavy until the streaking lights of the Solar System filled with stars, raced past me. I was hurled toward an unknown target. At least, it was unknown to me at the moment. I was fired into the night to another world. Maybe it was another time. It did feel real!

Things began to slow down. Then, I was gently caressed under the most comfortable sheets onto a soft bed, with my face resting on a familiar pillow. Released from the grip that tossed me into the darkness, I relaxed with my eyes closed. I was relieved that it was over. Whatever it was, that just happened, outside of my ability to control, was more than a memory or a dream. Every muscle released the tension and my mind told me I was going to be OK. I was used to getting bad cramps at night when I worked all day.

I was suddenly pulled into this young man. Fused into a teenager who was sound asleep. Whatever just happened was real. It felt real. My ability to control my own actions returned and I found myself under the sheets lying in darkness. Something smelled so familiar, as I breathed the air deep into my lungs. At first, I did not want to move. I savored the moment, letting my brain adapt to my situation.

### Back Home Again, Farther into the Past.     Home Sweet Home!

With the ability to fully think for myself again, I suddenly pulled back the sheets and the blanket to stand next to the bed, where I was resting. The launched missile feeling left me. Panic returned to my consciousnesses. I began to evaluate my position and create a response to what happened. I scanned the room looking for tools that I could use if there was a reason to defend myself. I am good at using tools when needed. Anything can be used to defend oneself. I learned a lot in the military. I trained with soldiers.

But as I visually looked at every detail, I realized that this was home, my childhood home. My brothers were still in bed and I was looking down on them. We shared

*Memories of Loving You*

one small room. I was in the lower bunk bed and my little brother was on the top. My older brother had his own separate single bed and he was snoring. I took some time standing there. It was so serial to experience the moment, but the present reality of the wonderful smell from the other room pulled me away.

I opened the squeaky door slowly. Looking down the hallway I could see the light in the kitchen. I knew it was my mother, Virginia. I was home! This is the place I always considered my home. I grew up here. This was my first family. My brothers were still sleeping and my sister was still in her room. Dad was out the door with his lunch packed by Mom, and he had already had his breakfast. Mom was frying mush on the griddle. The same griddle was passed on to me and I had given it to my eldest daughter in the future. I rushed into the room and threw my arms around my mother hugging her like I never did before. I did not want the moment to end and she snuggled me in her arms, wondering what was happening.

I told her it was great to see her this morning and I just needed a hug. After a strong embrace, I stepped back to look into her face to tell her how much I loved her. She returned her love with a big smile and a kiss. Then she returned to the mush frying on the griddle. I sat and we

*Memories and Reality*

talked as she continued to prepare breakfast for us kids. At the moment, I was the only one there and had her completely to myself. She was happy to talk with me because I was a normal cantankerous 15-year-old rebellious teenager and she did not get this opportunity often. It was just me and her. I was happy at the moment!

As the smell of bacon filled my nose and the vision of my mother at the stove cooking continued to press the reality of the moment into my thoughts, she asked me how Sally was. In my mind, I remembered the question she asked me, as well as, the original response I gave her when I was a boy. The memory was clear. The first time I responded to my mother, back in the past, I said, "I don't like Sally anymore. We broke up. I don't want to see her again…" My mother responded to me, "But she is such a nice girl. You need to call her." "I don't want to call her," I answered.

My response this time was tempered by my life experience, as I said, "We are not seeing each other. I guess she is mad at me." "Well, you should talk to her," Mom advised. "I don't know if she wants to talk to me," I muttered sadly. "So, you still like her?" Mom questioned. "Aghhhh, I don't know." "Well, when you see her, you should go up to her and ask her to go out again," Mom coached me. "She won't talk to me. I would be wasting my time," I whispered, as if not to respond. "Well, that's what I would do," she advised.

By this time, my sister and brothers came barging into the room and I lost my private session with my mother. It became a family time, which I also relished in the moment. Joanne pulled a chair up to help Mom at the counter and Rex and Mark peeked around Mom to see the food they would soon consume. The smiles and the chatter filled the kitchen as we settled down at the table for the first meal of the day. Mom always made sure we had a good breakfast before going to school.

***Back to School.*** *Another experience of high school.*

It was the first day back to school and I walked the half mile, with my backpack, down the sidewalk on Church Street, to the Swanton High School, home of the Bulldogs! It was my Junior Year and I was planning on making it my final year. I had taken my Government Class at Bowser High School in Toledo over the summer and I had all my credits needed to graduate at the end of the school year. I graduated at age sixteen from high school in 1973. I wanted to get on with my life! Maybe I should have taken things slower.

My friends joined me as I walked to school. Randy, my next-door neighbor, was waiting for me at my door. David, whom we called Ox in high school, ran to catch us as we walked by his house. I could see Kevin and Jeff way ahead of us, so we ran to catch them. We talked about our first day of school and how it would be great to see all the girls again. Our guy friends too, but the girls were on our minds. These were the guys I hung out with through the summer. So we were focused on what was ahead and not what we had done during the summer break. We knew what we did all summer, but now, we were going to see everyone we missed all summer, and the girls were the primary subject. Just like teenagers always do, we talked about certain girls, who stood out. We laughed. We smiled. We joked and teased each other, as we crossed Cherry Street and entered the school property.

### *A Long and Winding Road* *Then I saw her face!* *Back to Her Door Again.*

Busses were lined up on the street in front of the school. Juniors and Seniors had to be there earlier than the lower classes, so the busses were there to take Juniors and

Seniors, who went to Penta County Vocational School, to morning classes in Perrysburg, Ohio. They returned after lunch for the normal classes. As we approached the main entrance on Cherry Street, greeting friends and pointing out new faces, I noticed Sally as we passed her bus. I saw her standing next to the bus. Long blonde hair and big brown eyes caught my attention, as I walked past her with my friends. It was the beginning of the year at Swanton High School and Sally was going to Penta County Vocational School a few mornings each week, to study office management and secretarial skills.

I turned my head to get a second look and she saw me smiling. *Then I saw her face,* and I believed she was happy to see me. I secretly waved to her and kept going. All my guy friends were in the door starting to split up. I turned and told all those who could hear me still, "I got to see Sally." I rushed out the door and down the sidewalk catching her just before she got on the bus. Everything about her caught my eye. Her long blond hair and those brown eyes gazed at me. I fell into a trance looking her over as I approached. Bell bottom blue jeans, and a blue turtle neck sweater, darned by a dainty neck-less. She was holding her books against her with both arms. She looked so cool and I was captured again.

We talked briefly because she had to go. I asked if I could call her and she said, "Yes, call me tonight." As she stepped up the steps, I watched and she turned with a smile. I continued to watch as she sat down looking out the window at me smiling. I recalled the moment from the past, as it became fresh again, my heart melted as the bus drove off. It was more than a pause that made me stand still waving. There was a sadness in my heart remembering what was going to happen many years into the future. Boys don't cry! A tear swelled but I retained it. Turning away to the school, I slowly dragged my feet to the first classroom. I was a little late but the teacher just smiled with a nod to sit down.

***Multi-Tasking Brain at Work.*** *Distracted during class.*

Was I dreaming? I participated through the day but my thoughts were racing with Sally on my mind. I was anxious for school to end, so I could call her, and maybe see her. The day moved slowly as I was rethinking everything from my past. The classes I did extremely well in were those classes when I liked the teacher. If I liked the teacher I paid attention and enjoyed learning. When I did not like the teacher, or I was bored, I did not apply myself.

*Memories of Loving You*

I knew I had the potential because in my future I earned an Associate, Bachelor of Science, and Master's Degree, all in Civilian Education and I had my Basic Officer Training, Advanced Officer Training, CAS3, Command General Staff College, and several certificates that certified me in my field, but back then I did not care. I was not encouraged by most of my teachers. I remember being treated like I was not as capable as other elitist kids in Swanton. I felt this way.

Some of the high school teachers had favorites, whom they catered to. Some of the men favored the girls. I did not like some teachers because they were not good teachers, or they just acted like jerks. I remembered the principal, who did not like me. He told me one day that I was a loser. I would never make it in life because I was trouble. It seemed to me that they failed me in those early years. I believe some of them had arrogant condescending attitudes. Maybe it was more me but I don't think so.

That day during various classes, I ran intellectual circles around the teachers, challenging their understanding and knowledge of each subject. It felt good. I was different, and they knew it.

However, there were those wonderful teachers who took the time and allowed me to excel, who were surprisingly happy. Those teachers always gave me good grades, because I earned good grades, based on their ability to keep me interested in the topic. They are the ones who influenced me to use the skills I had when I went to college and graduate school many years later.

***Remembering those*** *Remembering my youthful past.*
***special times.***

I was really there again, reliving the memories of high school. My thoughts played in my mind as youthful ability and increasing potential. My favorite sport was wrestling during the season. I also played football, and I was even in the band. Late spring and into Summer, I was on the Delta Swimming Team. I was a high diver, and relay swimmer, and even competed in the district in the back-stroke. The coach grabbed me at the meet and told me to join the lineup for the backstroke. I responded negatively. I never swam backstroke. The Delta team member was injured and the coach threw me in. She gave me a quick demonstration and told me to do my best. The starting gun fired and we were off. Down and back in specific lanes. I finished second place, which was unexpected. My placing gave the team more points than the coach thought and we stayed in the top competition.

I had the chance for a redo! Names and faces ran through my thoughts as I looked around during class. My memories reminded me of the wonderful adventure of growing up in the small town of Swanton. It was a great place to raise a family! All day long I was anxious. I was not sure if I would see Sally. The experience might end like last time, suddenly with no control. I did not want this dream to end. It felt real. Maybe it was real! To have a second chance, to do things better than the first time, intrigued me. If so, that would be an amazing gift. To have the opportunity to get a good old "Army Redo" was definitely welcomed. (The real first time it was my fault for not applying myself but the encouragement and influence of teachers is important to a child's education.)

All day long I questioned my heart. Why was I here? Was I dreaming? It seemed real enough. Did I have a purpose? Was I supposed to do something, like on Quantum Leap, one of my favorite series when I was older? *(Sam Beckett had to complete a task before he leaped again.)* Would I Quantum leap somewhere else, or would I go back to my "Time Tube?" Would I stay in my First World, or find myself in the Second World, where I had already made great friends? The uncertainty bothered me.

After school, I ran back home. Rushing into the kitchen, where the telephone was on the wall, I waited with anticipation. Sally's bus left before they released me for the day. Her stop was one of the first on Mink Farm Road. I stood next to the phone waiting. Was she going to call me? I waited for several minutes. Nothing but silence filled the room. I was impatient! I remembered her phone number after all these years. I dialed it: 419-826-2866. Ring after ring I waited until the line clicked and her voice said, "I'm here don't hang up." I said, "Hello."

There was a brief pause before she asked me how my summer was. We shared our stories and hearts because we missed each other. I think she missed me. What I knew now from my future experience, was she had seen Joe several times over the summer and they liked each other. He hitchhiked from Toledo to see her and even drove when his parents let him use the car. I knew this from future knowledge but I never mentioned it at this current time of the past. I also knew he already was in the Army and gone.

She never told me about him back then. Knowing and listening to her share her summer activities with family, caused me to feel the heartache of the future. I wanted to ask her about him but I would not let myself. I feared losing her again, which I knew was in my future. Maybe the "Redo" was not a good thing.

She invited me over. As I went out the door, my mother told me to be back before 5:30. "That's not going to happen," ran through my mind as I remembered these early days in my life. For many months I would stay for supper at Sally's. We spent a lot of time together. Helen, Sally's mother, would tell Sally, when I knocked on the door, "That's David. Set a plate for him."

Of course, when I got home late every night, my mother would mildly scold me about eating every night at Mikola's. Her mother and my mother were friends and they would talk. Helen would tell my mother it was alright because they liked me. So the scolding was tempered by the fact that my mother wanted me to see Sally. When we were not seeing each other, my mother would tell me that Sally was a nice girl and I should call her.

***Puppy love two timer.*** *Was I a two-timer because I liked two gals and two families?*

We were back together for a few months. Sally started having problems with an allergic reaction to metal and her skin would break out in a rash all over. There were times when I was turned away from seeing her because she was experiencing pain and was embarrassed about the severe rash all over. I would leave her house and go a few houses down to her friend's house, Polly Shishler.

Through Sally, I got to know Polly's family. Jo Shishler, Polly's Mother, was an amazing lady! A Godly mother, who was kind and fun to be around. Polly was a year younger but I liked her and I loved her family too. When I could not see Sally, I went down to Polly's house to see Polly. In time, Sally and Polly both dropped me because they said I was two-timing them. I guess that was not too smart. I made several attempts to get back with Sally but she was mad at me. Her mother and father liked me and would tell her to talk to me. But she started dating others and I eventually started seeing someone too.

***Another Love.*** *There were other girlfriends in high school.*

When I was fifteen, I worked for Jim Keller. He was a roofer and his step-son was David. David and I became friends and I started working after school carrying bundles of shingles up to the roof for various jobs. In time, I was taught to lay the shingles, which I was good at. David was two years older and his sister was a little bit older than me, but in time we started dating. Linda's parents liked me. I was a likable guy. Well?

I cared for Linda, and as we continued to see each other, I knew she wanted to get married. Her mother and stepfather wanted her to get married so she could leave the house. I was just a kid and eventually, this scared me. I broke up with Linda. This was a hard thing to do at the time and I took the cowardly way out. I sent a friend over to get my ring from her, which confused me and made her mad. Getting married at that time scared me. I was not ready! I was too young. During the time Linda and I dated, I would talk about Sally. I do not think Linda and Sally liked each other. Summer ended and school was starting.

# Chapter Eight:

# Reality of Finding and Keeping the One You Love

***There can be only one.***     *Finding the one you love.*

**THE MEMORIES OF** other girls flashed through my mind. I remembered other young puppy loves from high school. I liked Cindy Seal but I was too shy to ask her out or even speak to her. I thought Terry Bloom was the most beautiful girl I had ever seen, but I never approached her. Tony Brown was my friend, Scott Brown's, younger sister, and I thought she was cute and liked her a lot. My mother made me break up with her.

I reviewed my life choices, reflecting on the girlfriends I had in high school. There were a few more I have not mentioned, who were amazing. I know I could have loved another, and knew that at the time. I did have young love experiences. But as I pondered each beautiful experience from my past, I returned to Sally. Even though she got mad at me, I still loved her. I always loved her.

***A Promise to Keep.*** *A simple prayer changes everything.*

I have always thought about Linda over the years and carried feelings for her. I have thought about Tony and if we could have been together. I have wondered about a few others but I have always returned to Sally in my heart. There was a period when I worked at Hansen's Turkey Farm in Swanton, Ohio. I gathered eggs, fed hundreds of turkeys, cleaned, and did a variety of chores. After completing my chores on this job, I walked out into the open field. It was dark. I was alone. The sky above was the deepest dark blue that faded into a distant blackness. A blackness that makes you feel so small. At the time, heaven was filled with trillions of sparkling stars. I stood in the openness under this heaven and I prayed. Looking at God's creation of beauty, I asked God for Sally to be my girlfriend. I missed her. I think I was begging God at the time. My heart cried inside as I asked the Lord to bring Sally back into my life. I promised the Lord I would love Sally always.

The time went by so fast. I stood at her door and knocked. I was hoping Sally would answer but her father, Muggs, greeted me. He told me that she was out riding her motorcycle with her boyfriend. After a short conversation, I turned to walk away. As I stepped onto the side of the road to walk home, the powerful grip that transported me back through time, threw me back to the future. I felt my body become stiff as a rocket. I was shot back toward heaven into my future life. Crammed through this gateway hole, I fell back into the room where I lay in a bed soaked with sweat. It was cold.

**Who brought me back?** *Complications of these memories demanded my attention.*

The duality of my struggle became evident within me. I felt lost. I felt torn between two worlds. Ripped into two experiences. Both worlds pulling at my soul. Why did I just experience this second time traveling jump into the past? Seems like I was there for a few years. Was this experience forced on me to remember? What should I do now? What is expected of me? Man, I was tired and confused. I just lay there in a pool of sweat shivering in the cold for a few hours. Could I go back? Should I go back?

*Memories of Loving You*

Was I supposed to change anything? Why am I back here? I was happy reliving my young life. I could have done things better this time! I could have picked another girlfriend. I could have had another life. I could have avoided this terrible storm. Looking at the hole above, I shouted, "Who brought me back?" I yelled in distress. The pain of the heart is always hardest to endure.

I heard my owls outside join me in thought. "'Who brought you back?" repeating what I said. They questioned me, "Who do you think brought you back here? Who do you think has the power of the eternal?" They both hooted as they chuckled at each other and questioned me. The last thing I remember from the jump was my prayer to God. I promised to love her back then! I promised to provide and care for her until I died. I was still alive. What was I doing? Did I have any authority or control over what happened? My heart was heavy as I stepped out of this back chamber and tried to listen to the two busybody owls, as they chatter their many questions. These questions were really answers that made me think. *(The owls were really there. There were a total of six owls in the canopy above. Sandy said that four were young owlets.)*

***Trying to make***        Wrestling with my memories.
***better choices.***

I searched for wisdom to make the best decisions. Then, much later in the morning, I stepped outside with my cup of tea. I immediately looked at Heckle on the flag pole. *(I named the two owls, Heckle and Jeckle, like the two cartoon character crows because at first, they seemed to always bother me in the morning and evening for about fifteen minutes. They always made such a ruckess.)*

Heckle was the larger one of the two and always led the conversations. It was apparent to me that the smaller one was always repeating what Heckle was saying. She repeated each question with a chuckle as if to mock me. Heckle blinked his eyes at me and turned his head to the side to watch me. I greeted him with a smile and a welcoming, *"Good Morning Wise One." "What advice do you have for me today?" "Do you know what I have been through?"* I questioned my majestic feathered friend.

"Last night I went back and experienced my teenage years again. I relived two years in a matter of hours," I declared with a tone of questioning what he might know. "What is happening to me." Owls don't smile. They are always serious or sarcastic. However, I could see his smile through his eyes. "Yeah, you know, don't you, my feathered friend," I whispered. *(I really sat on my deck and spoke with these owls as they looked at me unafraid. They always asked the same question but I understood. "WHO?")*

Jeckle joined us from above, landing on the roof's edge. Her hooting begged for my adventure to be revealed. So I told them about my lost love and how my shipwrecked heart was heavy with sadness. I shared my heartbreaking experience, and the reminder of last night's adventure, which ended in my prayer as a teenager. They silently listened to every detail as I spoke. I had an audience listening to me. As I told my story, the forest came alive. The geckos gathered to listen. The Egrets and Ibis crowded together close by. Frogs came out of their hiding to hear what I was saying. The rabbits huddled with their ears stretched high to take in every word, and Momma Bear watched from the edge of the forest. It was story time. I was center stage and all eyes were on me.

There was no one else around to witness this gathering. No neighbor walked by and no friend came near, except these creatures who already accepted me, who let me live here. Finally, I told them I needed some sleep. My tea was gone and I could not utter a peep. My eyes kept closing and my head drooped down low. The story has ended and now I'll sleep sound, at least I think so.

I went back inside and laid down. Time passed with no memories because of the exhaustion. Eventually, my eyes opened again, but with some caution. "Where was I," was my first thought, for memories can take me away. This time I was still in my "Tube," all tucked away from reality, but here to stay.

**Another new day and my gift from God.**   *What next? Making myself clean again.*

The neighbors thought I disappeared. No sign of "Good Neighbor Dave" all day long. My Canadian, Scottish, and Irish friends kept an eye out for me to show myself. Judie wondered where I was. I seemed to have taken the day off and didn't tell her. Betty was worried when the "Tube" remained dark and no curtain moved. "Where was Good Neighbor Dave?" Their anxious worry was the talk of the day. Betty, my "Flower Girl," told me later she knocked a few times to see if I was there, but there was no answer from this one in despair.

I finally opened my eyes and landed my feet on the floor. Standing upright gazing at the scene on the TV that was still activated, I wondered how long it stayed on. The splashing water, dancing in the clear pool, poured out of the triple bamboo stalks, was still creating the ambient sound that pulled me away the night before. I looked down at the sheets, that were soaked in sweat earlier, and realized they dried around my body to a tight crispy stiffness. I lay there a very long time as my body recovered from the exhausting experience. There was also a stench that filled the place. I stunk like a skunk!

I rushed into the bathroom to take care of business and jumped into the shower. I shaved and brushed my teeth, which made me feel much better. The smell was still profound so I opened my windows to let fresh air circulate. I lit perfumed candles. Then I pulled all the blankets and sheets off the bed and took them out into the workshop, where my washer and dryer anxiously awaited the opportunity to become useful.

When I opened my door to go outside to the shop, I realized it was already late at night. I spent the whole day, after the meeting with all the curious creatures early in the morning, unconscious in bed. I was too tired to think or dream all day and into the night, but now I felt refreshed.

I caught up on the things that needed my attention like laundry, dishes, floors, and bathroom. I dumped the black and gray water and added the good-smelling stuff into the drains. I fixed a good meal to regain my energy and then sat in the chair alone thinking. Boy, did I have a lot to consider! But, I was no longer stinky!

***The Video of my life keeps***     *An acute focus on my*
***playing in my head.***     *personal space.*

Morning came quickly. I was anxious to get outside again. It was a cool still early morning with clouds holding back the light. I walked down the street, where about twenty other RV homes were parked, and all my TARA friends were still asleep. It was quiet in every direction. The edge of the forest was filled with shadows as if everything was trying to escape the night. I could sense that I was not the only one wanting the light of day to reclaim Tara.

I walked up and down the RV Park road and finally stepped onto the long double dock, lined with boats, reaching into the waterway. A chain of seven lakes was connected to this waterway. This tributary connected many rivers and canals that reached all the way to the Atlantic Ocean, 120 miles to the East, and all the way to the Gulf of Mexico, 110 miles to the West.

There were times I would see groups of Manatees. Other times I watched gators searching for their next meal as Egrets, Blue Herons, Ibis, Anhingas, Wood Storks, and a variety of beautiful fowls stalked the swamp's edge, along the flowing stream next to the dock. I loved sitting out there on the bench as the cool morning breeze passed over me.

The dock was about four hundred feet long and the swamp, along the edge, was always hiding the eyes of many creatures. They were watching. I sat down on the bench at the end of the dock to watch the morning give birth to a new day. It was a relaxing moment, as the world before me filled the creative canvas of the Eternal Master's gift to me. It was my moment of solace! I like my solace! It was everything that God designed within me to gather such an amazing picture before my eyes. My senses functioned perfectly as they drew me into this morning's gift. It was so much more than a gift, it was a testimony to God's glory: every living thing I looked upon was intricately designed to exist and contribute to nature's symphony of life! The morning theater was accompanied by the natural orchestra of all creatures beckoning for the glory of light to overthrow the darkness. I had a front-row seat. It was nice to rest and think of other beautiful things!

***Good Morning Nature.*** *The world was alive and evil hunted for prey.*

For me, the moment was mine. I did not have to share it with any other human being. I just absorbed it as my gift. The smell of the forest's fresh air was mine. The glistening mirror of water flowing past me with all the reflecting images from the sky above to the swampy forest that contained the earth around me, were mine. Every majestic tree stretching far into the atmosphere pointing up to heaven, were all mine in this moment. The longer I sat there the more I realized that I was inside this picture I enjoyed. I thought I was alone, but this experience was shared by other creatures besides me. Some of these creatures did not see it my way. Some creatures existed without enjoying themselves. Life passes too quickly when there is no joy.

My instincts became very aware, grabbing my body to alert my focus. I was not alone. One creature in my happy moment was stalking me. After sitting for about 10 minutes scanning the environment, I stood up. I noticed movement in the water and walked over to the rail to search the water's face. I was trying to see below the still surface that was reflecting the world above it. The glistening picture I just received as a gift was looking back at me. Deep under the beauty of this image, which just filled my heart with joy, there was an evil presence lurking. I felt this evil threat. A predator was watching me.

Peering deeper and deeper into the dark waters I looked for this hidden threat which made my skin crawl. Finally, he revealed himself. A seven-foot gator peeked his eyes out of the dark water. At first, I did not know how big he was because he kept his tail deep. He was in a position to lunge and his eyes were on me. He too was in my morning picture, but he was hidden. He was there, but I could not see him until the picture became my video. He could see me looking back when he moved! My awareness forced him to change strategy, as I mustered my defense.

As I walked back and forth on the dock, he followed me. I felt like I was teasing him. I guess I was. However, I was keenly aware of his position. I would walk past a docked boat to keep him far enough away that he had to rethink his strategy. Almost immediately, I named this opponent, "Joe." "Joe the Pirate Gator," became his name! I gave him this name and my anger peaked in my taunting! I spoke to him like he was my enemy. He was my enemy. He became my devil to defeat. He took on the personage of my enemy. He was "Joe the Pirate Gator," who beguiled my love to steal her away and destroy my life. Finally, he shows up as the predator he is. I felt a rage within that hungered for appeasement. I wanted to shove my anger down his throat and choke this evil coward. I wanted to destroy him! I wanted to unleash my fury! *(I try hard to be a nice guy every day of my life. I am not always nice.)*

I told him I wanted to rip his skin off and make some boots, so I could kick (his !*& and crush his skull) him around everywhere I traveled. I told him that I don't eat trash, so no gator bites for me. I would skin him and throw his carcass into the water for other gators to eat. I told him I would enjoy cutting him into pieces to make this happen. As I carried on this conversation with this beast, I had my real enemy on my mind. Yes, the Narcissistic Evil Pirate Piranha Joe became Pirate Joe Gator, who attacked my family and caused the storm, that brought me to this place, was clearly seen in the face of the beast below me, hiding in the water. It seemed like I became a different person as my anger increased. *(I have said many times, "The thing that scares me the most is knowing what I am capable of when I am angry." I don't like myself when I get angry. The Lord helped me with this when I was saved and began my walk with Him a long time ago. It was* *back to negotiate my defeat. However, the Lord promises to never leave or forsake us when we are, "Born Again," filled with His Spirit.)*

The more I spoke at this beast, the more anger stirred within me. I stood at the dock rail, which was about two feet above the water. Gator Joe was about another two feet from the dock with his tail deep in the water ready to lunge at me. All I could see was his face. At that moment, I decided to do the "Scottish Thing," which I almost did one day, when I found the real Joe's place and waited for him. He never left and never returned that day. I was ready to do what the Lord kept telling me not to do, as I wrestled with God in prayer. I reasoned (Imagined) within myself the evil of ripping his heart out and other actions that he would always remember.

The memory of that long day of waiting, when I was going to mark my territory at his threshold, continued to be recalled. The memory always stayed the same. The Lord kept me from trouble that day. I finally drove away. However, Gator Joe was not so fortunate. He received my disdain, as my eyes were locked unto his and he received my gift. I felt bad later that I did this to the beast. It felt amazing, as I did it because in my soul I projected my action against my real enemy. Oh, how I wanted to hurt him in reality. It is not the right thing to do. I almost did it anyway. I'm glad I stopped. Thank you, Lord!

***First world storm brewing inside me.***   *My story about "The Scottish Thing to Do!"*

## THE SCOTTISH THING TO DO

*"I ------- on his door."*
*"I marked my territory to show him I was angry!"*

Many years ago, I was counseling a young soldier in my office. He was distraught over the discovery of his wife sleeping with another soldier when he was deployed. I was helping him deal with his anger and his decision about what he should do.

During the first session, I learned a lot about the circumstances that led up to the situation. He wanted to work things out and was struggling with forgiveness. I explained that forgiveness was a gift that the person who was hurt gives to the person who violated him/her, after the violator takes responsibility for the act, apologizes or restores, turns away from the sin, and confesses the wrong done to the person hurt. I explained that mercy is treating someone who has sinned/hurt/violated someone else but has not changed the behavior or acknowledged his/her responsibility for causing the harm/damage… *(This is a kindness given by a believer in Christ to an unrepentant sinner, but it is not FORGIVENESS.)*

Mercy is a gift given to someone who does not deserve to be treated better than deserved because the person has not repented or acknowledged the sinful behavior. So, often, mercy and forgiveness are scrambled together by believers and they do not understand true forgiveness. Forgiveness includes mercy but mercy is limited when the violator has not taken responsibility for the action that caused the harm. God Almighty does not forgive anyone until the sinner repents/acknowledges the sin and asks for forgiveness. Repentance is a personal act of the will. Confession is the act of the sinner who knows he/she has caused harm/sin against another.

I further explained that we have a responsibility to tell the person who has harmed us that we are hurt. When we let the person know we are offended/hurt, we allow them to see the harm/sin, that the person has caused, and, it raises the opportunity for the sinner to accept responsibility, and acknowledge the personal responsibility that leads to repentance and forgiveness.

*Reality of Finding and Keeping the One You Love*

The first session ended and the soldier was going home to work on his marriage. I set another appointment with him and invited him to bring his spouse.

A week later, he came back alone. We met in my office again and he told me that he did it. I said, "good." As soon as I said this, I retracted by asking what did he do. He immediately said, "I did the Scottish thing." "What is the "Scottish Thing," I inquired, feeling a little lost in our progress and his progress in his marriage.

The soldier told me that his wife knows he is angry and hurt. "She knows that I want to save the marriage and she must stop seeing this guy." "That is good," I said. He immediately declared that he did do the "Scottish Thing." Of course, I was lost in understanding his comment and I asked him to explain.

"I pissed all over his doorway," he proudly declared. I started laughing as I asked where he got that idea because I did not tell him that. "I know you didn't tell me to piss on his door but that's what we Scots do." "He knows I know and he knows I am pi--ed at him." (Sorry but I must be clear.)

Well, we continued to talk about things and even met a few times after this. I am not sure how things ended up for this couple but I always remembered what he told me, which became a reality in my life many years later.

I retired from the Army after a total of over thirty three years of military service. I moved to Tennessee to be with my family: children, grandchildren, and wife. Things started to become different after a few years and I did not understand why my marriage was stuck. I think we both gave up on some things. The reality is that I had medical/urological issues and we were not close like we were. My wife seemed to be different too. I just gave up. We were together but not intimate like before. Seemed like she was always upset.

In December 2019, she confessed that she loved another man and she wanted to be with him… Of course, much more was said. She wanted a divorce, which I said I would never hurt her and if she was leaving it was her choice. Over the next few months, she went to be with him and returned three different times. The next fifteen months the drama continued and I took her back seven times, but she continued to call him and talk to him and even meet him once. I learned a lot over these many months, which explained to me why things were so hard after I retired. Yes, it happened to a preacher!

*Reality of Finding and Keeping the One You Love*

Me!!! I thought we had a good marriage, even though there were issues.

After the sixth time, she went to be with him and she returned to me, I took a trip to Michigan to drive someone home from Florida, and then I stopped in Toledo. I had this guy's address because the Tennessee divorce paperwork had his address. (Paperwork I withdrew when she came back to me.) At this time my wife was with me in Florida. This was a last attempt to reconcile, so I thought. I also thought we were starting to heal our relationship.

I found his apartment. I walked around feeling nervous because I was about to do the "Scottish Thing." I was mad at this twit and wanted to make sure he understood me clearly. I was even ready to physically ensure he understood. He never came back or left the apartment that day. I looked for cameras to make sure I was not recorded. A few hours went by and my consciousness worked on me. I knew that I did not want to get angry. In the past, I have become so angry that I could not stop my behavior.

I was angry but I believe the Lord kept working on me, even though I tried to ignore the voice within me. If he had shown up within the first hour, I was ready to do what I knew I should not do. I even blocked God's voice out as He spoke to my heart to restrain my vengeance. The still soft voice kept saying, it is not worth it. You will hurt yourself and your family even greater. It went through my head time after time, maybe hundreds of times. "You're a pastor to many over the years and you will hurt them knowing what you have done. Don't do this… You will hurt your family." The wise patient voice of the Lord kept whispering in my ear.

So, I calmed down and never did do the "Scottish Thing." I never saw him and therefore never physically touched him with anger. I still wanted to, but I drove away never seeing him that day. I returned to Florida.

Well, after many months of dramatic emotional pain, we were divorced. I have made it clear to him that his behavior has hurt our family. I struggle every day, knowing that she is hurting deeply now because of her own choices and his sinful unrepentant persistence.

The "Scottish Thing," as I learned it to be, is the wrong way to make sure the person causing the harm understands your anger. Showing this coward that his behavior is sinful and wrong was important. However, getting to forgiveness includes the sinner's acknowledgment of the responsibility of the sin and the contrition to apologize and make it right. Sinners must sincerely ask for forgiveness. The Lord invites us to confess our sins and call upon Him/Jesus to forgive us of our sins. *(1 John 1: 9)*

Jesus paid a debt for sin to forgive us of our sins and cleanse us of all unrighteousness. The shed blood of Christ on the Cross was for atonement. "Whosoever calls upon the name of the Lord, will be saved." Forgiveness is a great gift! The old gospel song, "What can wash away my sin? Nothing but the blood of Jesus." *Chaplain LTC-R David Druckenmiller*

| | |
|---|---|
| **Refocus on Second-World Reality.** | *No closure keeps me from moving into the future.* |
| | *Living in the reality of this world.* |

Walking back from the dock I was smiling. I left the confused gator in my swoller. Returning to my "Tube" I walked with a spring in my step and the smile of victory on my face. I was laughing at myself. "Did I do that?" "Yes, I did!"

The sun rose above the clouds. An eerie dawn filled Tara. Shadows formed upon everything that the breaking light exposed as if to keep the darkness of night involved. Defeated once again, after the long night of hiding the beauty of the day, darkness fades into a dull shrinking grayness. The darkness of night continued hiding behind everything the light touched, creating the reminder that it was still there. The spies of the night refused to crawl into the cracks and crevasses, even when the brilliance of the light illuminated creation. Dark clouds infiltrated the skies to provide cover. Darkness remained in a fallen world to remind creatures of their inability to remove the darkness themselves.

Darkness regrouped to plan a strategy for the next battle because it was going to return with vengeance. Shadows are always present during the day, but this day a covering shadow filled the sky. Shadows move around as the sun forcefully chases them. They shrink and lose power to the beauty of light until the power of the light disappears over the horizon. But this day the gloomy force of darkness remained heavy to the world. The power of the light keeps chasing darkness into the next day. Darkness is a coward that runs away from light, but this enemy is growing with hate. The creatures of the day were now hiding inside their crevasses of safety.

The light rose slowly into heaven before the drizzle fell from above, drenching the earth. Everyone stayed inside and I retreated into my tube. I felt like I was forced to stay alone for a while to battle with my memories and to wage war with my darkness. Was this retribution for my disdain for the enemy? The enemy never forgives.

Heaven was pressing me to do what was right and good, as I kept making excuses and running away. Every time I escaped the night, hard painful memories followed me into the day. I wanted a redo of life but my heart always brought me back. Persistent unrelenting life experiences and moral responsibilities climbed back upon me. I tried to run away from my past. I tried to hide from life. There was a still small voice speaking truth and honor into my ear. Should I listen to my thoughts? Must I react to my memories? A great friend from my childhood past always called me to check on me! He reminded me of the goodness of life and the love of God. He called me "The Church Street Pastor," because I grew up on Church Street as his neighbor and friend. He is a Godly man from a Godly family! He reminded me of my life and love for the Lord.

Patiently, I waited for life to return in Tara, as the steam from my hot tea dissipated into vapor upon my face. Sipping my very strong brewed "Scottish Breakfast Tea," accompanied by a mind full of memories and regrets, the past rolled through my head on fast forward. I had to return to the present but my heart remained in the past. I needed help to find my present reality. Was I stuck? Would I always carry this gloomy heartache? Will I ever find peace? The record was scratched and the revolution continued in my head.

Thoughts about wanting to change my past, as well as, wanting to find closure, so I could move ahead, wrestled each other in my confusion. I just wanted to find happiness. I just want to find love. I want to hold a hand that holds me back. I want a hug that pulls me into her soul. I want to see the good in life and experience the joy of sharing everything I have, and who I am, with a lady who wants to be with me. I want a lady who completes me and helps me to be the "GOOD," which God Almighty did not say about Adam until He created Eve. When God brought Eve to Adam, He said it was good! The two became one! I want the good me. Is it possible to be the person the Lord wants me to be? I hope so. I need the Lord's help. I knew the answer but still struggled.

***The Real First Family Foundation.*** *The force of evil to destroy families.*

Adam and Eve became the First Family of all humanity. They are our greatest grandparents, created by

*Reality of Finding and Keeping the One You Love*

God. Every human being, procreated by love, between a man and a woman (ONLY TWO GENDERS), throughout human history shares the same ancestry. There is only one Human Race and we all are linked to the past by God's design. The idea of evolution allows anyone to formulate opinions of differences in human value. This leads to aggrandizement strength for some, and weakened values that create excuses for using and misusing others. It formulates elitism privilege, the accusation of elitism privilege to manipulate outcomes, and multiple excuses of misuse in our day that cause hate and division. Evil is the source of hate that hungers for destruction. Deceived children pick up the baggage of hate and participate in their own destruction. The failure of the family creates the conditions for their assimilation of evil.

Evolution, the self-theism of becoming your own god, is the beguiling lie spoken by the serpent. This lie becomes an excuse for someone to manipulate relationships, enforce cast systems of social values, royalty elitism, and serfdom, and enslavement of those who are valued less than another just because someone is stronger or has mustered more power in some way. It leads to murder for enrichment in many ways. It keeps humanity on the edge of hate, anger, and the excuses for war. It builds bombs to destroy others. The growing idealism of control, power, and superiority finds origins in basic evolutionary tenets. This hate grows because a creature rejects the Creator.

This devilish manipulative scientific hypothesis is the dross of lies behind everything that divides with hate. It is the shadow that falls under every excuse to hate and abuse others. It is the excuse of man to hide from his Creator and make himself his/her own god. The original sin of self-theism that was used to manipulate Eve to disobey the Lord is interwoven in every lie evolution formulates. If you do not believe in God, you try to understand why or how you are here. So, evolutionists, let us make up our stories. Ignore God when you observe the micro and macro facts of the universe, which clearly reveal intelligent design and God's power to sustain. On the other hand, many who believe there is a God develop a concept of god that makes them feel good. Their construct fits personal ability and capability of their comprehension. Then they place their god in a box so they can satisfy their understanding and/or manipulate their control. Two extremes are crazy. God is real and He is the Creator of all things.

Almighty God is much much more, way beyond comprehension by any human mind. In Him, we live and move and have our being. He is not so distant and unconcerned as some define. He is in everything. His power sustains all we know in life. Just because your immediate senses can not see does not mean that God is not known. A good scientist observes every lead. A good scientist looks at every element and thinks deeply about what is observed. A bad scientist will reject the most involved and powerful element within anything observed, as a foundation for their investigation, which leads the science to a false conclusion. I say evolution is the evil explanation for rejecting God's existence.

The genetic pooling that created specific recognizable ethnicity over time, happened when Family groups spread out after the **FLOOD**. Isolated families became community tribes, and marriage within these groups created specific DNA markers with distinct dominant qualities. Noah's sons migrated away. Seth moved Eastward toward Asia. Japeth moved North and Westward into Europe. Ham moved South toward Africa. (Three basic groups within a "Kind" and many traditional ethnicities became reality.)

At first, they did not move far. They remained close until after the Tower Of Babel. Evil was on the rise and hungered to control all mankind. Nimrod rebelled against God's command to fill the earth. As a potentate, he establishes forces (government, media, military) to control all humanity. With this self-appointed power of elitism, Nimrod enslaves the people. He does this to defy God. He rebels against God's purpose.

Children born to each of the families, that walked out of the Ark, feared the destruction of the flood. They listened to the media rhetoric of their day, saying it could happen again, even though God promised Noah that He would never destroy the earth again with a flood. The "Rainbow" was used as a seal of promise that God would not destroy the world with a flood again. *(It is NOT the symbol of unnatural gay activity. Anyone who uses God's truth for immoral purposes will someday stand before the God of all creation to give an account of personal behavior. I do think that when you see a rainbow it is a reminder that God is being patient with His judgment for the increasing wickedness upon the earth. He is reminding us of His current mercy, but, it is also a warning that His judgment will be poured out upon those who sin.)*

Sin began it's work to destroy! Destroy freedom and dominate all humanity with world control. The beginnings of the same destruction that caused the FLOOD, were already working in the minds of the children born. Evil was forcing itself into the hearts of man like it did before the flood. The condition of humanity, when the flood occurred, was the result of sin because man's heart was evil continuously. *(Genesis 6:5)* There is wickedness on the earth. This wickedness slithers into the hearts of humanity through fear and hate. It manipulates truth for it's own strategic outcome. Evil wants everything.

The tower was built tall. It was very tall. It was built by slaves of all genetic variations. It was built to enforce the *elitism world control* of a self-appointed narcissistic evil man and his cohorts. Nimrod was trying to reach into heaven to defy God. He wanted every human to see the tower from a great distance to remind them of the Flood, so he could force his control. It was/is about power, prestige, and self-aggrandizement elitism. (Like our world today.) Nimrod was the enfleshment of evil to rebel. He hungered to enslave others. The same evil works in our day to control everything. Evil hates freedom. Evil is a soul prison.

This same idealism led to the wickedness before the flood. It was happening again. History repeating itself. Families were torn apart by the fear pushed by evil's agenda through the media and government. Yes, evil had a face at that time. Evil was Nimrod! At all levels of control, evil forces itself upon the weak-minded. Shallow thinkers allow others to think for them until they are enslaved. Evil has many faces. The evil of our day is the agenda of world domination with forced compliance. The "Borg" is here.

It is the System of the "Beast." Artificial Intelligence dressed up as convenience becomes the master of evil. Someday soon the AI Beast will control the world economy, transportation, and world government. The village of the beast will control everything. The seven years of Tribulation is almost here. It is a time of God's wrath poured out against sin. Believers are not appointed to wrath but unto salvation. Therefore, the "Rapture" of all believers in Jesus Christ will take place before the anti-Christ takes control. If you miss the Rapture you will face the beast. Are you ready? *(Romans 1: 18-32, John 3:36, I Thessalonians 5:9)*

Like in the past, families are being forced into village control at local levels. Villages then are forced into

National Control. Nations are pressured into global control. World governments negotiate for influence and positional participation within a global system of evil control. Those who have some wealth and power want to keep their ability to thrive under this growing transformation. Just because it is happening does not mean you have to participate! Fear pushes many lies in the war against humanity. We are facing another global disaster foretold in Biblical Scripture. This world system will cause the most destruction ever. It will be **The Great Tribulation.** *(Remember, help is on the way! The Savior returns and His Kingdom is established! The Word of God gives believers HOPE for peace evermore.)*

***The Control of Evil.*** *The works of evil are known.*

In our ancestry, where we do have a common human connection in our human family, the genetic pooling of our families became tribes, as ethnicity defined diversity. Tribes grew into states. States grew into nations. Nations created alliances in time because evil in this world causes division. Sin causes hate. Hate forces wickedness, which is willful evil actions toward another for selfish gain. Evil destroys. Evil must be dealt with.

Evil will be judged and destroyed someday. Until then, Evil enters and resides in the hearts of men and women. It crawls into the mind subtly. Then, it networks throughout the needed micro-strategic operations of thought and understanding of each soul to capture the individual. The takeover, and system development, for evil purpose, takes place over time. Before standing up fully: committed to an evil agenda, with the purpose of rebelling, hating truth, and despising Almighty God, evil networks a misleading agenda as a trap to capture and control the soul. (Your soul)

The Borg assimilates the drone into the collective. Drones are activists of the collective, controlled by the same evil that has always hated mankind. They hate others. They hate all creation because they hate God. They hate personal freedom and they advocate for collective control. I think some drones do not realize how quickly and easily they have been absorbed into this evil network. I hope the truth rescues them before it is too late. Eternity is closer than we think.

Evil attacks what is good with lies. Evil does not want what is right. Evil wants to force it's power on all to destroy what is right. Evil tries to control others to dominate their lives for self-gain. Evil wants to destroy what God has created to be good. Evil wants to manipulate sovereign creatures, created by God, whom He said were created good, after Adam and Eve were one in Love and Marriage. Evil works to destroy family!

Marriage is a man and a woman united together in a loving covenant. It is this bonding relationship of the intimacy of a man and a woman (a husband, and a wife) that bears the fruit of generations to come. Marriage is a loving responsibility of commitment between a man and a woman who love each other, and have children together, which form family into oneness. This pleasuring love bears children into a family that nurtures them until adulthood. This connection of love continues to create ancestry. It is a love of generations to come. Evil works to destroy families. Evil is actively fighting God's plan for families.

Freedom is God's design. Government control (elitism, superiority, domination) is the work of a dominant evil. No one owns another person! Families are for nurturing the health and welfare of humanity. Villages are where families reside together and share in the community. Community is born out of unique families sharing space. Families build communities and societies together, but when evil takes over and forces itself from the top down by potentates and tyrants, families struggle to maintain autonomy, and the "Village" forces power over the family. Evil wants this control.

Evil builds a collective to force it's agenda. Evil wants to assimilate or destroy every person. Compliance is demanded on all, or death will remove you. The evil collective before the "Flood," caused all humanity, except Noah and family, to only believe in evil's agenda. Their hearts were evil continually. Scripture reveals that this will happen again. As the days before Noah, so shall the coming of the Son of Man be. *(Luke 17:26-30, Matthew 24:37)* Evil will be worse in this future time than it was before the flood of Noah. We are told that "Perilous Times will come…" It is at our doorstep now! *(2 Timothy 3:1-5)* I believe we are already experiencing perilous times, which will get much worse. I also think we are very close to the time of TRIBULATION. It will be worse than any previous period of humanity. A dystopian struggle becomes reality. We might witness this soon! Those who know scripture understand this. We do not know the day or the hour when this unfolds. Days and hours are fine-tuning to the precision of a moment. These defining time tools are used within the concept of years, decades, centuries, millenniums…

Jesus answered the disciple's question about His return someday. He revealed many prophetic signs over 2000 years ago, which we are already observing. He told them that these signs are given so we, who wait for His return, can be ready. He said we cannot know the day or hour, but we understand when the events are at the door. I believe Jesus has the door knob in hand and is ready to twist it open. Even so, come Lord Jesus!

**Hate is growing around the world.**  *Self-theism and false Science takeover.*

Activism, based upon evil lies, lashes out against truth. The lies have been told for so long that children are educated with these lies. Brainwashing and manipulation of the truth crept into the education system for many decades. Recently this <u>lying false wokeness agenda</u> of God hating and Faith hating is boldly forcing compliance upon all humanity. People are deceived into trusting the government more than family or God's truth. The government is bribing the weakest among us. They are forcing evil's compliance and hate: hate for the Savior, hate for Christians, hate for Jews, hate for truth, hate between ethnic groups. This evil force persuades hate into families, communities, and politics. It destroys friendships and alliances to establish control.

***Destroying truth.*** *Sin's grip of hate tightens slowly until capture.*

Evolution is forced by self-theists to educate their social and political agenda of hate. A Marxist social control over all humanity is the end state of evil. This devilish evolution lie was a strategy of the slavery excuse. It is a foundation of the sexual revolution and makes excuses for the lies of contraception, which has murdered multiple millions of innocent babies for the sake of convenience. Convenience became more important than responsibility, which resulted in the rejection of the most innocent life. Helpless babies continue to be slaughtered and the choice to lay down in bed for the sake of pleasure has robbed innocent children of living their lives. Pleasure before the protection of the innocent is the foundation of the sexual revolution and the refusal of personal responsibility. (If it feels good, do it.) Men and women must protect the gift they share when love binds them!

It is because of self-theism, individuals who think they are smarter and teach their limited free-thinking, based on their rejection of God, or the concept of God of their own making, that evolution has led to corrupt science used to educate the children that are born into this world. Children are taught to ignore evidence and/or only accept the manufactured or twisted evidence these selftheists observe. They also form a system that rejects any evidence that does not fit their criteria or agenda. Rejecting any evidence results in a manufactured lie.

They are lost in their understanding because they reject the Lord God. Their "god in the box" fails them because their false god is a liar and a weak coward, who will grovel at the feet of the Almighty on Judgment Day. Evolution has dug a trench into the minds of the last 20+ generations and has poured an elixir of hateful disdain and rejection for God. This evil agenda against humanity is manipulated into the innocent minds of children until they are absorbed into the collective of social hate. *(Philippians 2:9-11)*

They are taught to reject what is obvious and true. They are told what to believe and what they should never consider. They are told to listen to their voices/agenda only and to never listen to the opposite truth. They are instructed in how to think. They are threatened not to believe certain things, and they are directed to accept things that are not good. We live in a fallen world. We live in a world where people lie, cheat, steal, murder, and struggle with evil every moment of every day. Their truth is control.

This is the world I find myself in. Both worlds struggle with the same reality. The reality is that evil is working against goodness. Evil attacks at every level and leads to destruction. Evil attacked my family. Evil attacked me! Evil is attacking you.

***Dreams end and reality*** *Why do I struggle so much?*
***moves back in.***

Life in Tara slowly emerged around me as I remained inside the tube. All these ideas and the reality of my understanding were still negotiating inside my head. On the second day after my return from my first-world childhood, I eventually emerged again. It was late morning and my neighbors were relieved to see me safe. When I was gone they talked about "Good Neighbor Dave." I became the subject of their conversation. My car remained in the driveway while I stayed hidden inside, which caused even more concern. They all wondered where I was at or even if I was still breathing.

Once on the outside, I joined them. Morning after morning I was once again stepping out into the freshness of a new day. I enjoyed my early solace with nature, as neighbors slept until life returned to the community. When they emerged from their homes, I would sit with my wonderful friends and talk for hours. Sometimes we planned our day. We would take trips. We would go out to eat. We would help each other accomplish needed tasks. Our close community of friends shared time and resources like a family. They became another family to me.

Time and situations kept moving along. Hearts became close and an openness of friendship drew us close together. It was hard to hide anything. The only problem with me was I kept most of my heart hidden in the pain I carried inside. Pain from the raging battle of my first world that still was active. Inside, I was sad. I wanted to escape this so I could move on, but my soul held my heart to my convictions. I worried about the lady who was my life for over fifty years. I remembered our family, our love, and our promises. Even though I wanted to move on, I did not have closure in my heart. I still investigated my thoughts and choices, which contributed to my life being shipwrecked in my first world. Even when I was with my friends, this situation haunted my thoughts. I think some of them could see this in me as time passed. I was just stuck.

A few months went by rapidly. I was so busy that time seemed to fly. I kept busy building decks, sheds, and carports for my friends. I would cook and share my limited culinary experiments, which normally turned out great. We had fish fries together, spending several hours as a big family. My brother joined us in the community and he provided the walleye, and homemade hush puppies, as others brought their specialty dishes. We always had a good time. However, the attempt to move forward became more difficult. I guess I ran my mouth sometimes, expressing my concerns about what I did not know. For such a long time I assumed there was no return to what I once loved. I thought I had to move forward in this new life, with my new wonderful friends. I honestly was trying.

## Chapter Nine:

# The Commander's Mission Intent

***What Does the Lord***     *Battle-ready armor forced to fit.*
***want me to do?***

I STRUGGLED IN prayer. It was as if I was stunned. The "Why" questions ran through my head because I did not understand how the storm could do this much damage. Why was my heart ripped open like this? It seems like healing evaded me. When I woke up every day, I felt abandoned in the storm without anyone to rescue me. Was I already too deep for a hand to reach me? There were no emergency crews to sweep in and rush me to an emergency room. Spiritually, I was still sinking deeper into the black depths of despair. I could not keep the ship afloat and I certainly could never walk on water. In my nightmares, I was still being tossed around like a toy in the tempestuous sea of darkness. Hungry monsters circled me for another bite of my soul. I was so tired that I just wanted to get it over. I felt like giving in to the predators, hoping it would end fast. I was physically and spiritually tired. *(I am not saying I was suicidal. Life is a precious gift and we must always be there for others!)*

So many passing thoughts and feelings ran through me when I was alone. The paradox inside my soul struggled between wanting to be alone, in my suffering, and being alone. I braved this battle almost every day when I charged back into my "TUBE," where I knew another battle awaited me. The tenacious enemy always had another angle of his assault ready. He adjusted strategy for his mission success every single time because he wanted to obliterate me. *(Luke 22:31 -Sift me like wheat on a threshing floor.)* He wanted to destroy me and he was willing to do anything to make this happen. He wanted to see me suffer. He wanted to defeat me and take his prisoner into the dungeon of torture. The face of my enemy, *Pirate Piranha Joe*, waited for me at the door each night. I would lunge forward with all my strength to rip his face off. I could not get my hands on him.

I knew he was there. My anger pushed me to engage in every battle. I wanted to destroy him. I wanted to make him suffer at my hands. I wanted to see his eyes fade from life with my hands around his neck and his squirming flesh under me. I wanted to be the cowboy who defeated this evil enemy. I wanted him looking into my eyes as he was dragged into hell. I wanted vengeance. The Lord kept telling me, "No."

After each battle, the next morning I awakened in the same place in a pool of sweat. Looking into the hole above me, as the light of day returned, the memories and dreams of the night faded. The joy of Tara, my peaceful shore, with all my friends, pulled me away from this spiritual "Theater of War." They always helped me recover from these battles, and I was able to experience some R&R, a military term for "Rest and Relaxation." The emotional scars from fighting must heal and my physical strength regained before another battle could be fought. I knew that I would fight again and I had to be ready for combat. A warrior knows how to draw the enemy close. He knows that he must be ready and stronger than his enemy but, he acts vulnerable and weak to draw the enemy close before striking with overwhelming force. *(I learned a lot from Dave Ferris, 7th-degree Black Belt trainer, and friend. I never earned a belt but I learned enough to be cautious about what I did know more than an opponent could cause fear.)*

The spiritual battle inside me remained fluid. My heart struggled with excuses because I wanted to see this enemy suffer. I was not listening to the Lord. At least, most of the time, I was not paying attention. The "still small voice" whispered in my ear, but I fielded every excuse in my head, sending my hate for the enemy into the open, where the spies gathered intelligence to use against me for the next battle. For the longest time, there was no offensive strategy in my mission planning. Everything I was doing was reactionary. You cannot win a war when you are always surprised and your enemy has a plan. I was determined and strong enough but I was outwitted, and each battle weakened me.

| | |
|---|---|
| ***I Fought the Battle Every Single Day.*** | *The strategy of my enemy, who continuously attacked.* |

My personal determination weakened in my new Tara life. Seemed like my health weakened as my worries from the past increased. My friends could see that I was worried about what was happening back home. They could also sense my inability to move on. Honestly, they were right. My nights were occupied with nightmares and my days were a struggle to prepare for the next battle with my enemy. These dreams became nightmares of engagement,

*The Commander's Mission Intent*

as I self-evaluated my capability based on my past actions. My adversary, the devil in this story, Pirate Piranha Joe, loomed on the perimeter of my safe zone, waiting for another opportunity to attack. He sent mortar rounds into my safe zone during the day, as I attempted to keep busy. I wanted to forget. I tried to find closure to move on with life. He still attacked to remind me of my failure and weakness. In time I realized it was not the physically weak coward Joe, but the evil spiritual narcissistic demonic creature, within this fallen person, who was the enemy. This fallen creature enraged me.

I was allowing this loser to continue his evil attempts to destroy me. It was as if I wanted to keep fighting. I wanted to keep the war going. I wanted to p--- on him. I wanted to take his territory and strip him of any power he thought he had. I wanted to hurt him myself. So, I prepared for the battle each night. When it was time, I rushed in with all my anger and strength. I tried to bring sudden and overwhelming force against him. I used tactics to outmaneuver this enemy but he seemed to have the ability to eventually regain his strength to keep fighting me. Fighting a spiritual war is exhausting.

A physical war would be easier. There is no doubt in my mind about being able to defeat this evil person. I know my physical and intellectual capability but I also know what is moral and right. Sometimes I want to ignore my faith and ask for forgiveness later. However, there is a friend within me, who will never leave or forsake me, pulling me back onto the path that leads to righteousness and eternal peace. I have to live with myself, and this wise and dearest friend always reminds me to be strong in the Lord and wait on the Lord. He speaks in my heart to direct me in righteousness. *(Ephesians 6:10-12)*

I am still a work in progress. Too often, I only move in my strength and end up molting like an eagle. When I get weary and worn from my own failing strength, it is necessary to "renew my strength like an eagle," so I can soar once again. *(Isaiah 40:31)* This friend will never leave me or forsake me. The Holy Spirit of God leads believers into all truth. "Jesus is the way, the truth, and the life," Whoever believes in Him, Jesus Christ the Lord, will never perish. He is the Champion who defeated death and offers forgiveness! This dearest friend reminds me of God's promises and God's Commandments. (Proverbs 3:1-6 is my life scriptural text to live by.)

My friends at Tara knew that something was different about me. Time seemed to pull me away often. I tried to escape my angst to keep fighting this war within me. It is hard when you really want to fight. I wanted to fight. It is even harder when you desire vengeance at your own hands. I guess it was good that I was shipwrecked on this peaceful shore so far away during this difficult time.

***Memories become dreams***     *Lord, help me!*
***and dreams can turn to***
***nightmares.***

I made it through another day. I was tired but I was able to keep busy all day and there were no thoughts from the past. I dragged myself into the "Tube" as the sun was setting over Tara I needed my rest from all the physical stress of the day. I remember eating a hot dog with a lot of yellow mustard. This made for a quick meal so I could lie down and turn on the TV in the front room.

It was a few months since my last time transport into my youthful past. Those experiences recalled my youthful life with Sally. The fact that she was always the one I came back to, even when I tried to move on with life, I came back to the skinny blonde I fell in love with. I remember the struggles we experienced back then, but I also remembered my prayer under the star-filled universe, as I begged God to allow us to have a life together. I promised to love her then, and I guess I loved her still.

***The Notebook* by Nicholas Sparks.*** *The dramatic story of a living love.*

I watched the movie, "Notebook," by Nicholas Sparks. The story of youthful enduring love in the midst of struggles, posed by family and hardships through life. This love remained through it all. As I watched, I could only think of my love for Sally. I felt responsible in some way because things turned out so bad for us both. The drama of his enduring love for her touched me, as I thought to myself how much I have in common with this story.

In this story of love, he loved her even until the end of their lives. I did see many things I had in common with this couple, but I did not want the same ending. In the story, he buys and rebuilds an abandoned mansion they played in as children. It was here they fell in love. He promises to rebuild it for her someday and they can spend their lives together. Of course, the tragedy of this love takes over, as family rips them apart.

Her parents wanted her to marry a boy from a rich family. The parents keep obstructing her relationship with her first real love. She gives in to their pressure. She marries the rich boy, who becomes a worthless failure as a husband. They struggle as a couple all their lives together. The poor boy works hard and eventually becomes successful.

He buys the old abandoned mansion and rebuilds it. In time, she hears about his success and the rebuilt mansion and goes to visit. They revisit the young love briefly. In time they both get old. She is living in an "Assisted Living Facility" for the elderly.

An older man, her age, visited her every day. He would ask her if he could read to her. She would respond at first with, "I don't know you," rejecting his proposal. She would be persuaded and listen to him read. Every visit he hoped some light of memory would return to her. Maybe sometimes a glimmer of hope emerged, but often, she just listened and asked questions. The next time he visited, he had to start over again but he kept going back to her.

She got very sick as time passed. He still read to her and took walks with her, just to be with her. He even became a resident at the home, just to be close to her. He would sneak around sometimes just to be with her. One night, when she was deathly sick, and he knew it, he snuck down the hall into her room. For a brief moment, she remembered him as he expressed his deep enduring love to her. Then he laid down next to her on the bed holding her tight. That night and that moment they died in each other's arms. The staff found them the next morning.

*Memories of Loving You*

The ending of this story reveals that they did eventually have a life together. They even had children together. She was in the nursing home after she lost her memory. He remained faithful and always visited her until the day they left this earth and walked into glory. Their love remained! The movie forced me to remember what I was trying to forget. I had a lifetime of love for this lady. I missed her. I worried about her all the time.

I was physically tired as I watched but I could not fall asleep. I watched every moment absorbing the heart-felt drama within. I bawled my eyes out as I thought of Sally. It reminded me of our lives together and our tragedy. Some things were different but the deep love and concern for a lifetime rang the bell of reality within me. I worried every day for Sally. I knew the harm this guy caused. I knew she was still suffering. My heart could feel her sadness for over a year after our divorce. I knew something was not right.

***My Own Notebook.*** *Why do I remember these things?*

Once again, I crawled into bed in the back chamber of the Tube. My thoughts were overwhelming as I turned on my "Ambient Sacred Sounds," on the TV, which usually helped me relax and go to sleep. I needed to rejuvenate my mind and my aching body. Laying on my back and looking at the hole above me, I wrestled with the pain of the storm that separated us two years prior. When I finally closed my eyes, and my mind shut down the memories that were swirling around me, a sudden jolt of power grabbed me again. A crushing violent force pulled me through the hole above and cast me through the universe of time into my past. This was the third time the "Tunnel" forced me to go back. Back to the past to face my choices.

***Home Sweet Home.*** *This is where I should be!*

I landed in front of my beautiful home at Garrison Cove in Tennessee. Arriving on my hands and knees, I awakened on a thick cushy yard of fescue grass, bending over into the flower bed, by the front entrance. As the fog of confusion dissipated from my mind, I realized I was in front of my home in Murfreesboro. The lilies I planted four years ago were beautiful, and the jenny undercover was filled in, around a gorgeous bed of flowers. The butterfly bushes, and the wisteria draped over the cedar garden bench and gazebo. The sitting bench was full of clusters of purple flowers hanging through the lush vines to shade a place for rest. The idea of just resting in this special place I created just four years earlier was inviting. My sore sleepy soul begged me to just sit down for a while. "Don't be in such a hurry, there is plenty of time ahead," a quiet voice spoke from within me. "Pay attention and learn," the voice inside me whispered.

My adrenaline spiked within me. The excitement of being back here in the place where I thought I would live the rest of my life, enjoying my family, was right in front of me again! This place was my home when the storm began. It was the place I felt was my real home and I wanted to be there. I was there!

I stood up and stepped back to the street, where I could see the bigger picture. It was fulfilling to know that this home was being taken care of and all my hard work was blessing the family that bought it from me. The trees, the bushes, and the flowers were beautiful. Just as I designed it after I purchased the home. The eight regions of the watering system for the yard and flower beds ran their cycle every other day, allowing life to thrive. I remembered people, who walked by when I was working in the yard and commented on the beauty. From time to time they would tell me it was the most beautiful yard in Murfreesboro. I thought so too!

After my front yard fulfilling examination of my former home, I just had to trespass. I walked around the house.

The fence I rebuilt and stained with Australian Timber Oil stood tall and firm. The back gate was still amazing. But when I entered the backyard and turned to view the East Coast Red Cedar pergola, and the back porch, surrounded by flower beds that created the sense of ocean beauty at the base of the Boat Dock, which I created, tears swelled. Oh, how I wanted to live there again. Too much was taken from my family by this storm of life. (Correction: taken by this evil narcissist.) It was a place my grandchildren loved to spend time with us. It was a place where we shared our lives and enjoyed our happiness. It was also a place where rising marital and family tension started to increase.

I walked away at first, but something pulled me back. I walked up the back steps onto the deck. The hot tub was just as I left it. The octagon cedar table, where I used to study and write early in the morning, was in the same place. I could hear the anger of my wife and daughter through the porch door but I could not get inside.

**The Argument of loved ones.**  *Reliving the same painful arguments again!*

I went to the front door to knock. When my knuckles struck to door, I was pulled inside. I was witnessing an argument between my wife and daughter. I remembered this argument from three years prior. I was standing here again in the middle of their vitriol. I walked past my granddaughter who was hiding in the dining room. As I approached the stairway, where they were arguing, I noticed that I was walking out of the master bedroom. I merged into myself. I became me from that moment with all the memories of the next three years after this incident. Not again, I thought to myself. I was right back in the middle of it all. "Lord help me," I prayed in my heart.

This was the day when the last argument exploded between mother and daughter, which irrupted into the raging storm that assaulted our family. The storm had been brewing for almost five years before this torrid lightning and explosive thunder rained down its destruction. I was reliving this same event. I did not want to be there. I was once again witnessing two bipolar women hurling anger at each other and I walked into the middle of it. I wanted to run away. I wanted to go back to Tara, my other world, where I lived a simple life and had marvelous friends. Sometimes you cannot get what you want! I was there and there was no escaping the heart-felt pain. Again!

I remembered how Sally and I worked hard to avoid this conflict for many months. We would go to our master bedroom and watch a movie, to be isolated from the

*The Commander's Mission Intent*

ensuing conflict every day. But the conflict could never be avoided! Our daughter came home from work and immediately confronted Bethany about homework, chores, and anything else that was going on. She always started the tension by yelling at her daughter. "I'm the mother," she would tell us. I would agree but respond, "We are the Grandparents. As grandparents, we are parents with experience and we have the responsibility of parents when you are working. We are helping you both."

*(I was the one that was there for Bethany the most. I helped her in the morning get ready for school. I helped her with her homework most of the time. I was there when she got off the bus and I was the one watching out for her until Sarah and Sally got home from work. I loved being a grandpa! Bethany was hurting inside because her daddy left them when she was six. I think she was mad at men for a long time. I wish I could have taken her pain away from her heart. However, It has made her tough.)*

PS: My nickname for Bethany became "BB Gun." Of course, there is a story to this nickname. Her cousin David could not say Bethany when he was little. He called her "BB." In time, I called her "BB Gun" because she was always a pistol. Tenacious and aggressive in her adventure of life. She pushed the limits of everything. Stubborn sometimes but always inquisitive. She was good at manipulating those around her! A good quality if mentored right, but it could become a terrible character trait if influenced by selfish or neglected motives. Yes, she is my "BB Gun," and I love my granddaughter!

I was retired with over thirty three years of military service and I was able and willing to be a good grandpa. I wanted to be there for my granddaughter. I loved my family and wanted the best for them all, but Bethany, my oldest granddaughter was special to me. I knew she was hurting because her daddy was gone. He only visited briefly when he was able. She was growing up with only her mother. Of course, she had us and we were doing everything possible to help. We loved her. I love her. She needed her daddy. I tried to be there for her.

Sarah lived in our home with her daughter, whom we also provided and cared for. We love them both. Sarah had to work but she could not afford a place. We had a four bedroom, three bath, two dining rooms, two living rooms, and a Florida porch with a covered back deck that was a four thousand square foot home. The daughter and granddaughter had the upstairs but also had access to the whole house. We provided a place to live, and the care, for our granddaughter to go to school. We helped her with resources, and we helped "BB Gun" do her homework. I prepared breakfast every day and watched my granddaughter get on the bus. I was there when she got off the bus.

When my daughter got home every night she immediately jumped on her daughter about homework and chores, which always turned into an emotional fight. Bethany would run to Sally and to me to be defended. She was crying out for help, and we wanted to help her and most of the time we did help her. Sally was always protecting her granddaughter. I would pray for wisdom every time.

This specific argument, the day my "Tube" brought me back to the past, escalated immediately between Sally and Sarah. I stayed back, trying to avoid getting involved at first. No such luck. I heard things that mothers and daughters do not say to each other. It was only getting worse.

I went out into the living room to the base of the steps and tried to calm things down. I was ignored and the hurting words continued to fill the air. Everything was on full display before BB Gun. I could see the pain in her eyes as she tried to hide once again. I spoke up, demanding that they stop. "Mothers and daughters do not say these things to each other," I escalated my volume above their anger. "Stop!" "Both of you stop," I repeated. It continued and became worse. I walked up the steps with my hands slightly raised as if to back someone up or direct the action for Sarah to back up into her bedroom, which she finally did. I asked her again to relax and calm down. "Please stay in your room until you can control yourself," I spoke with a much quieter voice. "Please!" Then I shut her door and focused on Sally, who was still downstairs yelling.

I walked down the stairs, asking her to calm down. "Go relax on the back porch until you feel better," I begged her. Then her anger shifted to me. "I hate this place." "I'm gonna leave." "I want a divorce…" She rushed away into the kitchen continuing her words of anger. Then I responded, "I'll help you pack." Followed by, "I haven't felt loved for a long time anyway." "Just please calm down and stop saying things that hurt." "Your mean tongue is going again," I reminded her.

She went to the porch and shut the door. Things quieted down and I went back to the bedroom. I sat down emotionally exhausted and tearfully prayed. Brokenhearted again, I asked God for wisdom to deal with this continuing problem. I was worn out and disappointed. I wanted to run away and hide from all this. I really did not want to deal with this anymore but I could not escape. Sitting there groaning inside with a begging heart before the Lord, I cried. I felt broken, which seemed to happen over and over again in the last few years.

I was so absorbed into the moment of reliving this painful event, that I forgot that I was reliving this past moment. It all happened the same way. It was a "redo," as we say in the Army. It was a redo with future experience and understanding but with the inability to make any difference. I was forced to relive this event. I wondered why I was reliving this moment. Then I heard the security alarm for the garage. I remembered that Sally left the house and went to our oldest daughter's home, just a mile away. She stayed there until Sunday.

***Calm Down.*** *Take a break to reflect on what happened.*

Sally went to Christa's and stayed a few days. She brought Christa with her to talk to me on Sunday, 20 December 2019. Sally began by saying she spoke to a lawyer. I listened and did not say much. I never got mad. Sally said many things. Christa was there at the table listening to it all. There was a lot said and I listened. I was shocked but not surprised.

The roller coaster ride of our marriage/relationship has been rocky for forty five years. Sally was the last of five children. Her mother loved her but also regretted having a child at her age (30s). There was this conflict between love and regret between mother and child on display when I first started seeing Sally at thirteen. Sally's oldest sister, Sharon, was fourteen years older when Sally was born, and she had a little living baby doll to take care of every day. Sally and Sharon became very close (Like a mother-daughter relationship), which became the reality of a lifetime. Spoiled would be the defining term to explain how our relationship developed. I do have to say that Sharon is an amazing lady. She was a great mother. In fact, I have always said that Sharon is like my second mom. I love her as a mother.

***The Admission.*** *Confession of truth takes ownership of guilt.*

Sitting at this revelation table of accusation and confession, I listened to her explanation of things from her perspective. I heard something in her words that made me think, "She is seeing someone." "No, it cannot be," I thought, but, I had to ask the question anyway.

I took in every word and finally interrupted as politely as possible. As she spoke, she only made eye contact in passing, looking away most of the time. I looked directly into her eyes to force her to look into mine as I said, *"Is there someone else? Are you seeing someone?"* She looked down and away. No longer keeping eye contact, she became silent. After about ten seconds, I re-engaged eye contact by moving into a facial position that forced her to see me again. I asked, *"Is there someone else involved?"*

Sally responded, "Yes." We sat for a moment in silence. I was shocked. I asked her, "Who is it?" She refused to give a name. Sally explained that this guy was the "Love of her life." "We have common interests and we want to be together." "He loves me and I love him."

The conversation continued. She explained that she had been talking to him for over three years. (Later she said he first called five years ago. I feel she was not honest with me.) At the time I was not sure it was only phone calls.

She said they want to be together. Much was said, that I do not fully remember. I guess I was surprised and did not really believe this could happen. I think I was understandingly hurt, but civil. I expressed disappointment but was kind. I told her, "I choose my family." My children and grandchildren are important to me. She asked me if I had a girlfriend several times and I said no. She said I took too long at Lowes shopping, and I must have a girlfriend. I did not! I do not. *(Nothing worked anyway so why would I have a girlfriend? I had prostrate cancer and urological problems for the four previous years and she knew it. The problem was solved/overcome with great success at The Nashville VA and Vanderbilt Hospital.)* It is amazing what Doctors can do today!

It is my opinion, I thought, from observation and remembering many issues from the past, that it might be Joe. I looked at her again and asked if it was Joe ----. She was shocked and said, "Yes, we love each other. He is the Love of my life but our parents would not allow us to see each other because we were cousins." It all made sense at that moment. Years of emotional struggle and isolation all came into focus for me. The many times she said, "I should have married Joe." Of course, I was deeply hurt but not confused. As it seemed to make sense looking back at things, I had to finally end the conversation. In my mind, I kept hearing, "Forty five years flushed down the toilet."

***The Pain We Bear.*** *Our actions affect others.*

In the moment I was reasoning: Forty-five years of emotional pain. Forty-five years of not feeling fully loved sometimes. There were times I did feel loved but too many times, I felt used. I think I was always trying to patch things up when she was upset. I was trying to make her happy. Sometimes I was fed up with things. If I had known this, it would have been better to leave a long time ago. As I said, my daughter was there and could fill in what I was forgetting. I know she is hurting too and has been a strength for me during this storm. She does know it all because she was there.

Reliving this nightmare event in my life forced a heaviness of silence in my soul. As I regained some sense of self, I sat in the recliner for hours, as I did the first time, with thoughts arguing in my memories. This dream became the nightmare that ripped my family apart. Humbled so deep in my soul, I questioned everything that came into my thoughts, trying to make sense of it all and find the right path to take. "Figure it out… figure it out!" my heart screamed within me. No one could hear my cries. "There is no help. There is no direction to escape. This battle is at my threshold and it affects everyone I love." "My only path is to engage with overwhelming and sudden force." My anger returned. Reliving the pain of the past is hard to do. (Struggling with anger and pushing the Lord back to handle things myself was a mistake. I never did like inner rage when it revealed its ugly face. It was all over me again. Thank God, He never leaves or forsakes His children. He never let me get away!)

## Chapter Ten:
# Thinking Deeper for the Battle

***Return to the***      *Life continues and pain follows.*
***present reality.***

I WAS SO tired, as I sat in my old recliner stewing over this revelation of infidelity. "Who are you?" "Who are you?" "Who are you," echoed throughout the Tube, until I woke from this nightmare past. Once again, every drop of energy left me. I was lying in my sweat looking at the open electrical hole in the ceiling cavity above.

Back in Tara, I passed out. Blank mind and ambient noise, from the Sacred Sounds on TV, held me in stasis for several hours. Weak and confused, I finally crawled out of bed. Trying not to remember what happened back then and even now, I stood in front of the mirror gazing at the face I did not really know. "Who was this old guy looking at me?" I thought. Seems like my feathered friends outside wanted to know too.

"Who are you?" I heard several of them hooting together in harmony from above. They gathered on the deck to harass me. Trying to pull me into their conversation, they relentlessly called me back into reality. The wisest one sat upon my flag, as always, and the others gathered close to listen. Their owl language chatter transformed into understanding their intent. I knew they were curious to know what happened. I cracked the door and whispered, "I'll be a few moments." "I'm coming."

They impatiently waited like cackling hens. Ruffled feathers and interrupting hoots, they competed to dominate their questions for the upcoming interrogation. Curious and full of questions, these wise birds prepared for my trial.

Inside, I brewed my tea. I cleaned up in a rush. Continuing my anxious hurry to get outside with my audience, I threw on my clothes and stepped into the morning freshness. My anxiety level was elevated because these cackling hooters were stirring up a fuss and the neighbors might just hear them. I wanted to talk to anyone who would listen, but I was not ready to tell my neighbors. I guess I was still keeping my worlds apart.

***Parliament Investigation.*** *Inquiring minds want to know.*

All eyes were on me, as I exited the motor home with a hot cup of tea. I was ready to disclose what happened again. These curious hidden creatures did not hide from me. They all perched along the gazebo and awning looking down upon the deck where I sat down. Only Heckle sat upon the American Flag, which was positioned the closest to my chair. His wide demanding eyes focused on mine, as if to say, "Get started and leave nothing out." The silence of demanding eyes surrounded me. All the animals gathered.

***Opening remarks.*** *I was defending myself.*

With a rushed tempo and elevated tone, like Russel Brand, I started from the beginning and yammered my thoughts and memories, as the morning darkness crawled back into it's hiding. The joy of a new day revealed hope for what lay ahead. I told them what just happened, what happened before, and how past and present realities merged inside me. Not a feather moved until I was done. Then silence took over and I sat there motionless. The birds were stuck too. Beaks dropped down and wide eyes stared at me for several minutes, as the questions and explanations of my experience were filed in their brains. I could see the analysis process at work in their minds. I could also see their summations forming in the silence of their individual investigation of my story.

I moved first. Raising my cup of tea to my lips, the slurping of my brew broke the silence, as a segue to allow discussion. All at once, they pounced with their inquiry like a self-appointed rabid cackle of media journalists. The questions rolled freely into a competitive mass of meaningless inquiry. I answered the best I could.

***Adjournment until later.*** *Take time to think deeper.*

During the upheaval of commotion, I looked at Heckle and shrugged my shoulders. This wise feathered monarch stretched his wings open to dominate the space and silenced the parliament. Things settled down quickly and Heckle issued an edict, "We will come back again. For now, everyone leaves this man alone. Think about what he said and we will discuss it later." Slowly each one launched from the perch and soared into the sky above. The spectators that gathered around the deck also scattered away. The gathering of a parliament always draws a crowd.

The sun was already above the tree line. The creatures fled into the surrounding foliage. The canopy above-created shade and disguised my feathered friends, who kept watch. But, the little invasive dragons (tiny lizards) came out from hiding. I knew they were listening earlier but did not come out when the predators were perched around me. I stayed on the deck until my cup of tea vanished. Then I walked down the long boat dock to sit on the bench. I was alone for some time cherishing and regretting memories. Time travel is hard on the mind! Explaining yourself to yourself is even harder!

Sitting in a numb state of reflection on this bench, I watched the active morning life of creation. The ripples of water spread across the surface each time a fish jumped. Each splash reveals the active life under this smooth mirror, reflecting everything above it, like a beautiful upside-down painted picture of the morning for just me. This morning scene was mine. Clouds floating in heaven's domain over the earth brought a peace that relaxed me. Time vanished from thought. The presence of mind occupied my thoughts. Curiosity investigated. Honesty prevailed. Safety was lost. Vulnerability opened danger's door. I just sat there enjoying my moment of reprieve while I could.

***The Enemy is always there.*** *The enemy is waiting to attack at vulnerable moments.*

If you sit there long enough, the enemy will find you.

He was there. Hiding, but still there! I sensed the danger. Awareness transformed the peaceful scene and restful moment into a threatening tense situation. My morning invader became threatening to me. He was stalking me again. I assume he was angry about our last encounter and the swoller *(stinky body liquid waste excretion)* I discharged in his face. Narcissists always want the last word, the last victory, the last self-indulging act of aggrandizing dominance: At least in their minds, they want to pat themselves on the back to feel better about their pitiful situation/existence.

I scanned the scene before me and searched around me slowly with a keen alertness. I knew he was there. I waited. Hidden at the water's edge, across the inlet by the dock, I saw a slight movement and ripples ran across the surface. Toward me. I watched. Then the surface became still again. I still waited in motionless silence, fully aware of his approach. Then two eyes broke the surface staring right at me; piercing past my eyes into my being. I was staring back at him and he knew it. There was no surprise today. The enemy was revealed! The scope of my awareness was dead center for the kill.

I finally spoke, "You back for more?" "I can give you more." "Swoller is never a good thing, is it?" I pressed my anger with a sneering smile. Then I stood to face the creature. Advancing to the deck's edge, I stared back. I knew he was there to antagonize me again. He wanted to rip all hope from my battle-weary soul. He was there to press for my surrender and claim his victory. It will never happen.

My thoughts became words. I challenged this evil being with all the truth I knew. He heard and understood what I was saying, and I knew it. The face of my real enemy transposed onto this evil predator. It was Pirate Piranha Joe, a coward of many battles. He came to hurl his darts of sinful hate and lying accusations. I thought I was ready but his deception was full of twisted lies. Yes, he got me angry but I stood my ground. I thought I was ready.

**The tactic used to capture and enslave.**  *Father of Lies uses temptation to attack.*

The conversation with this beast remained in my mind. I did not have to travel or dream. He brought the fight to me this time. Was it a spiritual fight? Was this real? Who was this creature staring at me, as I stared back with disdain? He artfully crafted his words to stab at my soul. Relentlessly he pushed every button to destroy any thought of what was right and good. He liked the fact that I was running away from my problems. He wanted me to keep running. Running away would cause more harm to more people. He is the prince of darkness and he revels in destroying the lives of men, women, and children. The evil within him wanted to destroy me so he could totally possess Sally.

He wanted to take my family into his dark hole of lies and destroy their souls. He wanted friends to forsake me. He wanted me helpless. *(Luke 22:31-44, 1 Peter 5:8)* Just like a Lion, he was seeking whom he could devour, and his focus was upon me. His end-state vision, of his attack on me as an apex predator, was already engorging my flesh and crushing my soul within his mind. He was salivating with evil intentions to satisfy his hunger.

Hate is a hunger that is fed with disdain and lies. Hate is always void of truth. It is founded in jealousy, revenge, unforgiveness, uncontrolled anger, and a weak mind filled with partial truths and twisted understandings. Hate is the battle cry of foolishness. Foolishness is taking action against what you know is true but you still want a different outcome. Hate is a rancid poison that spreads from one kill to the next until it destroys itself. Fools just keep doing the same things to their own defeat. It is little victories that fools live for. They never see the big picture because they are self-thesis, and they are convinced they have power. They are weak.

All humanity destroyed with eternal death is the mission success for this devil. "Freedom" is the cry from the heart when the devil attacks and eternal salvation is MISSION SUCCESS for believers in Jesus Christ. "If the Son shall make you free, you are free indeed." *(John 8:32-36, Galatians 5:1)* The standoff on the dock became a challenging examination of true faith. The attack happened when I was beyond tired. I had to trust the Lord. At first, I was not trusting. I was failing.

**Attack or defend.** *Trust in the Lord with all your heart...*

I sat down on the bench and the beast held his position. He wanted to play with his victim. I listened in my mind to all the insidious attacks he fired at me. He knew already that I just relived the last event. He grimaced at his success in tearing my family apart. This evil pirate posing as this gator reminded me about the many attempts I made to reconcile with Sally over the next year, after the revelation of infidelity. He was trying to get me to hate her all over again.

He reminded me that three different times she went up to Ohio to be with him. I countered saying, "But she returned in a week." The first time she went, she realized that he was a slob. He was a hoarder. His apartment was cluttered and trashy. She called me to beg to return, which each time I allowed. Each time she was up there she experienced his narcissistic control and manipulation. She became afraid of him. It hurt me to see her suffer. I really did not understand what was so bad about me that she would keep running back to him.

This hateful beast continued to force me to remember: The last time she was there, she called me after a week. She was whispering in fear that he might hear her on the phone. She begged me to take her to her sister, Sharon, in Florida. She told me she was going to tell him that she was going to visit Sharon. The next day she left. She came to Tennessee, where we met at our daughter's. I told her I would drive down and she could follow me in her car.

I packed and we left the next day. When we finally arrived, we stayed with Larry and Sharon. They have always been like parents to us both. Within the next week, we were starting over again and I was looking to buy a home in Harbor Isle. Which we moved into. I canceled the divorce filing in Tennessee and we were together again. I thought.

***Anger in the heat of battle rages on both sides.***   *Shifting strategies and unknown terrain.*

The devil in this gator countered this redirection and taunted his possible success. He snarled at me to recall after several months, how she was crying about missing him and loving him. She was saying she wanted to be with him again. I thought we had overcome and were doing extremely well, but to my surprise, she was talking to him again and she missed him. His persistent narcissistic control was beguiling her once again. He found a way to contact her and she gave in to his controlling persistence.

Every detail I was trying to forget was resurfaced. Fighting with evil thoughts, as the fiery darts of this devil were hurled at me, forced me to counter react to defend my position. (Ephesians 6:16) I was losing the battle. Wounded severely by every weapon and tactic he used, I lay bleeding within my soul. His twisted lies got under my skin. His accusations surrounded me, as he demanded my surrender. "Give her to me," he snarled. "I'll take her in a New York minute," he pushed every slimy angle to negotiate his victory. "Why, we can even share her, if you will," he chuckled hissing through his snarly sharp teeth. His perverse immoral hunger revealed his evil intent.

Hateful things were raised to remind me of the details I knew about the kidnapping and abuse of Sally. Sin is evil and sinners need a champion to rescue them from the eternal defeat of the soul. I needed my Champion, but at the time I was satisfied with my anger. This devil knew I could not find closure with Sally. He knew I worried about her every day. He rubbed it in my face so I would move on and forget. He hungered to possess her. He wanted a slave. He also wanted to destroy me, and destroying me would destroy others.

Then he poured salt into my wounds just to see me suffer. His narcissism boiled out to infect my mind and separate me from hope. Sordid twisted details were cast at me to ingest. Unimaginably vile and abusive lies were shot at me to kill my love for the mother of my children, and the woman I loved. He wanted me to kill and bury my love in my mind. He wanted me to walk away from my calling and service. He wanted to force his evil destruction throughout my family and friends, to smear any hope. He wanted to totally kill my reputation and bury everyone influenced, by his destructive beguiling, so he could throw accusations before others and destroy them too. He is worse than the evil trolls and hyena activists on Ticktock, who try to ruin Christians and their political enemies. These imps are foolish drone activists that eat the slop of the media and potentate beguiling deception. They are possessed by evil rhetoric and hate.

I stood up and walked to the water's edge. A large anchor lay next to the boat. I lifted it above my head, ready to throw it at this accuser. I froze in place, as a still voice spoke to me, "Go home. Do not lower yourself to his level. You are my child and there is always hope." I threw the anchor on the dock next to the boat. I turned and walked away. The angered beast roared his hate at me, which faded in the distance until I fully withdrew from the battlefield to regroup.

***Uncertain Information needs investigation.*** *A command decision must be made.*

Back inside the Tube, I sat arguing with myself. Curtains all shut and lights all off, I argued in my head. Debating the first traveling dream to remember my love for Sally and my prayer to God that we be together. Comparing my dream of love against the dream of the tragic storm. The storm that destroyed our family and brought me to Tara was the heaviest on my mind. I laced my arguments with the friendships I made in this community, against how I cared for them too. However, I always came back to the fact that I really have not moved on. I worried about Sally. I had to find out why I was so worried.

I was lonely, even though I had wonderful new friends. I would hide inside my bubble to avoid hurting myself and others. Matters of the heart are emotionally powerful. I wanted to feel loved. I wanted to go back to my home and family. I wanted what once was. I felt responsible for the failure. I felt weak because I lost my love to a narcissistic predator, and I did not understand why. Why would she leave me? What did I do, or, what did I not do? What was so bad about me? Why was I alone in this "Tube." I should be with family. I should be blessing my grandchildren and enjoying their presence. Man, I am a mess!

From time to time, I mentioned some of my problems to my dear friends. It was hard to keep up the pretense when I knew they could see I was hurting inside. They care for me too. I just felt stuck sometimes between my two worlds. Both of these worlds had my heart!

***The world back home.*** *I was sheltered from knowing.*

Back home in Tennessee things were returning to a new normal without me. For months, Sally was living in an Assisted Living Home. My children tried to protect me from knowing details. A few months after our divorce, which I filed for in Florida, Sally was living in an apartment and Piranha Joe came down to stay with her. I found out that she ran him off. Her eyes opened to his controlling narcissism.

Sally was drowning in her sorrow every day. Regrets for what happened and how it hurt us pressed deeper into her heart. The whole family was in pain. I was on the distant shore at Tara, but I was suffering too. Sheltered from daily details and then lost from knowing what was normal every day in the past, I swam in my own regrets, trying to breathe. Moving on became difficult for me, but I tried and tried so hard.

My cell phone rang. Reveille sounded loud and clear, calling me to attention and formation before the command, as my mind jumped to action. Charging into the front quarters of the tube, I answered the call. "Reporting as ordered," rang inside my head. It was my daughter. She reported to me that Sally was taken to the hospital. "What happened? What's wrong? How is she?" rolled out of my mouth. A moment of silence and tears drew me close to her heart. "Mom was taken to the hospital because she took too many pills. She had a breakdown and is depressed. I listened with a broken heart as she filled in details of the incident.

Sally was watching the grandchildren, who were playing games in the living room when she took too many pills. She could not remember taking them earlier and she was confused at the time. She was in the bedroom and she sent Christa a text. Christa said, "I called 911 immediately." "The kids were terrified when the ambulance arrived because they did not even know what grandma was doing in the other room. It was a cry for help." "She feels like she has ruined her life." Christa rushed over to the apartment to be with the children, she informed me. We hung up. A flood of emotions filled my heart. I felt so broken inside. (Sally told me later that this was not an attempt to commit suicide.)

At the time, I was devastated! Immediately, I sprung into action. I was going up to Tennessee. I had to be there. Mobilization and deployment experiences in the military put me in the car quickly. I told a few of my neighbors, as I started to drive away, that I would be gone for a while.

No details were revealed at the time but I said I had a family emergency. The winds of turbulence filled my sails as my car raced up Interstate 75. A heaviness filled my soul with a mixture of regret and anger. Compassion, fear, and vengeance accompanied me along the way, pushing me faster as I sailed down the highway. I was the guy others stayed away from on the road that day, as road rage was pushing its ugliness out. I was sorry but I am not the same person anymore. How I survived for 11 hours on the road, without having an accident or receiving a ticket escapes me to this day.

I arrived at Christa's home exhausted. She updated me. Sally was OK, but they were keeping her for evaluation. I slept for several hours. When I woke up, Christa, Jeramie, and I spoke about everything. I was told I could not see her. I could not call her. Our conversation transitioned into, where will Sally go when she is released, and who is going to take care of her. She needs a caregiver.

I asked if "Bozo," Pirate Piranha Joe, was out of the picture, or if he was still around/involved. They told me that he left some time ago and Sally has been having delusional dreams. They had her on some strong drugs, which contributed to her delusions. She felt like she was lost forever because of her sin and she was scared. She told others that the devil told her she was dying in a fire. The walls were burning and evil spirits came to her when she was in the apartment alone. She did not want to be in the apartment anymore. The grandchildren were visiting Grandma when this happened because she did not want to be alone. She was deeply broken and felt helpless in her situation.

My heart sank lower, as I found out what was going on. It seemed like, over the next several days, everything kept falling deeper into the hole of despair, for Sally, and, me. I felt responsible. I was always responsible for her and my children. This time, I was deeply broken.

As we discussed Sally, and what to do, I told them I would move up here into the apartment and pick Sally up when she is released. "I will stay with her and help her," I said. Jeramie questioned me, "You going to be her guardian? She is having mental issues and psychotic episodes, and you are going to take care of her." My response to him was, "Yes, I will be there for her. I can't stand seeing her suffer like this. I don't understand how this all happened but I will be there for her because she needs help." They agreed with me, and I started to fix the apartment up, thinking that we would be back together.

I set up the other bedroom with a nice double antique bed and dressers. I bought sheets and bedspread, room covering carpets and runners, kitchen decorations and utensils. In a few days, the place was looking marvelous. I waited to hear from Christa. I was hoping to visit Sally at the hospital. I called the hospital but I was told I could not speak to her or visit her. I just wanted to know when I could pick her up and bring her home. Days go by slowly. I wait. Finally, I was told she would be released the next day. My anticipation cup was full, like an experienced thoroughbred stallion behind the gate prancing to spring forward into the race, I was waiting for the shot to fire and, the gate to spring open, so I could use the adrenaline surging through every muscle.

**D-Day was launched and my enemy attacked.**   *Overwhelming forces were brought against me.*

Then, Christa called me, "Dad, you can't get mom," she told me. "Why not?" I questioned. "She made some violent gestures and threats toward staff and she is in lock-down. "Sally?" I questioned with a sudden burst of doubt. "Sally would not do that," I fortified my argument. "She is not a violent person," I declared from my 50 years of knowing her. "She would not hurt anyone – ever," I declared with certainty. My daughter told me the case worker called from the hospital to update her on Sally's status. She was not being released today. They had her on some strong medications that cause delusions.

The caseworker was looking for some extended medical care for Sally because she had to be moved. The hospital could not keep her there because of the harmful intentions made to the staff and toward me. "Toward me," I repeated with exclamation. "She threatened me?" My daughter reluctantly responded, "Yes." "She said things they consider HI, Harmful Intentions. "I'm sorry Dad. They are keeping mom. You can't pick her up," Christa said with a heavy heart. We both cried as we hung up.

It seems like the storm became a violent hurricane, and my heart was back out on the torrid sea sinking deeper in the darkness. Terrifying predators circled me, as they fought each other to claim their prize. Helpless to escape, I continued to fall deeper and my breath diminished from within. I felt dead, as I watched myself being destroyed.

The phone rang again. It was the case worker at the hospital. She affirmed what I was told. Sally was on medication and was delusional. She is making threats toward the staff and toward me. The Case Worker said, "Sally is having harmful intentions toward you." "I'm sorry to tell you, but, no one can see her at this time," the lady informed me as we hung up. I sat motionless, trying not to believe what I heard.

I was stunned for several minutes as I sat motionless on the couch. The cell phone in my hand rang loud, breaking my motionless blank mind into alertness. I answered the call. It was Sally, "David I'm scared. I'm really scared." She explained her actions and said I needed to move on. "I would never hurt you. I want to protect you," Sally assured me. A fearful shaking voice told me that she was afraid that she would hurt me. "I had a vision. The devil told me to hurt you." "I would never do it," she said with brokenness from within, which I had never heard from her lips before. "I don't want to hurt you. I would never hurt you," she said. "You must move on without me," she cried in the deepest sorrow I have ever heard. "This is not you," I said in disbelief. Then we hung up. *(Sally was on medication that made her delusional. This was not normal.)*

Still, on the couch, I just sat there. A whirlwind of memories and thoughts swirled inside my skull, as I tried to understand what I just heard, as well as, tried to form a plan of action. Just a blank empty skull and a motionless body occupied the space where I sat. Some time passed and nothing formed inside my soul. Just a void of existence occupied my heart. When my intelligence returned from scouting this void, I felt the relentless attacks of evil pressing forward upon me to bring overwhelming force against me. The army of my enemy was pushing with everything he had, bringing overwhelming power onto the battlefield. He was pushing his force through the objective and beyond his mission intent to defeat me and declare his victory.

My resources were depleted and my allies were scattered. I felt alone. I felt defeated. I did not want to surrender to this enemy. I cried out into heaven for help, bowing before the Lord, as saints, cherubs, and angels listened around the throne to my pleas for help. Suddenly, I was pulled out of this prayerful briefing and sat on the same couch.

Then, my cell phone demanded my attention again. I received an email from my enemy, the cruel narcissistic Pirate, Piranha Joe. It was the same day I was informed of Sally's delusional threats. It was shortly after the hospital case worker hung up. How could there be any more drama, than already loaded upon my shoulders to bear? This evil narcissistic creep of a being knew when the knife was plunged into my heart with this message, and now he was going to twist it within me to make sure any hope to rescue Sally, from his grip of destruction, was dead. He salivated in his assumed victory, as he was positioned at the table of spiritual consumption, ready to devour his prey. It was not just Sally, it was me he wanted to spiritually murder.

I read his lengthy message. It was a typical narcissist stabbing of his enemy because he was losing his "Precious" object of affection, whom he was trying to kidnap. His words were evil. Details of his immoral delusion spread throughout the document to humiliate and discredit my desire to rescue Sally from his hunger. He wanted to possess her soul. He started this message by blaming Sally, to remove any responsibility from himself, just to shame her for rejecting him. Laced with twisted information and lies, he was making himself feel better about his heinous actions. It took him five years of hidden beguiling to set the hook of capture, by calling a married woman night after night and speaking into her ear for hours each time.

He took advantage of their memories together as her third cousin. He relived the young idealistic affection they shared when they were very young. Memories tempered with the knowledge of her naivety, and their years of recent conversations, which slowly poisoned our marriage, were revealed in his vindictive message to me. It was all her fault. Not his fault. It was my fault, in his mind, because I stole her from him forty seven years ago. He also rubbed the immoral acts he forced upon her, both real and vengeful lies, in my face to cause his damage. He did not want me to be there for Sally. He wanted to destroy any feeling I had for her, so I would never want her again. (Evil only destroys.)

The beginning of the message was filled with his insinuation that Sally wanted to divorce me. He wrote, She wanted me dead. *(What she said was that my health issues concerned her and that I was having health issues after retirement that were concerning.)* He said she wanted me to die many times, during their early conversations. He even said her words scared him. He knew about my medical issues, which they talked about, which kept him waiting for her. He said he even stopped calling for a while because her words scared him. Everything he said was twisted into his vindictive lies to run me off so he could claim her. This diluted womanizer concluded that he would take her back in a New York minute. Sally had already told me that he was lying. She said she would never hurt me. His vicious tongue used every angle to be vindictive against me. I know he was trying to force me away forever so he could captivate her.

Then he poured his venom unto the page by revealing things between them, which I had a hard time believing about Sally. He was trying to infuriate me. If he did care for her, how could he say the things he wrote? The only reason I could construct in my thoughts was this was his narcissistic way of viciously attacking me. He wanted to make sure I never had feelings for her again. No chance of that.

***Real spiritual warfare.***     *The devil in my story is Pirate Piranha Joe.*

Seeing his victory within reach, the enemy had one more objective to launch forces against me, as he pushed for his triumph. My cell phone vibrated with a beep to indicate I had a voicemail. 205-201-0231 called and left a message. The date of the call, still saved on my phone, was August 18, 2021.

*(This happened. Telling this story is from my heart, laced with some imagination, but founded on real events. This is my honest attempt to share with others how evil creeps in and hungers to destroy. This is a real story and this .*

*The truth is this evil, in a variety of ways and through all kinds of situations, has attacked men and women since the Fall in the Garden of Eden. The enemy hates God and hates all who are created in the image of God. This demonic one wants to destroy. He works through those who open up their lives to the influence of sin. He beguiles the heart and glorifies death. The Lord Jesus offers LIFE, hope, forgiveness, love, and eternal joy. Be careful what you receive in your life. Be careful who you listen to! Be careful how close you wander to evil!!!)*

I listened to the message. A brief silence followed by two minutes and thirty one seconds of heart-beating. That's all, just a heart beating. The heartbeat started strong. It sounded like it was recorded by ultrasound. The heartbeat was strong for a minute and then it began to slow down. Over the next minute and a half, the heartbeat became slower and slower until it was faint and eventually stopped. I listened for several seconds after the beating ended and heard a voice very distant and inaudible. I called the number but it was no longer in service. Who sent this message and why? This whole day was filled with the accusation that Sally and whoever wanted me destroyed. That's my understanding. This became the worst day of my life. Even more than the revelation.

*Thinking Deeper for the Battle*

***Defeated but refusing to surrender.***  ***I needed a Champion to rescue me.***

I knew that I needed someone from above the treacherous waters to rescue me. I cried out for a "Champion," to walk down into my battle-weary soul to fight my enemy. I needed to be saved from this evil foe. I needed the hand of a Savior who could pull me away from the monsters. A Savior who stood upon the water reaching into the evil world that was pulling me deeper. I needed this powerful Savior to pull me out of the storm and put me back into a safe ship where a calm breeze would sail my vessel through calm waters to a peaceful shore. I realized that I could never accomplish this for myself. I needed the Lord's help.

Withdrawing from the day's battles, I retreated from the theater of war. I was battle-weary from the fight and I needed to withdraw, regroup, refit, rest, and rally my allies to fight. I assembled a small staff, the crew of my life ship, my children. I explained my withdrawal from engagement in this fight, and they understood my decision. Like me, they were confused by the struggle Sally was facing. I called my best friend, Chaplain Colonel Steve, my mentor and Army Buddy for over twenty years, for his advice. The consensus of agreement was I must leave. I had to go back to a resting place, evacuated to recover from my deep wounds.

My crew sent me on my way saying, "We got mom. We will take care of her." "You need to leave today!" I was ordered. Wow, how positions can change quickly. I was proud of them! My adult children assumed roles I thought I would always maintain, but I felt so defeated by everything. I was glad to have such wonderful children! I told Christa, "You realize that you are now the matriarch of the family. You are the wisdom of a mother we all need." Then we cried together.

I packed things up. The car was bulging, when I drove away. I had to remove what I put in the apartment and I got some things from storage, which I was going to need back in Florida. Sally did not want to live at the apartment so Jeramie was going to rent it. Christa became the guardian for Sally, and when she finally left the hospital, she was living in an Assisted Living Home, 2 hours away from our children.

I withdrew back to Tara, the peaceful shore, where my amazing friends were happy to see me again. I revealed very little of what happened. I kept hidden, the sorrow in my soul. I honestly tried to move forward once again, but I still did not have closure. I tried to have a relationship but in reality, my heart was still in the First World. I think my dear friends could see my struggle, the conflict in my soul. I know my life would be amazing going forward, but for some reason, my heart would not commit to another. I wanted to find love. I could have found love! I think I would have been very happy! I was for a while, but my promises held me captive. My responsibility pulled me away. I even thought there was an opportunity for an amazing relationship, but my heart kept me from moving forward.

The storm of my life has become the most difficult struggle for survival I have ever experienced. I just wanted to go back to my life with my family of forty six years. I missed my family and the time at Garrison Cove, even though this was the time that Piranha Joe launched his assault. I miss being close to my children and grandchildren. How I ended up here is beyond my comprehension! I felt like Job in the Bible. Why did this happen? What did I do? I believe in the Lord. "Why me?" "What have I done that she wanted to leave me?" How did this happen to me? I was now the enemy of a spiritual narcissistic evil minion.

***Scripture life verse.*** *My prayer many years ago was to live for the Lord.*

A few years after accepting my call to ministry (1978), I declared that my life verse to live by was Proverbs 3:1–6.

*"My son, forget not my law; but let thine heart keep my commandments: For length of days, and long life, and peace, shall they add to thee. Let not mercy and truth forsake thee: bind them about thy neck; write them upon the table of thine heart: So shalt thou find favor and good understanding in the sight of God and man. Trust in the Lord with all thine heart; and lean not unto thine own understanding. In all thy ways acknowledge him, and he shall direct thy paths."*

I prayed that this would be true for me. It continues to be my spiritual challenge that keeps me looking for the Celestial City, whose builder and maker is God. Knowing my weakness in the flesh, this challenge continues, but the desire to walk with the Lord keeps me living with hope! Knowing I'm saved and in Christ is my power to overcome.

***Living for the Lord.*** *A sermon I preached after a year of retirement:*

I feel like the Tin Man in *The Wizard of Oz* after several hard rains. Not only are my muscles and joints sore from the daily maintenance I currently do, but my mouth seems too rusty from these many months of not preaching. I always loved my preparation and study, as I prepared to preach the Gospel of the Lord Jesus. I miss my studies and I miss preaching.

I retired in April 2011 after serving in the military for thirty three years eleven months and twenty five days. For the last twenty two years, I have been a United States Army Chaplain. As a Lieutenant Colonel, I had the joy of pastoring and preaching at some of the premier pastoral positions in the Army. My service as a chaplain allowed me to preach or lead worship almost every Sunday for over twenty one years. It was a joy serving soldiers and their families, and I miss those amazing days. Yes, amazing days and wonderful soldiers and their families. They are the Patriots who sacrifice and serve freedom and moral responsibility!

My last two years of service was at Fort Bragg. Two years prior I was at European Garrison Command, two years with Recruiting Command, two years at NATO

Mission to European Union and Delegation to NATO Tri-Mission, and much more: I served two assignments with the 101st Airborne Division, Fort Campbell, Kentucky. I served five tours overseas: two with family, one without family, and two hardship tours in Korea. I served at the end of Vietnam but did not go to Vietnam. I was with the Infantry when the Gulf War erupted. I was sent to Fort Sill to serve as the chaplain to the 1-78 Field Artillery, preparing soldiers to deploy for Desert Storm. I remained on active duty, serving with Field Artillery, Infantry, Mechanized Infantry, Aviation, four Garrison Commands, and one Recruiting Command until 2011, when I retired at Fort Bragg. *(Fort Bragg – Not Fort Liberty. Why do we allow inexperienced activists to have any say in who our heroes are and how we operate our military? Why do we tolerate the destruction of monuments that represent truth in history?)*

If I was young and healthy, I would do it all over again! The position of a chaplain is a staff officer for religious support to the commander. Not only does the chaplain have a duty to teach and preach (Running the religious program), he has the staff duty as an advisor, trainer, counselor, and all other commissioned officer duties as any officer. The position is much more complex than just pastoral duties. It wakes you up at four in the morning for physical training and might allow you to come home in the evening. You sleep on the ground; you run with the young soldiers; you plan, you train, and you constantly prepare for any mission. Then when duty calls, you deploy with your unit. Chaplains are Soldier Pastors! I had the pleasure of being one!

***My life verse sermon.*** *Looking at my life verse deeper for understanding. (Proverbs 3: 1-6)*

As a leader, you are responsible for those under your command. You are also accountable to someone higher. When you receive an order you execute the mission. Certain expectations must be met. Leaders have a responsibility for those under his/her command.

A **good leader** communicates his expectations. Subordinates, followers, will carry out those requirements because there is a level of respect. Leadership is earned! Those who willingly give allegiance to someone normally, do so out of respect and duty. So a great **leader communicates his expectations**. He tells his subordinates what he wants. Then he clarifies the "END

*Memories of Loving You*

State." This means, "What things should look like when expectations are met, and victory is realized."

After communicating the mission clearly, the **Commander will train soldiers** to ensure they know how to accomplish the goals established. He will clarify objectives and milestones to reach the "End State" of the mission. **Faithfulness, Loyalty, and hard work** are all elements of success. Personal responsibility and a good work ethic will always bring personal honor and respect from others and leaders.

ILLUSTRATION: After twenty five days at Fort Polk on a training mission with the 101st Airborne Division, I was attending the Battalion Awards Ceremony. Soldiers were receiving awards for their honorable duty. At the end of the ceremony, the Commander called me forward. I was not expecting any award. He held a plaque with the back facing toward me. He explained to the battalion some of the things I accomplished which contributed to the mission's success. I was humbled and honored. Then he presented me with the plaque.

It was a picture of me preaching in the Old Fort Chapel at Fort Polk. I was in my older BDUs with soldiers in the pews. I was animated. Mouth open wide and hands gesturing as if on the attack. The caption placed over the picture read, *"Preaching the Hell Out of Them!"* This has always been my favorite award! I was honored to receive it! I even hope it was true.

**In Proverbs Chapter three, we read God's Mission Requirements for faithful servants.**

Young Solomon prayed to the Lord when **he became the Commander and Chief of Israel**. He was the King. He was humbled at the time because he was young and inexperienced. He prayed to God Almighty to help Him lead the people of Israel. God told him to ask for anything and He would give it to him. Solomon asked for wisdom to lead. He wanted to serve the people of God as God would have him. God granted Solomon his request and declared that he would be the **wisest man to ever live**. Being the most intelligent does not guarantee you are the wisest. Therefore, I direct your attention to the book of Proverbs, and the words of wisdom.

If you want to **live for God in this difficult world** during the increasing times of narcissistic evil, I suggest you read and hide the words of wisdom in your heart. To live by faith means you always press forward in righteousness. You trust God's leadership. In this passage of scripture, we find God's expectations for us, as we live our lives for Him. The expectations that will lead to success in your personal life.

As a young pastor many years ago, I struggled every week to study and prepare sermons. I wanted to do my very best! As I prayed and studied scripture one day, I read this passage. God spoke to my heart and I prayed that God would make this true about me! I share my life verse with you and I pray that you will see the truth of Christ within! The first thing I want to declare is that God's EXPECTATIONS are made clear in this passage. We will begin your mission journey to accomplish God's Mission Requirement!

The First Mission Requirement that must be met is the **personal identification of standing**. You cannot go with the Army unless you join the Army. *This identifies which side you are on.*

God makes it personal! He says, *"My son."* The word "my," means ownership – personal relationship – family! Are you a child of God? Do you know the Lord as your "FATHER?"

The second Mission Requirement is a **command to know**, understand, and remember God's expectations. Know the mission! You must know God's law! "My son, forget not my law; but let thine heart keep my commandments." The word for "Law" in Hebrew is "Torah." This means God's Word. The scriptures contain God's instructions, expectations, and commands. The Word of God is given for instruction in righteousness so the man of God is thoroughly furnished in all good things! God Almighty wants you to know His WORD! God makes it very clear! Keep His commandments!

The word, **"but,"** contrasts with the idea of just knowing and understanding God's requirement. He is telling us that He wants us **to know and to live** according to His Holy Word. The idea here is to learn God's Word and to live by His Word. **Make righteousness your way of life!** Be good. Be Holy, as He is Holy. Live for the Lord because it is within you. Living for God is a way of life. Make it personal!

The Third principle of God's Expectation for your life is the "End State." God tells us **what the benefits are!** "For length of days, and long life, and peace, shall they add to thee."

1. Every day is valued! Every day is full of God's blessings! Long Days of living! Long Life! Full and rewarding! Abiding in God's joy!

2. The benefits of peace with God and with others. Contentment with others. The word is "Shalom," which means peaceful friendship!

The Fourth principle is the training! God not only tells us what He expects, but He also tells us how to accomplish the mission! God clarifies **two mission elements** to ensure success!

1. Mercy – loving kindness – forgiveness – undeserved politeness.

2. Truth – veracity, honesty, genuineness, honor… Reputation

The word *"forsake"* means to walk away from or neglect responsibility.

How can we accomplish the mission? "Let not mercy and truth forsake thee: bind them upon thine neck; write them upon the table of thine heart:"

1. Bind them – tie securely – hang openly – live outwardly – be proud of living for God! Meditate on His word! Live your faith openly for others to see!

*Thinking Deeper for the Battle*

2. Write them – "Kathav" to chisel into granite. Make them permanent qualities in your life!!! Live for the Lord because it is within your soul.

3. Table – polished or cleansed area where you feast/eat. Where you feed your soul!

4. Heart – Soul – inner being – the core of who you are! Created in God's likeness and image. We are required to live in God's glory before the created world! But it must come from within!

The "End State" of God's Expectation for you is found in verse four. "So shalt thou find favor and good understanding in the sight of God and man."

**You will be blessed by God**– His favor will be yours. This is a promise! You will find His favor in every situation you find yourself in. This does not mean you will never have difficulty. In this world, you will find hardship. You are not greater than your crucified Lord!

1. Favor – acceptance – elegance – grace!

2. Good = excellence – ethical – righteousness

3. Understanding = prudence – insight – good sense = *"shekel"*

4. = vision – being seen – others watching – witness to what you are living!

Yes! God is watching us! But He is not at a distance! He is right here with us. He is intimately involved in our success. He wants to bless His children and He desires to bless you. Let Him by trusting and following Him.

I testify to you that when you work hard and accomplish the objectives of the mission, you will be honored! Scripture tells us that Jesus is "The Way, The Truth, and the Life." He is grace and truth. He is Emmanuel = God with us! Trust in His truth and follow Him. Learn of Jesus and follow Him.

"Trust in the Lord with all thine heart; and lean not unto thine own understanding. In all thy ways acknowledge him, and he shall direct thy paths." He did not say maybe. He said He will!

The **final admonition** of wisdom is clarified: Trust the Lord with your entire being! Give Him your soul – your thoughts – your understanding = belief.

Acknowledge God = Emmanuel… Jesus said, *"My sheep hear my voice and they follow me."*

Your mission is: **"Give your life as a living sacrifice to God." Live for the Lord and be His glory in this present world.** Run the race for God/Christ/Jesus – and one day you will be present at the award ceremony in the eternal! Hopefully, you too will preach the hell out of someone's life, as you witness for Christ and others get saved. CH Dave

***Discharged from service.***   *Retreat from the battle.*

I stayed away. I remained out of touch for months. Anything I was told was filtered through "the need to know." My children protected me from a distance, filtering all intel available about what was happening to Sally. They became the perimeter fence guarding the safe zone. I remained in my safe zone, Tara, healing from my infected battle wounds. Disabled in my heart, and lonely in my soul.

Hidden deep inside me were my memories of a life devastated. I wanted to move on. I tried to move on. My mornings were spent with creation, as a new day awakened before me. I watched nature open a new day of life, as the sun revealed the heavens above, and the creatures in the forest and waterway around me scurried about their business. My nosy friends above began their chatter, hooting their questions, wanting to know my most recent journeys filled with tragedy or triumph. They kept bugging me because all I could do was sit mindlessly in my silent pain. My little dragons scampered around me as I tried to relax drinking my morning tea. I watched their playful dance. I think they were entertaining me to keep my mind away from my troubles.

Jeremiah, who was the bullfrog, came out every day to annoy me. He became a friend too, but what an annoying croak he was. He was always there in the evenings when I sat alone drinking my wine (Juice). Like my grandfather, I occasionally had a little bit of mighty fine wine to help me sleep. After I went to bed, he made such a ruckus outside, stirring up the crickets and other frogs in a musical annoyance to keep me awake. I eventually realized he was keeping me from the dreams and nightmares of reliving my pain. In time, this miniature symphony became a lullaby of joy to relax my soul to sleep. It reminded me of the many nights of sleeping on the ground as a soldier, and it helped me to have dreams of better days from the past.

***Back to the Past.*** *Visiting the past is hard to do.*

They say, "Time heals all wounds." Maybe time gave me a break for a while but, eventually, the past catches back up to annoy the present. Many months passed and the inner void of emptiness, which I pushed into the background of my existence, edged forward again. Covert operations were on the move to pull me back into the fight. Intelligence was received that drew me back into staff operations for planning a new mission. I was helpless to refuse the need presented to me. In reality, my soul was still running away from what I felt was the right thing to do. I was tired of the battle but I was called back into the fight because I knew what the Lord "would have me to do." Crippled and maimed from the previous fights upon the spiritual battlefield, I listened to the situation presented.

Yes, a still small voice infiltrated my life in Tara. This voice called me back from hiding. This voice awakened me slowly. Persistently pulling at my heart, this voice spoke to me within. Every time it interrupted me, I ran away. I tried to hide from the voice. I kept busy to keep from worrying. In time this recall affected my relationship with friends. The pulling me apart from both worlds stretched me beyond my ability to cope.

My friend Judie, whose husband passed a year and a half before I met her, and I spent a lot of time together. I was building a large "She Shed," as she calls it, and a carport for her. This kept me very busy. We both had military life and experiences in common, which made for good conversation. Her husband, Tom, was retired Army and they had a wonderful life. Judie was an amazing lady and I enjoyed her friendship. We watched movies, together and had supper often, after a long day of building her shed and carport.

She asked me again during supper one evening what I thought our relationship would be in six months. My answer was "We are friends." I knew she wanted more than friendship, but I was still trapped in the past. I was trying to overcome and find closure but this evaded me. Then at another evening meal, during our conversation, the issue was raised again. I told her I only wanted to be a friend. After a short while sitting at the table, she said, "Well, the one thing I do worry about is that you will go back to Sally." My immediate response to Judie was that I was not going back to her. In reality, I was conflicted within my heart. I knew I was still worried about the lady

*Thinking Deeper for the Battle*

I loved for so long. I was connected to family, which I missed. At the time, I was not looking to get married. This conversation was the segue within me that opened up my curiosity back to Tennessee.

I called my daughter to solicit what information I could about Sally. All I knew was that she was in an Assisted Living Home, under the care of a registered nurse. The money I gave her from my pension was spent on this care. She had a room with a bed and television. There were a total of three residents being cared for when she first got there. One patient died and the second patient was taken back to be with his family. Sally was all alone, except in the morning when she had breakfast, the chef came in to prepare it for her. Then later in the evening, when supper was made for her, a caregiver stayed through the night in a separate suite connected to the home. She was all alone most of the day. I envisioned her loneliness and sadness. This broke my heart. I guess I still cared.

Christa invited me back to Tennessee in March 2022. She wanted me to stay with Ella, my granddaughter, while Jeramie and her went to a conference for a week. I gladly accepted. I flew back the first week in March. While I was there, I took care of all the animals on the farm. I took my granddaughter to school and picked her back up. I worked on a few projects during the day, and I did some work at my son's home, which was about ten miles away. However, one day, Ella was going over to a friend's, after school, whose mother was picking Ella up and returning her later in the evening. This presented an opportunity to visit Sally.

I called the Assisted Living Home registered nurse, Veronica, to get permission to visit Sally. I was approved. It was a two-hour drive. I was nervously anxious because I worried about her every day. I was not sure of the situation. The nurse let Sally know. When I arrived to visit, Sally was happy to see me. She cried and hugged me. Telling me a hundred times how much she was sorry and needed her family. I hugged her back and told her I was sorry this all happened. Inwardly, I could not understand how she ended up in this place. She was frail. I could see that she had given up on life.

I took her to Ruby Tuesdays for lunch. We talked for a few hours. It was nice. When I took her back home, she cried and we said goodbye once again. I drove away with sorrow. How did she end up here? I knew but this was a spiritual inquiry about how could this have happened. What did I do? What could I have done better? What should I be doing? The questions rolled through my mind again and again during the trip back to the farm.

When I first saw her, I saw an extremely thin woman. Smaller than I remembered her. She always watched her weight, walked a lot, and rode her bicycle every day. She took care of herself when we were together. But, what I saw was a much thinner lady who was so sad that the muscles in her face were weak and her lips were drooping, unless she forced herself to smile. She had a pouting look that revealed to me her deep sadness. This made me sad too. Sally did not look happy at all. She was a broken shell, who sat in a chair and cried every day she was there. Well, I finally knew something about what was happening, and it disturbed me. She did not deserve to end up like this. Yes, she did sin, but this is why Jesus is the Savior we all need!

We said goodbye and I drove away feeling her sadness. The drive back seemed like forever. I was sad too. I felt sorry for her. I felt like I lost so much and would never be happy again. I knew she was not happy. Not only did she tell me she missed me and loved me, but she missed our family. She missed the grandchildren, whom she loved more than anything. She worried about them all the time. Yes, broken and alone, filled with regrets and painful memories. Sally felt lost and alone. She cried for help.

I have done more in my life than I ever dreamed I could or would, as a young man. I would do it again! Sally was at my side from high school, through College and Graduate School, and all the years I served my country. She served her country too! She raised our family and she moved every time I was reassigned. She sacrificed the opportunity to be settled in one place building a life of security. She stayed by my side through it all, and she did not deserve to be cast away and forgotten. This broke my heart and weighed heavy on my soul.

***Back to the future again.*** *Is this where I lived or am I living in the past?*

A day later, I flew back to Florida. My friend, Betty, the Florida Flower Girl, picked me up. I reentered my New World life with friends, who I enjoyed being with. I continued my same routine every morning. I worked on Judie's carport, knowing I had to get it done. We had fish fries together. We went out to eat and played cards. Days seemed to blend and time escaped me. Time could not heal my divided struggle within, as I still worried about the past and lived in this future among my dear new friends. I never really opened my heart fully, even though I wanted to. Inside I was lonely.

Christa checked on me often. The family, Christa, Ella, and Jeramie, came to visit me at Tara several times. My son called me often, and Sarah would text me. I felt loved but I felt like I lived in two worlds. I did. Both worlds pulled at my heart!

When I moved to Tara Village, I brought the motor home, which I thought Jeramie gave to me. I thought he was going to give me the title, but he was actually letting me borrow it. Christa told me one day, when I asked about insurance and title, Jeramie eventually wanted the motor home back someday. This changed my situation. I was not sure what I was going to do. They had done so much for me and I appreciated everything, but my uncertain future became even more unstable just knowing this.

A few months passed as friendships changed. Judie went to see family for many weeks and Betty spent time with me. We both agreed that we were only friends. We watched movies together and we would go out to eat. We even shared late mornings having tea and coffee on the deck.

## *Chapter Eleven:*
# THE RESCUE MISSION

*The next time travel experience becomes a road trip.*
*Traveling back and forth between worlds.*

**THEN I FLEW** back again to help my family. I was there for my granddaughter, while her parents were away, and then I spent time with them after they returned. During my visit, the fact that Jeramie wanted the motor home, "The Tube," back someday was reaffirmed. He sold the other motor home he owned. He bought it because he missed having a place to rest and use as an office after he let me have the "Tube," motor home. I was interested in buying the other one, but when I returned, he had already sold it. This created a new problem for me. Where would I live?

I also found out that Sally's situation was soon to change. The many months of her living in this home all alone were going to end. Veronica, the Assisted Living Home Owner and Registered Nurse, wanted to use her home for another purpose and Sally was going to have to

## THE RESCUE MISSION

be placed somewhere else. Sally still needed a caregiver, so her living conditions were going to change. Christa was once again directly involved in finding another home. She could not provide care because she was working at the school and she had a very active life.

Sally was so depressed and lonely. She had given up on living and just sat around in her sorrow. I was torn apart inside over it all. I worried about her every day.

When I returned to Tara, I put on a good face. The worry remained within me, but the happiness with friends kept me going each day. My uncertainty about keeping the motor home remained in my thoughts, and what was I going to do, kept me on edge. I wanted to know when Jeramie wanted the motor home and if he was going to help me drive it back up to Tennessee.

I even started looking for another place to live. I searched for an apartment or condominium around Englewood, Venice, Nokomis, North Port, and the surrounding areas. I felt like I needed to be closer to where I used to live for many reasons. One reason was I already had medical care, which I kept when I moved up to Leesburg. The problem I ran into was everything was already leased for one to two years out.

*Memories of Loving You*

Then, I finally found a condo in Port Charlotte, Florida. I spoke to the owner, Donald, over the phone and then drove down to look it over. I called the owner back and told him I wanted it. We agreed on a lease and I signed the paperwork. Just in the nick of time.

My daughter called to inform me that Jeramie wanted to fly down to drive the motor home back to Tennessee. She wanted to know if I was coming back with him. I told her, "Yes." He came down. I picked him up at the airport, and we spent the day preparing the motor home and the car to return. Everything was moving so fast.

I already packed everything up, many days before Jeramie came, and even sold the shed and deck to Betty, who was going to move a new RV in the space and sell hers, which was next door. Seemed like all was working out, but my uncertainty remained within. My worries continued to invade me. Worries about moving forward to help Sally and worries about leaving my precious friends. What to do?

***Good Counsel.*** *Discussion of mission needs to explore mission capabilities.*

We drove away from Tara. The "Tube," was full and the journey would take about twelve to fourteen hours.

*THE RESCUE MISSION*

Cruising highway I-75 from Florida to Tennessee allowed time for detailed mission analysis. We discussed the whole situation, and the issues created for future planning. Sometimes I felt like I was being grilled for information, and yet, I was given advice about actions and possible end-state responsibility. Yet, my heart was pulled in different directions because I was still living in two worlds with friends and loved ones I cared for. It was hard to drive away from Tara. It was stressful driving into the storm of uncertainty that lay before me. My son-in-law, Jeramie, is a Life Coach to many Aspiring Realtor Agents. He helped me to think deeper, as we traveled back to the first world, my first life.

Did I have the willpower and the energy to take on responsibility? Was I ready to launch a rescue mission? Did I want to rescue her and be responsible for her? What did this mean and what would life be like? Was I setting myself up for the same painful results? What should I be responsible for? What does the Lord want me to do? Once again, too many questions. Where are those pesky owls when I need them?

I had opportunities to move forward. A good woman would love me. A good woman would share her life and I could be happy again. I think. But, this heartache would always haunt me. I wonder how many suffer in their experience of starting over and having regrets. How many just run away? I'm too old to start over. I am too old to take on another family and to love the children and grandchildren of another man. I am a good guy. I could love another and could love their families. Do I have the energy and willpower to do this? I do love life and I love people, but starting over at my age is harder than I could ever imagine. When there is no closure in a relationship, it is hard to move forward.

Loving someone from a young love experience, that was lost many years ago, creates heartache. Even if the feelings are real, it becomes difficult. Making a new relationship become a reality, that divides feelings and energy, is difficult. I love my family. I want my life back! Was it still there?

I love my grandchildren. I love my children! I love the life I had before the storm. I love the young lady who became my wife and supported me through life. Even with all the hardship and struggles, I wanted my life back. I also wanted the friends and the love shared with me during my hardship. People who cared and helped me survive during difficult times are in my heart and deep in my soul. Loving somebody is loving the life you have together. It is loving each other and loving family.

I come back to my faith. Even when I failed, I wanted to walk with the Lord. I struggled to find forgiveness and I struggled to be forgiving. There was anger still inside me. I wanted my enemy narcissist to suffer. I wanted him to be pulled into his darkness. I wanted the monsters from the deepest darkness to feast on him slowly to prolong his pain. Hate was trying to pull me to the dark side. In some ways, I wanted to go there just to hurt him. I wanted this evil one to suffer. The desire for vengeance kept me on the battlefield of hate. Did I lose something precious and can I get it back?

"What would Jesus do?" To be honest, I struggled with my heart. I was still uncertain about what I should do. Maybe I was selfish. I know the enemy kept up the assault against me. This enemy kept shoveling his lies and deception onto the heap of my struggles, even when he moved on and left her helpless and alone.

The journey back home was long. The challenges upon my heart were exhausting. What was the right thing to do? If she had moved on to be with him, I might be on a different path already.

Jeramie was mind-provoking as we discussed options. He needed to protect his family too. Both he and Christa took on a responsibility that became overwhelming and directly impacted their family. I realized this fact and it was heavy on my mind. What should I do and where was my heart in this?

Constantly I realized I cared. I cared for my children and their families and I cared about her. I knew that I needed to make a decision. As an Army Officer, I was good at making decisions. I was good at seeing the big picture and organizing things. I was good at making things happen. Seems like my abilities were lost in all the confusion. The enemy knew where and how to attack me.

### *The Slow Return to My First Life.*

*We arrived back home.*

The time-traveling "Tube," got us back to Murfreesboro, Tennessee. We drove straight through. There was one detour, which caused us to travel over fourteen hours. We made it! Jeramie parked the motor home in the same spot on the driveway, which is where he kept it in the past.

The next few days I cleaned it inside and out. I took everything I had to the storage unit. Then I focused on

Sally. I called her and found out the details of her situation. I spoke to Veronica, the Director of the Assisted Living Home RN Nurse, about what needed to happen, and I continued discussions with Jeramie and Christa. Sally had to leave the home where she was staying. I was ready to be a caregiver because I could not stand seeing her like this. I could not stand the hurt my children and grandchildren were experiencing and the bad example we were. I could not stand the emotional pain I endured for so long. I wanted it to end. It had to end! Will it end?

Sometimes we need to be reminded of things we forget. We need to be reminded of the promises we make. We must learn from our failures to experience our success. Most of all we need help to overcome. We need a Champion to stand before us! I needed someone above the troubled waters to pull me out and take me to safety. A Champion to put me back in the boat and put my feet on solid ground is who I needed. The battles of life can destroy what is good.

**Remembering the Savior.**  *My Champion walks on water!*

I finally understood that the victory was easy because my Savior, who walks on the water, was reaching out to me all along. He fought the battle and secured the perimeter of God's Eternal Peace. His power of redemption\* is placed around all who are rescued from the wages of sin. His eternal barb wire fencing, keeps the glory and peace of the Eternal Space, Heaven, from the evil conflict. Those outside the "Safe Zone" of His redemption remain at risk. Unless they find their Champion, Jesus Christ, they will realize their "End State," defeated in eternal death. Only His power and His truth offer hope. There is no such thing as "my truth," or "your truth." (*1 Peter 1:3-5 is my favorite scripture*)

There is only real truth, which is **God's truth**. *(John 17:17)* Truth always remains the same. It never changes. No one can rewrite it. It must be embraced! No attempt to mislead "free thinkers" or convincing "wokeness" can alter the truth. Wokeness is a self-aggrandizing deceitful edification of the distortion of truth for mental captivation to a lie. It is the serpent hissing in the ears of the innocent. Real "WOKENESS" lies are realized when sinners cross over into eternal death, separated from God's truth. Imagine, eternally dying, cut off from the power source of real life, which comes from God Almighty. Unless the problem of sin and evil is defeated in your lost soul, your power source of life, which goes back to God breathing this life into Adam, the first man, will eternally run down. *(Revelation 21:8)*

Waning away through eternity, as what little bit of life's power is continually exhausted. Weaker and weaker you become as the battery of life in your soul is used. Remaining in sin and rejecting the Savior keeps destroying any capability you have to function. Destroying energy and removing the ability to enjoy life and happiness is constantly ripped from your soul as you are eternally reduced as a being. Suffering in the fire of exhaustion. Hell is real. *(Matthew 13:50, Mark 9:48, Revelation 14:10)*

Imagine stepping into the eternal space. There is no time measurement. There is no end, as we understand. The "Worm (soul) dieth not, and the fire is never quenched." The consideration of "eternal death" should be terrifying for anyone lost in their self-theism, without God's forgiveness and reconciliation.

The reality of truth for believers, rescued by the only Savior, Jesus Christ the Son of the Living God, becomes eternal rest in the Lord's presence FOREVER. This truth, when embraced through faith in the work of redemption, is a debt that no creature could ever pay for. Jesus invites you to find and embrace His rest. *(Matthew 11:28-30)*

*Memories of Loving You*

I am not sure how many times I have stood before others to declare that Jesus is the way, the truth, and the life. No one comes to the Father unless they come through Jesus Christ the Lord. *(John 14:6-11)* The reminder of this truth echoed in my soul. Drowning in the darkness of this storm, with deep wounds and surrounded by more enemies ready to attach my soul, I remembered I had an advocate. I had the Champion walking on the water who was ready to put me back into the boat of safety and deliver me to my destination, the eternal peaceful shore! *(1 John 2:1-12)*

Someday, heaven becomes a reality for believers in Jesus Christ. The invitation is real! Faith is not complicated. Sin is complicated and exhausting. Jesus Christ offers rest for the soul! He will not force you to believe and He will not force you to accept His invitation. He created you in His image and likeness, which means you have freedom of choice. To take freedom away would make you a slave. This is what evil does. *(1 Peter 5:8)* Evil promotes and feeds hate. God is not the author of confusion and there is no evil within Him. *(1 Corinthians 14:33, James 1:13, Hebrews 6:18)*

Freedom is what made America Great. YES, AMERICA WAS GREAT! It was founded by those who hungered for FREEDOM. Those who love freedom still defend America. Compare evil's desire to control everything and how evil promotes hate and discord, and you will understand the enemy of all that is good. Our forefathers, of this idealism of the "Free," formed a Constitutional Republic to stand against the forces of evil, which hungers to enslave. I say again, "It's not the village, but the family, that nurtures the soul in goodness." The social village wants to enslave and control because those who hunger for power over others are the elite slave masters of the fallen. "If the Son shall make you free, you are free indeed." *(John 8:36)* I hope you find freedom for eternity and walk with God someday! Ask Him to take over and lead the way! Trust the Savior and believe!

***Reaching out for help.*** *We all need the Lord's help! Great song of faith:*

"I see the hand of mercy, and I hear the voice of cheer, and just the time I need Him, He's always near! He lives, He lives, Christ Jesus lives *today..." What a great Christian song of hope! (Matthew 14: 22-23)*

I returned to the Assisted Living Home in Hartsville, Tennessee to visit Sally. She was happy to see me again. I smiled when I saw her. Nothing else mattered. All of the hardship, the bad decisions, and the violations of our love evaporated the moment I saw her smile through the frail pain she suffered. She was reaching out to me with her heart. She needed a Champion too. She had suffered too much and was holding onto the little bit of hope available to her. Me! I missed her and still loved her.

My heart told me that I needed to live what I was also seeking. I loved her and I wanted to forgive her and be with her. I could tell that she wanted the same. We embraced and kissed through our tears. The world disappeared around us for this moment in time. It became the anchor point of the future together. It was a new beginning with the winds of hope filling our sails again.

I called Sally days before showing up after I signed the lease for the condominium in Florida. I told her I was coming to get her. On the phone, she sounded happy. I was going to be her caregiver, at the very least. But once I saw her and embraced her, I knew it was going to be much more.

Finally, after the revelation of infidelity and three years of suffering, we were able to love each other again. Her bags were packed. She left the lonely home where she survived each day. She drove her car back to Murfreesboro, Tennessee to meet me.

We visited our children for a few days and we prepared for the trip to Florida. They were happy for us. I think they were weary but hoped for the best this time. Imagine parents finding their healing after this storm and their grown children questioning possibilities. Will it happen again?

***Another Prayer of HOPE.*** *Prayer changes everything!*

The morning we drove back down to Florida, while everyone was still asleep, I stood alone under the dimming stars of the night, as the morning began to awaken. I guess I was in prayer but nothing was happening. I felt like I was inside of an emerging story. Everything outside was silent. No birds singing. No insects or frogs practicing their skills or warming up for the approaching performance. A pause of time took over the world around me. There was no pirate or evil devil to interrupt. There was not an enemy anywhere in sight or even in the world I dwelt in. No cause for being alert for danger and no reason to fear anything at all. I had no sorrow at the moment. No tear formed in my eye. No pain pressed me to suffer. No failure was pushed into my face. Just that moment of pause that welcomed the voice I needed to hear. *(1 Kings*

*18:20-40, 19:12, Psalms 29:3-9, 68:33, Matthew 3:17, John 12:28-30, 2 Peter 1:1-18, John 10:27)*

I am not sure how long I stood in this silence. It felt good. It was what I needed at that time. It drove away doubt and welcomed me before the throne. This was my moment. This was my audience before the ruler of all things. I was frozen and yet bowed my heart and soul before the Lord. The silence was immensely full of my memories. Not a word crossed my lips. All my failures were within me, as a universe of wonders slowly faded from my view. The darkness withdrew from the morning light, as it pulled the shadows back from under every living thing. Pulling them into full view. Shadows that remind us all that the darkness is still in our world, even when it is day.

For the darkness reveals sin, and sin is still in our world, even when the light shines. Shadows hide behind what the light exposes, as darkness runs away like a coward. It hides from the light, but the light reveals darkness's evil intention, to hide behind its cruel purpose to return. Sin is evasive and persistent. Sin presses against every weakness to invade the soul. It is relentless and powerful. Sin will hunt you down. Sin will hurt you. When this predator takes control, it will grasp and squeeze until it destroys

*THE RESCUE MISSION*

you with its darkness. Sin is like a strong grasping hand that lays upon the flesh. It begins with the gentle touch of welcome, and you know it is there, but the slow grasping clutch reaches deeper and deeper until the grip is overpowering. Sin will destroy you.

It will squeeze until the breath of life is gone and the flesh of this world lies motionless. The breath that God breathed into Adam, which has been passed with life to us all, is extinguished from the body. At that moment the Spirit is separated from the flesh, and the Soul is released into the eternal space, where walking with God can only occur if sin has been dealt with. For God does not allow sin to remain before Him. His glorious light drives sin away.

The darkness is cast away from His presence forever. The only way any man can ever walk with God is to have a Savior, who advocates FORGIVENESS! A Champion, who is stronger than any enemy, is needed. There is only one Champion who is stronger: the Savior, Jesus Christ the Lord. *(Job 26:7-14, Psalm 71:18, Romans 5:10, Hebrews 1:3, 1 Corinthians 1:18, 2 Timothy 1:7, 2 Peter 1:3, Matthew 1:21, 22:29)* "There is no other name given among men, whereby we must be saved." *(Acts 4:12)* Only His power can save!

The sun rose slowly over the horizon. There was a dark bluish-purple haze of light that burst forth at the point where the sun would break through the long night. Like the announcement of the King in all His royalty was almost here, the purple mantle revealed the golden lining of His glory. The shining gold with shades of red and orange encircled the power of His might as the light resurrected before me. I watched as the Lord drove the darkness away and His glory filled the sky. The beauty of the **Created Garden** reemerged before my very eyes. Yes, the one that was without form and was void because darkness filled the earth, was being illuminated before me into God's Glory. *(Rev 4 & 5)*

God Almighty did speak. My ears did not hear but my faith listened to truth. He said, "Let there be light." and "There was light." He created a division between the light and the darkness and he called the evening and morning the first day. The Lord God Almighty said this was good. This was the first day! *(Genesis 1: 1-5, John 1:1)* "In the beginning was the Word and the Word was with God and the Word was God…" I bowed before the Lord as I witnessed His power and glory revealed to me again.

I am telling you that His throne room spiritually emerged in front of me as I bowed before Him in faith.

Every shade of darkness fled away as He approached my heart. The beauty of all creation splashed the vastness of color throughout the world around me. The sky became blue with stratus white lining and cumulus clouds as far as I could see. The earth was filled with every shade possible and every color available as a beautiful living portrait of life was exposed. Contrasts of greens upon the trees and green spread over the meadows with reds, yellows, whites, pinks, and more. His beauty decorated the floral decor to highlight the hope and promises of God. To me, the heavens declared the glory of God and this created world demonstrates His handy work. *(Psalm 19:1-6)* Just the awesome faith in Christ became my experience, confirmed once again within me this beautiful morning.

I humbly bowed before the Lord and rested in my faith during this amazing moment. Then He said, "Walk with me." He lifted me up, taking my hand, and the moment was at least a day in my heart. When I returned, I was in the same place standing before a new day. Some say we have a purpose. Maybe some have more purpose than others, and some drop the mantle of responsibility in weakness, but all things work together for good if you love the Lord. *(Romans 8:28)* You see, every day of creation, He said it was good. The Lord does have a plan and purpose for the ages, and He has a purpose for me. He has a purpose for you too. I pray you find Him and trust Him. *(John 3:16)*

The earth awakened with beauty and the sounds of music filled the world around me. The garden came alive with activity and I reacted to my morning experience with the Lord. I remembered the prayer standing under the dark universe of sparkling stars when I was a boy. I remember begging the Lord for Sally to be mine and my oath to always be there for her and provide for her. I promised to love her! I promised God, my Heavenly Father. This promise created my family and their future. I hope they know this. This new morning, I asked the Lord for the love of the lady who is the mother of my children. I asked God Almighty for the girl, who came with me on the journey of life when I was just a boy. I promised to love her and share my life with her again if He would bless me with her love. That morning, I witnessed heaven in my soul once again.

***The human experience of this story is reminiscent of every story.***

*Back to the Garden.*

Like the story found in Genesis, the Garden of Eden was the world God created for Adam and Eve, and all human ancestry. The Human Race is the ancestry of everyone born into this world. We are all the children from the garden. We are the children of our Greatest Grandparents, Adam and Eve, who fell into sin. They had to leave the Garden and walk out into a difficult and dangerous world. They walked into a world that has grown in hate through time. They were separated from God because of sin.

Before they stepped across the line into this world *(Romans 8:22),* which was corrupted by their sin, God gave them hope. Those who once walked with God in the beautiful garden had to walk alone in the fallen world. What a sad day and a sad life for the first couple, who once walked with God in the garden. To have the memories of what it was like to spend time with the Creator, and now being driven away to walk alone, must be a weight of heavy sorrow upon their souls. They carried this burden with them as they entered a world unfamiliar to them. It was a world of hardship, where evil would stalk them. Where the garden became hostile with thorns and thistles. A world at enmity with God. *(Romans 8:7-10, James 4:4)*

It was a world where self-theistic aggrandizement would develop narcissistic beings, who would rebel against their Creator. Narcissistic creatures who would invade and destroy others at will. Souls of invading mischief for self-glorification and satisfaction, where they are the authority and the bullies for self-gain. A beguiling narcissist who captures the weak and innocent for self-gain, building their potentate power over others to control with evil intentions. The accumulation of power and wealth to dominate others for personal gain and self-elevation became dominant, as some rebellious narcissistic potentates built empires and forced control over others. These creatures made themselves into gods, the sin that was used to beguile Eve in the garden.

In the end, it is the rebellion of the "Beast," a one-world system of control. The "Borg Village," not the family, is glorified in this fallen dystopian future. This future of evil will not endure for long because the King is Coming. HIS KINGDOM IS FOREVER! *(Matthew 24:42, 26:64, I Thessalonians 5:1-3, 23, Acts 1:9-11, Titus 2:13, Revelation 1:7)*

In this evil future, narcissistic creatures would feed upon the innocent. This is a world where sin destroys individuals and enslaves the masses. Evil beings who enslave the innocent for personal gain and control are the enemies of humanity. It is the same world today, but it will be on a much larger scale. Evil has harnessed hate

*THE RESCUE MISSION*

to destroy what is sacred and good. As I already declared, "Hate is the result of evil intentions in our world." The Tribulation Period is coming. It will be devastating for sinners. However, the scripture reveals that God has not appointed His children to wrath but unto salvation. The rapture of believers, the Church, will take place before the Antichrist takes over. The Antichrist will rule the evil one-world government system. Are you ready? If you miss the rapture, you will face the beast! I do believe we will see the perilous times of evil, as it crescendos into what becomes the Great Tribulation. Believers will not experience the "Wrath of God" against sin after the Antichrist takes control during the Tribulation. Believers will be at the "Marriage Supper of the Lamb!" *(Revelation 19:6-9)*

Driven from the Garden of Eden, and away from the Tree of Life, the first family moved far away from their relationship with God Almighty. They had children as time became a reality. During this time, sin grew around them. Their children only heard about God through Adam and Eve, who became parents, grandparents, great-grandparents, and original ancestors to all men and women. Their children began to be jealous and angry. Cain, their son, killed Able, their other son and the heartache

*Memories of Loving You*

of sin became a reality that would grow much larger through time.

Sin became so bad in a few thousand years, of this new experience of fallen nature, that God Almighty exposed that their hearts were only evil continually. Evil became so bad so quickly that it filled the earth with violence and hate. The innocent were destroyed and the hearts of men were filled with immoral rebellion. Rebellion against the Lord God and all His glory and goodness. Beings of self-will and determination for self-theistic aggrandizement over others, as these elite fallen creatures, who make themselves gods before others, took control and built kingdoms. They built armies to protect the world they controlled, and accumulated powerful influence to enslave the hearts of men.

People forgot God, they stole from each other, and they violated their marriage covenant *(God's design for procreation to create families with children who would fill the earth with goodness. But rather, they rejected God's purpose and plan, for the health and welfare of humanity, so they could indulge in the pleasures of sin.)* Immoral rebellion filled the earth with hate, anger, jealousy, violence, lying, and cheating as the darkness of evil spread throughout the fallen world. I am sure that Adam and

Eve found their joy for their children become the deepest regret within their souls. Parents who care want their children to be the best and have the best of everything in life. They want their children to find goodness and success in life. The first married couple, Adam and Eve, want their children to know the God they walked with in the garden. The pain of witnessing the evil of sin in their children's lives was the worst suffering that sin could inflict. Heartbroken to the soul! God was heartbroken too.

There was one man of faith. His name was Noah. This one man believed in God and built the Ark. One man and his family, wife and three sons and daughters-in-law, were sealed in this Ark (A symbol of Salvation) until the destructive power of sin, and the evil of humanity that filled the earth with hate, was removed from world. A flood covered the earth to destroy the power of sin that day. *(Genesis 6-7)* A new opportunity for humanity was created. But as time slipped into the future, sin's influence continued to grow. It is still forcing its power and influence on humanity. Sin is a narcissistic power that hungers to capture, control, and eventually destroy what God created for good.

Almighty God loves the sinner but He does hate sin. He knows what sin and evil do to the soul and he hates what it does to the creature, man. God hates what sin does. His hate for sin is not a motivation for retribution against the sinner, but it is the reason why He hates sin because there are always consequences for sin. We are responsible creatures and we are accountable for our sins. We are responsible for our actions. Evil is willful intent to harm others. In our world, hate for others that motivates harmful actions that destroy others (Who are created in the image of God) becomes the rebellion of sin from the heart. When you see hate, as the result of evil, you know it is not good.

God, our Heavenly Father, hates what sin has done to man. He told the First Family, Adam and Eve, that He would redeem man from this fallen state of sin. He informed them of His plan of hope. He told them a prophetic announcement before they walked out of the garden into uncertainty. The Lord told them He would send a Savior, miraculously born of a woman without the seed of a man, to rescue man from the sin that separated them from Him. *I am coming to get you!* I have a plan and purpose for reconciliation through <u>forgiveness</u>.

The Lord told the serpent, and He told Adam and Eve, that the conflict would continue: the battle against sin would be relentless, as they walked away into this

*THE RESCUE MISSION*

fallen world. (Genesis 3:15) "I will put enmity between thee and the woman, and between thy seed and her seed; He shall bruise thy head, and thou shalt bruise His heel." All humanity is affected by this judgment of sin and the pronouncement of prophetic hope. The struggle between good and evil will persist against all who are born into this world. Evil and hate will constantly cause conflict and war between what is good and holy and what is evil and hateful. What side are you on? You must choose. Jesus invites you to come into His redemption power and find forgiveness.

This conflict is a war! It is a spiritual war. Sin is real and accountability is inevitable. There is a day of Judgment before God Almighty. You will not escape accountability. Sin must be dealt with. *(Revelation 20:12-13, Psalm 1:5, Acts 17:31)* The wages of sin is death. *(Romans 6:23)* It is appointed on all men to die. After death comes judgment. *(Hebrews 9:27) All who accept Christ, repent of sin and are "Born Again," become the children of God. They have the hope of God's promises for eternity. Forgiven!*

This was a sad and dangerous day, as they walked away from the Garden of Eden. The Lord had to place His powerful Cherubs with flaming swords around the "Tree of Life," to keep fallen man away. *(Genesis 3:24)* If they ate of this fruit, they would live forever in their fallen state of sin, and there would be no opportunity for redemption. The chance of forgiveness would die with them. God wanted man to understand the destructive power of sin, and He wanted man to understand forgiveness.

I felt this dreadful emptiness and lonely walk the first moment I found out what had happened in my life. I walked away from the kitchen table where my wife confessed her infidelity. Evil is a hungry predator. Evil desires to consume and destroy!

## *The Powerful and Perfect Champion.*

*The gate to the garden is open.*

The work of redemption demonstrated the power of Jesus Christ the Lord to forgive. His sacrificial atonement, and glorious resurrection, secured the Gospel truth for all who believe and trust Jesus Christ! He defeated the greatest enemy of man. He rose from the dead! The day that Adam and Eve ate the forbidden fruit, they died. The process of death, and separation from God, who is the source of life, began, as time ticked away their living. Jesus defeated death through His substitutionary sacrificial atonement at Calvary. It is this only act of redemption that led to the power of FORGIVENESS, because He rose from the dead, and He is alive forevermore. *(Romans 8:17, 1 Corinthians 15:20, Colossians 1:18)*

He set the example because He loved man, whom He created in His likeness and image. *(Once again, I repeat that the term man includes the completion of humanity as Adam was created and woman was created from Adam's DNA, and the two became one.)* This oneness of two in marriage became the completion of man, and God said it was good. "Male and female created He them in His likeness and image, and God said it was good." *(Genesis 1:27, Genesis 5:2, Matthew 19:4)* Anything else is an abomination to the Lord. It is not wrong to love anyone. What is wrong is when you pervert God's plan of procreation to fill the earth with righteousness and replace it with immoral perversions that are not natural. It is immoral to pervert what God had established as a family. Our world continues to pervert what God created. They rebel against Almighty God.

Father, mother, and children are an image of triunity. It is a picture of oneness. Children come from within their mother, where the life and DNA are passed from their father, which makes each child a unique individual created by God. It is God's creative power to fill the earth with human beings, who were and are, responsible for reflecting God's glory and purpose within creation. Man is the final capstone of all creation. Man is charged with stewardship over all the earth. We have a responsibility for goodness, not evil. We have accountability before our Creator, who demands holiness. If you ever walk with God, you must walk with a purity of goodness, which is found through forgiveness. We are not saved by any work we can do. But, when you are saved, you should grow in the grace of our Lord. It is the blood of Christ in atonement that covers sin. We have all sinned and come short of God's glory. We all need a Savior.

The only Savior is Jesus Christ.

"Look and LIVE!"

## *Chapter Twelve:*
# Mission Analysis and Understanding Success

> ***What I know to be true.*** *If God forgives us of our sins through the work of Jesus Christ, I too must forgive others their trespasses against me.*

**HOW CAN I** claim faith in the Lord Jesus Christ, if I do not have the same character and purpose of forgiveness? (Matthew 18:15-21, Matthew 6:15) The example of forgiveness is at the heart of the Gospel of Jesus Christ! It is because God loved the world, and humanity, and He gave us the Savior to redeem us through repentance. It is Forgiveness that creates the pathway to reconciliation with God. Being reconciled back unto the Lord, who is the power and source of life, is the only way to walk with God in His glorious Garden again. It is through

Christ alone, that we find the only eternal forgiveness that empowers the soul to fellowship with the Lord.

I must be forgiving like my Heavenly Father is Forgiving. I must be humble like my Lord Jesus Christ, the Son of Man- my Savior, is humble. I dare not cast a stone or point a finger! *(John 8:7)* I just need the Savior!

| ***What does forgiveness mean?*** | *Understanding forgiveness is important to reconciliation!* |

Many months of separation after the divorce, I visited Sally in the Assisted Living Home in Hartsville, Tennessee. My first view of her broke my heart. I saw a frail lady who was crushed with sadness. She was physically weak and mentally broken. She clung to me as if she could never let me go. She wept in my arms and I cried with her. The sorrow of time surrounded us with regrets. The many days of lonely sadness and worry for her welfare, that I experienced while we were apart, reminded me of the hidden pain I felt every day for over two years. I felt her pain too, as I held her, empathy filled my soul. She cried her sorrow and regrets upon my chest as she squeezed me with a fear of loneliness. She had lived in fear for such a long time. Her fears and loneliness drenched my heart with her sorrow. My shirt was wet too! Forgiveness is a "Love Gift."

***Back in Time.*** *One more memory to relive.*
*The assurance of good choices to live with.*

That morning, I spoke of earlier, I prayed. I bowed before the Throne and time stood still in my heart. My Eternal Heavenly Father took me back to another memory. Lest I forget a special day in my life, a day when God taught me a lesson I needed. The Lord reminds me of His love and purpose one more time. I did not forget this event, but it faded through time and remained deep inside me, filed away and not used for many years. He reminded me that I wanted this to be my reality because I needed to be a good father like He is our Eternal Father. I must reflect His glory again in my example before others. I must live this truth! I want my family to know this truth!

This life event needed to be recalled because the Lord wanted me to live my life as a child of God, who understands His forgiveness. He brought me back to remember a time when I needed to see His love. I was in Seminary working on a Master of Divinity. I worked the third shift at Liberty University from 11:00 p.m. to 7:00

a.m. I worked some weekends with the Virginia Army National Guard and I also worked for Kroger's grocery unloading trucks and stocking in the late day on Thursday and Friday before going into my full-time job. I also took a full load of classes during the day at the University and Seminary. I slept about three to four hours a day. I also took care of my children while Sally worked at the Old Time Gospel Hour. This memory was real and the Lord wanted me to relive it. How I survived this period of my life is only miraculous. Reliving this experience was refreshingly real.

Many years ago, in 1986, the Lord used a life experience to speak to my soul. He taught me a lesson that has taken me a lifetime to fully realize. I did understand the lesson when it happened, and it has illuminated my ministry throughout my life. The journey to comprehend what the Lord was teaching me began when my Pastor, Dr. Jerry Falwell, made a statement of encouragement to me. He knew that I worked all night because many nights I was assigned to guard his family residence. I was assigned to protect his family at night, during the darkness, while his family slept. Dr. Jerry Falwell was a great pastor! He was a great preacher! He was a great man! I respect him! Always will!

*Mission Analysis and Understanding Success*

I greatly admire Pastor Falwell. He started Moral Majority years ago, but he was also the founder of Liberty University and Liberty Baptist Theological Seminary. He was the Pastor of Thomas Road Baptist Church, where Sally and I attended for over six years with our children. During this time I finished a Bachelor of Science and a Master of Divinity.

Often, during the day, when I would see the pastor, he took the time to speak with me. The first time I met Pastor Falwell was while I was attending Baptist Bible College in Springfield, Missouri. He spoke at Chapel. After his message, I rushed forward to meet him. I told him my name and my calling. I felt called to serve in ministry as a pastor. This is why I was in school. He made this comment to me at the time, "David, God has something special for you to do." This was the only contact at the time.

Over three years later, when I was pastoring a small church in Ohio, I was involved in a Curtis Hudson Revival in Toledo. I was the newest and youngest pastor to be involved with the campaign. On the first night of the revival meeting, as things were being prepared, I walked into the sanctuary. I was at the far end away from the altar, when I heard a voice, "David Druckenmiller, how are you doing?" At a distance, I could see Dr. Jerry Falwell. I was amazed that he even remembered my name. I rushed forward and we talked. I told him what I was doing and where I was serving as a pastor. He encouraged me. Then he said the same thing again, "The Lord has something special for you." I felt blessed at the time but was not sure what it meant. I received it as a successful pastor encouraging a young pastor.

The revival was great. I went back to my church and three years later I went to Liberty University to finish my bachelor's degree and to go to seminary. I chose Liberty because I admired Pastor Falwell and I knew that the school was the best education for ministry I could attend. During my time at Liberty, I worked for Liberty University Emergency Services, which provided security for Old Time Gospel Hour, Thomas Road Baptist Church, Godparent Home, and Liberty University. I worked the third shift, went to School during the day, Virginia Army National Guard on weekends, and even worked at Kroger grocery store. Pastor knew the long hours and I am sure he saw me every night when I worked if he looked out the window. He knew I studied hard and encouraged me when he saw me. (If he liked you, he would surprise you by poking you hard in the stomach as he laughed. I learned to watch out for him.)

One evening, when he returned home from a trip away, speaking at another church, he stopped at the gate (His Home) when he knew I was there. He asked how things were going in my life. I told him where I was in school and what my plans were in ministry. He said it again to me, "David, God's got something special for you to do. Keep up the hard work." I watched until he was back inside his home for the night. I stayed outside in the cold, which was my job at the time.

I did not understand what this meant at the time. I always admired the pastor when he preached and encouraged others in faith. He was a great Man of God. *(Sally and I received Christmas cards for years, sent by Macel Falwell, Jerry's amazing wife.)*

As I finished writing my conclusion to this book, on July 24, 2023, His words came to mind when I sat down to write. That morning, I realized that this was what was meant to be special! When I completed my book, which I hope to publish, I remembered Pastor Falwell. This book has been my labor of love, as I have attempted to share the story of my failure and God's success in my life. It is about family! My family; our family; our humanity.

As I was reading through one last time and I was moving toward a conclusion, I recalled the incident that occurred, while I was working at Liberty. I call this incident that happened at home, "Ooki Gookie Mess." This incident happened the morning after the last time Pastor Falwell encouraged me.

***Covering up sin.*** *The memory of the Ookie-Gookie Mess!*

When I was in Seminary, I also worked the third shift on the Liberty University Security Department. I would get off work at 0700 and often spend an hour finishing daily logs and reports. Each morning when I arrived home, I would help my wife get our two older children off to school. Then my wife would go to work around 0845, leaving me with our youngest child, Sarah, who was age three. Often, I would lie down on the couch in the living room to rest, while my daughter would play. The routine each morning was the same: close all the doors to the bedrooms and bathroom, and lock the child gate to the kitchen. Lay down and rest before the busy day.

This particular morning, when I returned home after a long exhausting night, I was extremely tired. The same basic routine was followed to get my wife and two older children off for the day. Then I closed the bedroom doors and pulled the gate to the kitchen. However, this morning

*Mission Analysis and Understanding Success*

I laid down on the bed and left the door open to the living room. I was so tired I needed a good hour of sleep before I took Sarah to child care and went to classes.

About an hour later, I woke up because it was very quiet in the house. I walked into the living room. To my surprise, I saw white paper plates scattered all over the carpet, couch, and coffee table. Sarah was in the corner crouched down trying to hide from me. I said to her, "Sarah, you've been bad." Then I walked over and picked up one of the paper plates. I found a black pasty pile of "ookie gookie" mess. Anxiously, I began picking up the plates and found a black pasty "ookie gookie" mess under each strategically placed white plate. I panicked! As an adult, I knew that my wife would hold me responsible for this situation. Stains on the couch and carpet; messy black paste all over the table and chairs! What was I going to do? My focus changed quickly. I had to get this cleaned up before I did anything else.

As the situation unfolded, Sarah was crouched down in the corner watching with her big blue tear-filled eyes, wondering if she was in trouble. My simple chiding of my daughter turned into a personal panic for me. Grabbing Sarah by the hand, I led her into the kitchen to the sink. She cautiously participated in my hurried activity of

*Memories of Loving You*

securing a bucket, soap, and towels. Sarah watched my every move with some confusion.

She went from feeling afraid of being in trouble to a cautious anticipation of my response. Her tear-filled eyes transformed into bright happiness as we both got down and cleaned up each mess. To my surprise, every stain came out! As my expressions of anxious concern changed into happiness, Sarah's fear of being in trouble diminished. When we finished, Sarah was back to her joyful self. She was laughing and playing again!

My investigation enlightened me about what happened. Sarah crawled over the gate into the kitchen while I rested, and she raided the refrigerator. She poured grape Kool-Aid into a glass and dunked Oreo cookies. She spilled this black "ookie gookie" mess all over the couch, carpet, and coffee table. Knowing she was in trouble, Sarah placed white paper plates over each pile of mess she made. I chuckled as I realized her intent to cover her mess = sin.

After things calmed down, God spoke to my heart. I realized that Sarah was hiding her sin. Recalling what just happened, when I walked over to her and took her by the hand saying, "We better clean this up," I realized that God was teaching me a lesson about a father's love.

With the bucket of water and soap, we both went into the living room and got down on our knees to clean up the mess. As I helped Sarah, she began to smile once again. (Of course, I cleaned it all up.) God spoke to my heart as I realized that God is not a big bully waiting for us to do something wrong so He can punish us, but rather, He is a loving Father who kneels beside us to help. He can get the stain out of every mess we make! We just smear it around and make it worse.

Like my daughter, so often, we human beings do wrong and then try to hide the wrong from God and others. We take our white paper plates and try to cover the sins we have committed. However, God knows when we do wrong and when we cover our sins. As a loving Father, He is there to say, "I can get the stain out and make you happy again." *(The Atonement of our Savior – Psalm 32: 1-2, Romans 4:7-8, 2 Corinthians 5: 19-20)*

In Isaiah chapter one and verse eighteen we are invited to, *"Come now, and let us reason together, saith the Lord: though your sins be as scarlet, they shall be as white as snow; though they are red like crimson, they shall be as wool."* (Isaiah 1:18) There is nothing that you have ever done that God will not forgive you for. Just ask Him for help, for He is a loving Father who cares for you! He can get the stain out and restore hope. You can experience the joy and happiness of your Heavenly Father. You can know the truth and the truth will set you FREE. *(John 8:36)*

*[PS: I know the blasphemy of the Holy Spirit is unforgivable according to God's Word. This is the sin of rejecting God's Forgiveness, which can only be experienced after the Holy Spirit convicts the sinner of sin and the need for the Savior, Jesus Christ." If you reject the conviction of the Holy Spirit upon your heart to repent and believe in Jesus Christ as Savior, you can never be saved. He is the only Savior for all men and women who have ever lived. If you do not trust Christ, you will die in your sin for eternity. Rejecting the Savior is the work of evil. Evil's mission is to destroy you. Yes, you!]*

**Finding the Freedom of Forgiveness.** *The weight of sin once carried is unloaded when forgiveness is a reality.*

The value you place on your soul is measured by the weight of sin. You know what you hide from others and God. Your accountability for immoral acts will stand in comparison to the glory and holiness of God. This is

*Mission Analysis and Understanding Success*

inevitable. You might think you will avoid judgment for your sin but you will never escape your accountability. You might deny the reality of standing accountable because you refuse to believe in God, but wherever you hide and whatever you bury away to conceal, or cover with your white paper plates, you will never be able to run away from. Your day of judgment is coming. All of it will be revealed. *(Luke 8:17, Mark 4:22)*

You can know your sin is already forgiven *(Buried and never seen again)* through faith in the Lord Jesus Christ. The eternal Heavenly Father has made it possible to uncover and then wash away all your transgressions = Forever! You can experience the freedom of faith and live a life with God's blessings now. In Christ you become a Child of God and are secured by the Spirit of God through Faith unto Salvation, ready to be revealed when He calls believers into His presence for eternity. You can walk with God now! The next best adventure is yet to come.

I have known the good, the bad, and the ugly of living in this world of sin. I have a peace that passes all understanding because I am in Christ Jesus my Savior. Yes, I have a Savior because I needed a Savior. It is personal. It should be personal for you too!

***The Long and Winding Road back to her door became a straight path.***  *Finding my Love!*

We said our goodbyes in Tennessee and returned to Florida, the Sunshine State. This is where we last lived together. It was a long trip but I already had a place for us to start again. Much has happened since then. We eventually got remarried. We are happy and strong together. I think we appreciate each other more than ever. We are still healing from the injuries endured because of our enemy, and our bad choices. We have lost a lot. We lost our home, our furniture, our savings. However, we are together and we are happy. We have held each other often and find comfort. Some might ask, "How is this possible." True love forgives! God loves you, even as a sinner. He forgives us through repentance and redemption through faith unto salvation.

*My dear, forgiveness takes care of the past.*
*Love for each other directs our daily journey*
*together now,*
*and our future in Christ is full of wonders to share.*
*Making our love better than ever!*

The journey of life continues. We did not have much left after the storm. We no longer have our home. We have no furniture. Our resources were depleted. Bad decisions were made by us both. We have each other. Starting over again on our new adventure becomes the future we make, as we love each other again. Come sit with me in the garden my love. Let us walk with the Lord in His Beautiful Garden!

Sally and I are re-loving each other. We have been together for over a year now and we love each other more than ever before. We are married now and experiencing life as newlyweds. We got a Re-Do! We walk in our garden again!

**Forgiveness is God's tool for Reconciliation!** *Restoration of a relationship.*

At the very heart of Christianity is the virtue of forgiveness. It is a unique attribute that is difficult for humans to understand, and even more difficult to practice. When a person violates or hurts another person, either willfully or accidentally, pain and suffering automatically accompany the situation. This pain could be physical or even emotional, and it causes heartache and division in the relationship. Sin separates love.

God Almighty created us, human beings, with the wonderful divine qualities that He alone possesses, for He created us in His likeness and His image. Therefore, the emotions and feelings that we experience, are the emotions and feelings that God has shared with humanity. As divinely constructed creatures, who possess the qualities of our master designer, God, we have been entrusted with the gift of eternal life. We are eternal creatures! *"For whether we live, we live unto the Lord; and whether we die, we die unto the Lord: whether we live therefore, or die, we are the Lord's." (Romans 14:8)*

With this divine construction, God has given us freedom and liberty to make choices and decisions about our lives and our existence. This freedom comes with personal responsibilities. Responsibilities that hold us accountable for the actions that we take when exercising our freedom. This therefore leads us to the concept that we are individuals who have accountability and responsibilities for each other.

What I am trying to make very clear to you is that every human being is an individual who is divinely created in the likeness and image of God, and we are responsible for our actions toward each other and to our Creator. When you hurt or violate another person, you are responsible for your actions. God holds you accountable for everything that you do, whether it is good or evil. Listen to me! You can not escape the consequences of your actions/sin. You can be forgiven when you confess and repent. Jesus Christ is the one who forgives sin when you trust and believe in His substitutionary death, which is glorified by His Resurrection from the dead. His work is the Salvation each one of us needs.

If you remain unsaved, you will stand (actually you will grovel in the dust on your face in terror and shame) before God Almighty and give an account for everything that you have ever done. You will pay the penalty for every sin that you have committed during your life. "There is nothing hidden that shall not be known." Your sin shall be shouted from the housetops for all to know. Only in Jesus Christ is there any hope for salvation. Through confession and repentance for sin committed, and by turning to believe in the Lord Jesus, as your Savior, can you be forgiven of your sin. Jesus Christ is the only hope for everlasting forgiveness. When the Lord forgives, He removes your sin and buries it in the deepest sea, never to be remembered anymore. *(Psalms 103:12, Isaiah 43:25)*

The scriptures declare that it is a fearful thing to fall into the hands of an angry God, for God is angry at the wicked every day. **(Psalm 7:11)** Anger is an emotion that God feels! Just think, God is angry when you sin. *Think about that for a moment.* Let us not play with our standing before the Lord. **God gets angry!!!** When you sin you make God angry. "Vengeance is mine saith the Lord. I will repay/recompense."

If the message from God stopped there, we would all be in terrible shape. "For all have sinned and come short of the glory of God." Our sin has separated us from God, and the soul that sins shall die. "For the wages of sin is death…" This would be a tragic ending for each one of us if God did not forgive us for our sins.

When a person sins against another person, the person who is hurt by the circumstances feels the hurt and the pain that is accompanied by the violation. Anger, sorrow, grief, pain, depression, and many other emotions may result from the violation perpetrated against an individual, and the relationship between the individuals will always be damaged or destroyed. This painful experience will always remain in the heart of the one who is hurt unless there is reconciliation. The process of forgiveness leads to reconciliation.

*Mission Analysis and Understanding Success*

Reconciliation is when two parties/individuals can come back together in a new relationship. God has opened the door for mankind to enter into a new relationship through forgiveness. When the prophet Daniel prayed for his people, He said, "O lord, to us belongs shame of face... because we have sinned. To you Lord God belongs mercy and forgiveness, even though we have sinned against you." (Daniel 9: 8-9) Forgiveness is an attribute of God that is shared in the heart of man by repentance.

In the Gospel of Mark chapter two, Jesus spoke these words to a man who could not walk, "Son, thy sins be forgiven thee." When the religious leaders heard this they began complaining. They said among themselves, "Why does this man speak blasphemies? Who can forgive sins but God only?" Of course, Jesus pointed out the fact that He had the power to forgive sin on earth." (Mk 2:10) Then in Matthew chapter six Jesus teaches His disciples to pray. As He concluded His instruction to the Lord's prayer, He summed it up by saying, *"For if you forgive men their trespasses (sin), your heavenly Father will also forgive you: but if you forgive not men their trespasses, neither will your Father forgive your trespasses."*

The parable found in the eighteenth chapter of Matthew addresses the issue of forgiveness in the lives of those individuals who would live godly. In the first five verses, Jesus teaches that we must become humble as a child who trust in their Father if we are going to enter into His kingdom. In verses six through ten, He reveals the nature of sin and its destructiveness; followed by the nature of God's forgiveness and love in verses twelve through fourteen. Then just before the parable on forgiveness, Jesus commands His followers to seek reconciliation by confrontation. He emphasizes the need for confrontational reconciliation by saying that heaven and eternity are at stake.

Peter pulls Jesus to the side, because he is embarrassed to ask Jesus the question before the others, and inquires how often he should forgive. (Matthew 18:21) The Lord Jesus responds to Peter by saying, "seventy times seven." He continues the story by saying:

> *"The Kingdom of Heaven is likened to a king who wanted to settle his accounts with his servants. When he began to settle the accounts, one man was brought to him, who owed the king 10,000 talents (millions of dollars by today's economy.) But the man could not pay his debt. Therefore, the king*

*commanded that the man, his wife, his children, and all his possessions be sold for the debt to be paid. The man fell before the king and worshiped him, begging for the king's patience and time so he could pay the debt. The king was moved with compassion and forgave the man of his debt. But the man went out and found the man who owed him a hundred pence (about ten dollars) and he physically abused him by choking him around the neck, saying, 'Pay me the money you owe me.' The man fell before his fellow servant and begged for some more time to pay, but the man would not allow him any more time and he had the man thrown into prison.*

*Others who witnessed the actions of the man who was forgiven by the king went to the king and told him all that the man had done. The king called the man back before him and rebuked him saying, 'O you wicked servant, I forgave you all your debt because you begged me. Don't you think that you should have compassion on your fellow servants, even as I had pity on you?' The Lord was angry and delivered the man to the tormentors until all that was due was paid in full."* "So likewise shall my *heavenly Father do also unto you, if ye from your heart forgive not     every one his brother their trespasses."*

I do not want to exhaust the content of this story before you, as we search for the deep meaning of our text. What I do want to do is point you in the direction of a transforming journey. It is clear to me that Jesus was revealing something unique and transforming from the heart of God Almighty. Here it is: Christians are forgiven their debt of sin, and they are transformed into the Children of God. This includes the forgiving Nature of God when the Mercy of God is applied through Jesus Christ. In other words, as Christians, we have a new nature in Christ which changes us.

Therefore, we are like our heavenly Father, who is a forgiving God. If you do not have a forgiving nature, you must not be a Child of God. "Old things pass away and all things become new," when a person is born into the Family of God. There is a definite change. If you hold bitterness and hatred in your heart toward another person, you are not acting Christ-like. If you seek vengeance toward another, you are not living as a Child of God. Forgiveness restores a relationship fully. Mercy is just a kindness undeserved.

Forgiveness is at the heart of God and the center of the Gospel message. *"Forgive one another as I have forgiven you,"* Jesus said. Forgiveness can not be applied until repentance is enacted. In the Gospel of Luke chapter seventeen, Jesus teaches about forgiveness:

> *"It is inevitable that offenses will come: but woe to the person who commits offense toward another. (Sins against another person.) It was better for that person that a millstone was hanged around the neck and the individual cast into the sea than it would be to offend one of the least little ones. Take heed to yourselves: If your brother trespass against you, rebuke him (tell him); and if he repent, forgive him. And if he trespass against you seven times in a day, and seven times in a day turns again to you, saying, I repent; you should forgive him."*

What I am saying to you today is that forgiveness is an attribute of God Almighty, and He requires us to forgive others just like He forgives us of our sins! Forgiveness, however, has conditions. **First** of all, there must be an offense between individuals. Someone must violate the rights of another.

The **second** condition to forgiveness is that the person who offended, or committed the offense, must accept responsibility for his action and realize that he has hurt the other person. That individual must acknowledge the offense to the person they have hurt. We call this confession. Repentance is the action of the person, who has sinned against the other person, by confessing and changing the activity which offended. Therefore, repentance includes acknowledgment of sin, and the confession of the sin, to the individual who was hurt by the sin.

The **third** condition to forgiveness is that the person who was violated by the sin must accept the repentance, confession, and apology of the person who hurt them. This is where the new nature in Christ comes in. **As children of God, we have a new nature from God, which demands that we forgive others.** When we confess our sins, He is faithful and just to forgive us our sins and cleanse us from all unrighteousness. (I John 1:9) Forgiveness is God's method of bringing people back together into a healthy relationship, and His method for bringing men and women back into a relationship with Him, as their heavenly Father.

*Mission Analysis and Understanding Success*

"Blessed are they whose iniquities are forgiven, and whose sin is covered. Blessed is the man to whom the Lord will not impute sin." *(Romans 4:7-8)*

*** Redemption is at the heart of forgiveness!**  *Freedom!*

Scripture reveals that everyone born from Adam has fallen into sin. Sin separates sinners from the Lord God. To redeem something means it is purchased. It becomes owned by the one who pays the price. It is bought in the marketplace. When you own what has been purchased, you can walk out the door because you own it. What is purchased is no longer for sale. It is taken off the market.

The owner can use the property redeemed and do what he wants with the purchased item. He can set it free. Jesus Christ came down into this world and He purchased the souls of those He redeems through faith and repentance of sin, which forgives the debt of sin. He walked out of the tomb of death, by His resurrection, and He takes the repentant sinner off the market of this fallen world of sin. He takes those redeemed with Him and sets them FREE! If the Son of God makes you free, you will be free indeed!

I just have to say this: We are brothers and sisters of humanity! [*Multiple thousands of White Soldiers, and Black Soldiers fought slavery during the Civil War. Many died for freedom. They, in a real sense, were the redeemers for those who were slaves. (Black or White Slaves!) They paid the price of injury and death as a sacrifice for freedom. Ancestry of families, and posterity, were sacrificed as soldiers died to set slaves free. It is a shame that many in our day are beguiled by the lies of evil to hate. The majority of white people in the United States were greatly involved in fighting the enemy of slavery. They fought the enemy of segregation that raised its ugly head after the Civil War, and many believe that we are all equally brothers and sisters of ONE Human Race. The majority of whites today were never involved in the slavery of others. Many believe that we are all one human race: One family from the breath of God Almighty.* Only those who divide and hate continue the vitriol of evil's hate and destruction. Good men and women stand up and fight against evil when the innocent are harmed. Don't be deceived by those who distort history and propagate hateful ideology. Jesus told us to love others. PS: The Federal Government of the United States at the time, led by the GOP, fought the enemy of slavery and won! They liberated all the slaves no matter their skin color. We need to get back on track as a Free Nation Under God. Liberty and Justice for ALL. Freedom is the gift of God in Christ our Lord. Dr. Martin Luther King was right!]

***The END:*** *Or should I say, "My conclusion for now?"*

All of this has been about my faith and memories during an emotional spiritual battle. It has been a battle, which was fought over my deepest convictions and love. My love for God and my love for the woman I love. I always believed the enemy, evil, was there, but I realize now that evil knows I am here too. We are enemies. Evil fills the hearts of men and women throughout history. Evil surrounds us today and whispers the beguiling deception of hate into the minds of those who are assimilated into self-theistic rebellion against truth and goodness. It is the war between good and evil that continues to play out before us all.

I think I have some small measure of understanding about the wickedness of evil. It is spreading every day, as it takes more ground and captures more prisoners. Wickedness is evil that exercises it's willful violation of others for gain. It manipulates the battlefield and crafts the attack against all objectives. It is the Serpent Enemy, at a strategic level, trying to take control of all that is good

*Memories of Loving You*

and Godly. You are just one pawn on the battlefield of life. Evil will take prisoners or leave no enemy alive.

However, the Good Champion on the battlefield never loses. He stands in the face of the evil giant of darkness and rolls the stone away in victory. This Champion is my Savior Jesus. He fought the battle and won the eternal promise for me.

As I said, this story is shared from my perspective. It is a story about my memories as I struggled to find peace with the Lord. I struggled to forgive. It is a story of how the Lord opened my eyes to see His forgiving nature and my accountability. This difficult journey has led me to find my love and to love her even more. I hope you know the Lord Jesus Christ as Savior. His promises are true! He will walk in the garden with you when you trust Him as Lord. His love for you has been echoed since Calvary! You can find what you have lost if you grasp the hand of hope that reaches into the troubled waters of your life. He is the rock of salvation for all who believe.

> *"Believe in the Lord Jesus Christ, and you will be saved." (Acts 16:31)*

PS: Find a good New Testament Christian Church and attend faithfully in these days, which are leading us all to

*Mission Analysis and Understanding Success*

a period foretold, The Tribulation. It will be worse than man has ever known. Only the redeemed will be raptured before evil establishes its worldwide village of control. Sin and evil will erupt upon the face of the earth and the AI Beast (Antichrist Intelligence) will take control. The wrath of God will be poured out against the worst evil ever known to man. Jesus is the only hope and His Kingdom is eternal.

## *A LOST* **POEM**

When I look for something that I cannot find,
my anxiety level always climbs.
I'll search every drawer, and, look under the bed,
for that one item until I get mad.
I'll question my wife until she is sad, and the item
I search for just can't be had.

I'll look in the garage, three of four times, and pull
the cushions off the couch just to find.
I'll look til I'm frustrated, with the time I am wasting,
and blame everyone else for the misplacing.
"Where did you put this precious lost thing?"
"I've searched every corner and you are to blame."
"It's all your fault, and you know it, that I am
running this late.

I just know that you've used it, there can be no debate.
You know I am right, so, don't make me wait."

"It's not in my pocket. It's not in my drawers.
Not under the seat, it's not behind the door.
Where can I find this thing that I lost?
"Can anyone help me?" even at cost.
I've seemed to have forgotten.
"What was it I lost?"

*Poem written by David Druckenmiller, 15 August 2009*

Don't forget your soul!
Do not loose your soul!

# Chaplain Dave

## Biography of Chaplain (LTC-R) David Druckenmiller:

**RETIRED CHAPLAIN, UNITED** States Army, Lieutenant Colonel David Lee Druckenmiller, served in the Military for over 33 years. For the last 22 years of his Army career, he served soldiers and their families, as a Pastor Chaplain endorsed by Liberty Baptist Fellowship, and, as a Staff Officer to each Command assigned. To this day, David has soldiers and family Members still contacting him about his impact of ministry in their lives. He has friends around the world who stay in touch. Chaplain Dave served as Senior Pastor to five Army Congregations, and Assistant Pastor to four Congregations. He was also greatly involved in the planning and approval for the first new Chapel built at Fort Bragg, NC, since the Vietnam War. His nickname was "Chaplain Dave."

David was raised in the Lutheran Church in Swanton, Ohio. He made a public profession of faith in Christ in

1975 and Joined the James Lee Road Baptist Church in Florida. Two years later he felt the call into ministry and pursued his theological education: He graduated from Baptist Bible College in Springfield, MO in 1980. He pastored two churches in Ohio and then went to Liberty University, where he finished a Bachelor of Science in 1985. Continuing his education at Liberty Baptist Theological Seminary where he graduated with a Master of Divinity in 1989. He was endorsed by Liberty Baptist Fellowship to serve on active duty. He also served in the Virginia Army National Guard for 6 years while he attended College and Seminary, and then he re-entered Active Military Service in 1990.

David retired Army Strong on April 1, 2011, and moved to Murfreesboro, Tennessee to be with his family.

Printed in the USA
CPSIA information can be obtained
at www.ICGtesting.com
LVHW080711031123
762791LV00002B/6